LEGAL FEMINISMS: THEORY AND PRACTICE

Legal Feminisms: theory and practice

Edited by
CLARE McGLYNN
Newcastle Law School
University of Newcastle upon Tyne

Routledge
Taylor & Francis Group
LONDON AND NEW YORK

First published 1998 by Dartmouth and Ashgate Publishing

Reissued 2018 by Routledge
2 Park Square, Milton Park, Abingdon, Oxon, OX14 4RN
711 Third Avenue, New York, NY 10017, USA

Routledge is an imprint of the Taylor & Francis Group, an informa business

A Library of Congress record exists under LC control number: 97041408

ISBN 13: 978-1-138-33397-0 (hbk)
ISBN 13: 978-0-429-44562-0 (ebk)

Contents

List of Contributors

David S. Berry is a Lecturer in Laws at the University of the West Indies, Barbados.

Eugenia Caracciolo di Torella is a postgraduate student and tutor at the University of Durham.

Richard Collier is a Reader in Law at the University of Newcastle upon Tyne.

Mary Donnelly is a Lecturer in Law at University College, Cork, Ireland.

Junping He is an Associate Professor at the China Central Leadership Institute of Politics and Law, China.

Elizabeth A. Kirk is a Lecturer in Law at the University of Dundee.

Clare McGlynn is a Lecturer in Law at the University of Newcastle upon Tyne.

Katherine O'Donovan is a Professor of Law at Queen Mary & Westfield College, University of London.

Anu Pylkkänen is a Professor of Law at the University of Helsinki, Finland.

Fiona E. Raitt is a Senior Lecturer in Law at the University of Dundee.

Hilary Sommerlad is a Senior Lecturer in Law at Leeds Metropolitan University.

Jenny A. Tooze is a postgraduate student at the University of Nottingham.

Ian Ward is a Professor of Law at the University of Dundee.

M. Suzanne Zeedyk is a Lecturer in Psychology at the University of Dundee.

Introduction

CLARE McGLYNN

This collection of essays has its genesis in the Newcastle Law School conference *Women and the Law: from theory to practice* which was held at Grey College, University of Durham on 31st August 1996. The impetus for the conference was the perception that there is insufficient collaboration between feminists in the legal academy and legal practice. In particular, it appeared that the understandings of feminist academics were not reaching a practitioner audience, and vice-versa, where the dissemination of such knowledge could be most productive. That this absence of dialogue is considered problematic is premised on the belief that those engaged with feminist theories of law and articulating feminist perspectives of the law do so in order to seek changes to the ways in which the law affects and constructs women. Such engagements can be enriched by an understanding of the practice of the law. The corollary is that feminists engaged in practice might gain insights from an understanding of the work of academics undertaking research in similar fields.

In this sense, engagements with theory are pragmatic. Understood in these terms, 'it is not so much a question of application but rather of movement between 'theory' and 'practice'' (Bottomley and Conaghan, 1993, p.2). It is this on-going movement between theory and practice which underpins this collection of essays; moving away from the one-way track implied by the conference title 'from theory to practice'.

In addition to considering the relationships between theories of law and the practice of law, the conference aimed to encourage dialogue between feminist legal practitioners, activists and academics. Particular understandings of women's situations in practice were offered by Barbara Hewson, Joint Vice-President of the Association of Women Barristers and barrister of 12 Gray's Inn Square, Elizabeth Woodcraft, former Chair of Rights of Women and a barrister of Tooks Court Chambers, and Judith Willis of the Association of Women Solicitors. These contributions, together with those of delegates, provided a great insight into the role and status of women lawyers. The benefit of dialogue was evident in the discussion arising from the presentation given by Hilary Sommerlad, which also forms one of the chapters of this collection. Hilary Sommerlad draws on the results of empirical research carried out with women solicitors, sets the data in a theoretical framework, and identifies the means whereby the marginalisation of women in the profession is effected. Sommerlad argues that social closure against women in the profession is reinforced through a gendering of the concept of 'commitment', a core criterion for participation in the primary legal labour market. Thus, the experience of women in the profession, together with an understanding of a theoretical context to this experience, illuminates debates both in the profession and academia regarding women in the legal profession.

The chapters written by Katherine O'Donovan, Ian Ward and Richard Collier exemplify further such engagements with theory and practice. Katherine O'Donovan examines the concept of gender bias, particularly in relation to judicial education, suggesting that metaphor and fable may illuminate our understandings of the concept. In problematising the familiar concept of gender bias, O'Donovan encourages and initiates a more sophisticated understanding of the concept, and of bias itself.

In a similar vein, Ian Ward employs literature as a means to investigate some of the contemporary concerns of feminist legal thought. In particular, Ward examines the role of Portia in Shakespeare's *Merchant of Venice*, a role which has increasingly been considered to be symbolic of the situation of women in law, particularly by judges and practitioners. In doing so, Ward seeks to destabilise this symbolism, suggesting that this destabilisation itself reflects current trends in feminist legal thinking. Richard Collier, drawing on recent scholarship concerning the relationship between identity, subjectivity and corporeality, seeks to re-conceptualise the 'masculine' cultures of legal education and practice. In view of the lack of political will to address questions of transformative social and economic structural change, Collier suggests that it is likely that debates regarding men, women and the legal profession will continue to be marginalised. Further, an examination of the sexed specificity of men is required if the question of 'women in law' is to be more than a 'woman's issue'.

A further theme of the conference, represented in this collection, was to engage with, and develop, recent scholarship applying feminist legal analyses to areas of law hitherto free from the feminist gaze. In particular, the growing application of feminist analyses to international law is considered in the chapters written by David Berry and Elizabeth Kirk and

Jenny Tooze. David Berry considers the development of scholarship analysing international law from a feminist perspective, and how it particularly relates to the rights of aboriginal women, aboriginal communities and the wider Canadian state. In doing so, Berry argues that feminist theory at the international level offers one of the most exciting critiques of law, rights and culture. Elizabeth Kirk and Jenny Tooze focus on one particular aspect of international law, namely water law. In considering whether the legal regulation of the use of water resources has a gendered impact, Kirk and Tooze suggest further avenues of research, and possible law reforms, which may be necessary in order to ensure that the impact of this area of law does not adversely affect the interests of women.

In addition to expanding the boundaries of feminist legal analysis, it is important to develop and strengthen analyses of areas of law and practice of on-going concern. The chapters of Fiona Raitt and Suzanne Zeedyk, Eugenia Carraciolo di Torella, Mary Donnelly and Clare McGlynn seek to engage with and develop some common themes of feminist legal scholarship. Fiona Raitt and Suzanne Zeedyk bring an innovative, interdisciplinary perspective to our understandings of rape law, arguing that because of the inherent biases of the two disciplines of law and psychology, neither the findings of fact, nor the content of opinion evidence in cases which come to trial, are neutral or objective. The result is a powerful collusion between law and psychology which works actively against the interests of women. In developing this analysis, Raitt and Zeedyk advance a feminist analysis of some of the rules of evidence hitherto considered neutral and objective, demanding a more complex analysis of the effects of rape and rape trials.

Eugenia Carraciolo di Torella examines developments in the European Union to combat discrimination on the grounds of pregnancy and maternity. In comparing the case law of the European Court of Justice with legislative developments, Eugenia Carraciolo di Torella suggests that the approach taken by the Court of Justice has been the most fruitful and should be further developed by pursuing a litigation strategy. Mary Donnelly examines the way in which presumptions about women's essential nature, and assumed social role, dominate the debate regarding the non-consensual sterilisation of women. Donnelly articulates a feminist approach to the debate which is more centred on the reality and diversity of women, rather than being dominated by stereotypes. Clare McGlynn's chapter suggests that the dominant political strategy being employed to improve the position of women in the workplace is the business, or economic, case for sex equality. Having outlined the main elements of the business case, and identified its shortcomings, McGlynn argues that those seeking to improve the position of women in the workforce must recognise the inherent limitations in pursuing an economically-based strategy, be aware of the long term implications of the approach, and seek new ways in which to advance sex equality.

The diversity of women's experiences of law underpins each of the contributions to this collection, reflecting the breadth of approaches and experiences considered at the conference. The conference considered the dynamics of feminism in North American law schools, the rights debate in Canada, employment law in Sweden, women's rights in China and cultural understandings on gender in Finland. The latter two areas of discussion form contributions to this collection. Junping He outlines the development and nature of the special protection of women's rights in China, providing a fascinating insight into the protection of women in a legal system rarely examined. Anu Pylkkänen offers an understanding of the concept of gender in Finland through the lens of the establishment of a Chair in Women's Law at the University of Helsinki. In doing so, Pylkkänen, together with Junping He, encourage a deeper understanding of the role of gender and its relationships with law in diverse societies, as well as reminding us of the commonalities between all women.

This theme of diversity but commonality underpins this collection of essays, represented in the title, *Legal Feminisms*, as opposed to legal feminism. Nonetheless, I would argue that in recognising diversity, the role of feminism as a political strategy must not be lost. To this extent, it is hoped that this collection represents part of an on-going process of dialogue, with the insights of theory and practice informing all approaches to the theorising, problematising and practical resolution of the interaction between law and feminism. This book is a collaboration between academics of various theoretical perspectives, interests, nationalities and sexes, and therefore represents a wide variety of legal scholarship. It is intended that it be through such diverse understandings of legal feminisms that this collection draws its strength.

In the organisation of the conference, and the editing and production of this collection of essays, my thanks are due to many people. First, I would like to thank Caroline Graham. It was during one of our many discussions regarding the status of women in the legal profession that the idea for the conference evolved. The organisation of the conference was only possible with the help of many of my colleagues at Newcastle Law School. Particular thanks are due to the Head of Department, Professor Mike

Allen, for his support for the project before I had even arrived at Newcastle; to Alison Dunn for her valuable assistance at the conference; to Joanne Milne who helped produce all the documentation for the conference, and who formatted this collection of essays; and to Richard Collier for his encouragement, support and assistance.

Considerable thanks are due to all those who participated in the conference, in giving papers and contributing from the floor, who together provided a stimulating forum for the discussion of contemporary issues concerning women and the law. The conference provided an essential stimulus for the production of this collection of essays, and I would like to thank the contributors for the quality and diversity of the chapters and for their perseverance with the editing process.

My thanks are also due to Nina Hall for her encouragement and support throughout the life of this project and others. I draw great strength from our endless discussions regarding feminism, the law and legal profession. Final thanks are owed to Ian Ward for his support and humour, and for tirelessly listening to my splenetic outbursts on the trials and tribulations of conference organisation and the editorial process.

Bibliography

Bottomley, A. and Conaghan, J. (1993), 'Feminist Theory and Legal Strategy', *Journal of Law and Society*, vol. 20, pp. 1-5.

PART I

PERSPECTIVES ON SEX, GENDER AND THE LEGAL PROFESSION

1. The Gendering of the Professional Subject: Commitment, Choice and Social Closure in the Legal Profession

HILARY SOMMERLAD

Introduction

Recent studies of women in the legal professions of several countries have argued that whilst the proportion of women employed as lawyers has increased, their position in the profession remains marginal (Sommerlad, 1994a; Skordaki, 1996; Hagan and Kay, 1995; Thornton, 1996). This chapter examines this phenomenon in the context of the parallel changes taking place in the profession, and identifies the means whereby the marginalisation of women lawyers is effected. I will argue that social closure against women in the profession is being reinforced through the notion of 'commitment' as a core criterion for participation in the primary legal labour market.

The conception of commitment, whilst distinct from the altruistic dimension traditionally attributed to professionalism, is necessarily polyvalent, though its ultimate definition is in terms of a 'lack'; something which women cannot demonstrate. It is naturalised, through what Podmore and Spencer described as the dominant 'cultural mandate' (1982, p.28) of the profession, and through the crystallisation of this 'common sense' view in academic labour market sociology (Hakim, 1995). Consequently, the professional subject is gendered in such a way as to render women's marginal position the apparent consequence of their own 'choice'.

In developing a theoretical framework to support this analysis, I have drawn on feminist writers on social closure, on Pateman's work on the 'sexual contract' and on Bourdieu's concept of 'cultural capital'. The supporting empirical material results from research carried out with women solicitors in West and North Yorkshire between 1990 and 1994 (Sommerlad and Allaker, 1991; Sommerlad, 1994b). The study was concerned predominantly with women returners to the profession, and the means by which their re-entry into practice could be facilitated through training, but also considered the extent to which women solicitors experienced disadvantage in their careers. The principal research method was a questionnaire survey. In 1990, the sample comprised all senior or managing partners and all practising female solicitors in the sample area; the latter group being divided into two categories: those who had never taken a career break and returners. A third category of female respondents comprised those women out of practice who could be traced. In 1994, 50 per cent of the original sample received a questionnaire. Both surveys produced an average response rate across all groups of between 55 per cent and 69 per cent. The quantitative data was supplemented by in-depth interviews with a purposively selected group drawn from the questionnaire samples in both 1991 and 1994.

Professional Restructuring and 'Commitment' in the Discourse of Legal Employment

It is of course not new to argue that women are, through their life pattern choices, the authors of their own destiny. However, this approach has recently been revived through the curious coincidence of the publication of Catherine Hakim's assault on 'feminist myths' concerning women's employment (1995), and the election of Martin Mears to the Presidency of the Law Society with a programme which combined anxiety over the oversupply of qualified solicitors with explicit hostility to 'equal opportunities' in general and 'feminists' in particular.

The strategy by which women began to enter the professions in large numbers can be described, using Witz's terminology, as a credentialist usurpationary strategy (1992, pp.64-65), and coincided with the development of the solicitors' profession as an exclusively graduate profession (Skordaki, 1996; Burrage, 1996). The importance of credentialism as an instrument for formal equality is crucial. The classical 'knowledge mandate' of the legal profession was in large part a function of processes of socialisation; the imbibing of the mystical integrity of professional knowledge through the process of apprenticeship. There was no necessary link between professional expertise and 'hard work' in the classical model, except during the period of apprenticeship, and it does not merit comment in academic texts on professionalisation. However, the concurrent transformations wrought by the increase in women entrants to the profession; together with the expansion of demand for professional services, the development of the corporate model of lawyering and the increasing involvement of the State in the provision of legal services, have all combined to undermine the stability of the profession and its image of itself (Sommerlad, 1995). In this new world, credentials no longer stand as a proxy for conformity to the dominant male norm and the 'knowledge mandate' no longer acts as a satisfactory form of social closure, especially since women out-perform men academically (Lewis, 1997).

The emphasis on 'commitment' in career development in the legal profession represents a response to this situation. In its vagueness and flexibility, the concept of commitment recreates the almost mystical character of the classical 'knowledge mandate': it enables key actors in the labour market to discount women's formal credentials and expertise against this key 'deficit', without ever being explicit about how it can be demonstrated. Crucially, it enables the ideal type of the professional to be reconstructed normatively as male. In the remainder of this section, I will consider the discourse of commitment in the responses of employers in the research sample referred to above (Sommerlad, 1994b), and through a critique of the academic rationalisation of the concept in the work of Hakim (1995).

A longstanding response by employers to the charge that there exist glass ceilings to female career progression is that occupational segmentation of any kind is not a consequence of structural discrimination but rather a rational preference on the part of the discriminated. This explanation is sometimes related to the tendency to 'choose' (what have become) less prestigious specialisms, but is most frequently utilised in connection with career breaks for child-rearing. One employer therefore ascribed the continuing large-scale exit of female solicitors from private practice to 'nature - women bear children and men do not'. In 1995 the Law Society President reacted to survey evidence of slow female career progression with a denial that this was in any way indicative of discrimination, remarking instead that 'it is a fact that many women solicitors do ... put their families before their careers' (Ward, 1995). Hence, as Menkel-Meadow has argued, 'women are perceived as 'opting-out' without any examination of whether the work structure has within it impediments or obstacles that preordain the outcome' (1989, p.217).

Both in 1990 and 1994, employers tended to place all responsibility for their career patterns onto female solicitors. For example, in 1990 one employer stated that women had 'difficulty in long term planning caused by lack of ability to give total commitment to the career'. Commitment was named, by virtually all employers in both surveys, as *the* principal criterion both for selection for employment and for partnership. Furthermore, the central importance of commitment to professional inclusion and progression was confirmed by all three categories of female lawyers, in whose responses the term repeatedly surfaced. For instance, a returner argued that 'there should be understanding that just because you have children does not mean that you lack commitment'. Women who had never taken a career break noted that 'a request for a career break is seen to be a lack of commitment', and another observed that career breaks are viewed as 'a sign of a lack of commitment (the death knell)'.

The continuous need to demonstrate commitment also clearly affected employee behaviour. Many women referred to the need to obtain promotion or partnership before having children, because even if only a short maternity leave was taken, the perception of increased domestic commitment would inevitably harm career prospects. Part-time returners reported working regular and extensive overtime, partly because of pressure to prove their commitment. Thus, one commented: 'I am taken by those with whom I do not work closely to be giving less than a full commitment to the firm'. Another explained: 'it is very easy to feel that you have to do a full-time job in part-time hours ... difficult not to feel guilty about being part-time and feel as though you have to prove your seriousness about the job by over-committing yourself'.

Although professional fragmentation has resulted in an extremely varied demand side of the legal labour market (Flood, 1996), giving women a variable range of career possibilities and barriers, my research findings indicated similarities throughout the different variants of legal firm (for an international comparison, Thornton, 1996). However, it became clear that the larger commercial firms may be viewed as paradigmatic of the new approach to women solicitors. Hantrais and Walters (1994) have noted a connection between the rapid growth of such firms and the increased numbers of female solicitors. In my survey, such firms tended to be both the biggest employers of women and those most likely to shed women once they had family commitments.[1] In the words of one female respondent: 'all big firms have the reputation of being real hard nosed bastards - if you're a woman with children you don't have a hope in hell with them'.

Hakim's work on employment, referred to above, gives academic respectability to the employer perspective on commitment and choice. Her approach is firmly located in the 'rational choice' model. Indeed, rather than viewing occupational segregation as an aspect of structural discrimination, she argues that it 'has been reconstructed in the late twentieth century to provide separate occupations and jobs for women following the marriage career, which allows only non-committed contingent work and non-career jobs which are always subordinate to non-market activities' (1995, p.450). The concept of commitment is fundamental to Hakim's argument: 'criticisms of labour market discrimination as unfair and unjustified often rest on claims that ... women workers are just as commited, dedicated, hard-working and productive as men'. Hakim proceeds to argue that in reality there exist significant gender differences in the concept of commitment, which emerge particularly clearly with part-time workers: 'the commitment of a part-time worker to a part-time job is not equal to the commitment of a full-time worker to a full-time job. At the minimum, the two levels of commitment differ in degree, and arguably they differ qualitatively as well' (1995, p.434).

Despite the centrality of commitment to Hakim's work, there is no formal definition of the term. As I indicated in the introduction to this chapter, the very indeterminacy of 'commitment' is one of its most important features. In practice, Hakim, like the employers surveyed, sees commitment as coterminous with extensive working hours. However, the number of hours is not an objective measure across occupations or even employment sites: it clearly varies according to the cultural norms of the profession and of the particular firm.

A Critique of 'Commitment'

In this section I will consider this ideological construct of 'commitment': first in terms of its own logical inconsistencies; secondly by reviewing the alternative models of professional commitment, before finally theorising the use of commitment as a gendered device for social closure.

First, Hakim's measure of work commitment is unidimensional and based on a single question concerning desire to work in the absence of financial necessity (1995, p.435). Arguing from data which actually proves little gender difference between full-time workers, she claims that the demonstrated gender difference between the total populations of men and women are significant in looking at gendered attitudes to work. It could be argued that the findings are at least equally significant in measuring men's commitment to home, but clearly the gendered construction of the relationship between private and public spheres is accepted as a given.

Secondly, Hakim relies heavily of the views of employers about the 'instability' of women part-time workers, views echoed in my own research, and fails to examine the way in which the attitudes of employers are crucial determinants in the career decisions of employees. My own research provides clear evidence that employers' views result in a deterioration of working conditions and career prospects, which in turn contributes to women's so-called 'employment instability'.

Thirdly, the use of a single measure fails to encompass the *quality* of commitment offered by employees, which may also be gendered. A more exhaustive analysis of commitment than that offered by Hakim relates it to the 'unique constellation of (professional) traits' (Kaldenberg *et al.*, 1995, p.1359). Kaldenberg's study of dentists has approached the concept in terms of behavioural and affective commitment. Behavioural commitment is interpreted as the investment of a 'limited resource (money, time) ... in pursuit of an end' and is found to vary according to gender, largely because such an investment may be 'credited to several different ends' (1995, p.1372). The result is that the male work role is perceived as an aspect of the familial role, whereas in the case of women, such a work role is perceived as competitive with their ('natural') familial role. This was also a finding of Seron and Herris's work on law firms in the USA (1995).

In contrast to behavioural commitment, affective commitment represents a 'moral involvement to abstract principles'. The research of Kaldenberg *et al.* found that 'females are spending less time doing professional work than men, but tend not to differ from them in their attitudes about work. Likewise, females show less behavioural professional commitment than men, but do not differ from men in affective commitment' (1995, p.1373).[1]

The female respondents to my survey did appear to share a more generalised, altruistic notion of service and of commitment to the client in comparison to the responses of men I have surveyed. This was also the finding of a recent Policy Studies Institute survey of law students which reported that women were more concerned than men about the value of legal work to the community and that conversely men were more interested in their potential salary and the status of the job (Halpern, 1994, pp.59-60).

Finally, in an illustration of Marks' study of the stresses induced by multiple roles (1977), which noted that commitment in one field did not inevitably produce a lesser commitment in another, the majority of female respondents did not accept the orthodox construction of commitment as a finite quality. Most part-timers surveyed viewed themselves as just as commited as their colleagues. Given the obstacles of returning to practice (which frequently include the need for lengthy and expensive retraining), the generally lowly pay, status and prospects on return and the problems of combining domestic and work responsibilities - generally without the back-up of a 'wife' - it could be inferred that the commitment to, and interest in, work exhibited by a returning solicitor must match, if not exceed, that of the full-time solicitor who has never taken a break (Hagan and Kay, 1995, pp.153, 185). Furthermore, far from part-time work indicating a lack of commitment, 40 per cent of such returners stated that they still aspired to partnership. This conclusion is confirmed by Hagan and Kay's findings, especially with regard to women who return to full-time practice (1995). They found that role diversity in fact enhanced rather than diminished 'life experience', and that 'women who have children and continue to work full-time in private practice do not lose their commitment to their work, and they are often more satisfied with their work and happier with their personal lives' (1995, p.187).

The results of my study amongst others (*c.f.* Brannen and Moss, 1991) indicates that participation in the public world requires such exclusion of the private during the hours worked that rather than domestic commitments taking precedence over, and thereby reducing, professional commitment, the reverse is frequently the case. Many women returners claimed that such were the demands of work, and such was the pressure to demonstrate commitment, that to participate at all as a professional meant a continual relegation of the needs of the family: 'the extra hours were severely detrimental to me and to my daughter and eventually caused me to leave altogether'.

Commitment as Social Closure

The empirical evidence from my research, discussed below, indicates that this open-ended and ambiguous notion of 'commitment' is a central, if unwritten, term of the contract for the legal profession today. This contract is, however, not a neutral contract between two parties with equal power; it is profoundly gendered. Pateman's discussion of the sexual contract (1988), which is also cited in Thornton's discussion of women in the Australian legal profession (1996, pp.26-7), unmasks liberal contractarianism as constructed by and for men. In Pateman's view, women were excluded from the 'original contract' which formed the basis of the move from the world of status and the establishment of civil, contractarian society.

However, women *do* participate in civil society, and their participation, for Pateman, requires that they 'acknowledge the political fiction (of the original contract) and speak the language even as the terms of the original pact exclude them from the fraternal conversation' (1988, p.221). The relevance of Pateman's argument for the micro-world of legal practice is striking, and corresponds to the observations of many commentators in this field. For instance, Epstein, in her discussion of women lawyers in the USA, writes: 'there is a focus on women's family responsibilities which highlights 'difference', both biological ... and ideological (because there is a consensus that it is women's main responsibility to assume primary care of infants) ... problems are considered 'women's problems' and not family or social problems, and ... most women accept these role designations' (1991, pp. 332-3).

The construction of the ideology and material reality of professionalism is thus simultaneously antagonistic to and dependent on the social construction of the domestic sphere and of women. If women are to engage in this world, the terms of the contract into which they enter, whilst apparently neutral, are constructed on the apparent 'separateness' of these spheres, and, hence, of the distinctive and subordinated nature of women. Women legal practitioners therefore experience a complex form of exploitation. Female solicitors, if employees, are of course subject to this subordination, but their subjection is increased by the fact that the terms of that nominally free agreement have been written by and for men. Moreover the terms of the agreement have been constructed on the understanding that the male parties will have entered into what Becker saw as a 'long term contract', involving specialisation by women in 'domestic activities', in exchange for protection by their husbands 'against abandonment and other adversities' (1981, p.14). The resulting, specifically gendered subjection is then intensified, since, in order to demonstrate conformity with its terms women must, 'give sustained evidence, not required of men, of being prepared to fit their domestic and family life to the demands of the job'(Hantrais and Walters, 1994, p.29).

In general, in order to 'prove themselves ... [women] had to work harder and perform better than men in similar situations' (Caplow and Scheindlin, 1990, p.423). Bourdieu's concept of 'cultural capital' (1977, 1984) provides the conceptual link between women's skills and qualities, and their treatment in a gendered labour market. For Bourdieu, the concept of cultural capital implicitly postulates a differential valorisation, not just of the formal 'skills' and qualifications which are generally understood to be embraced by the term 'human capital', but also of other forms of 'practical knowledge' or 'knowing how things are done' which govern the distributions of rewards, the signs of eligibility for patronage, of 'background' or informal special languages and work-related behaviour. Hagan and Kay have utilised the concept in their study of women lawyers in Canada, since they note that 'because legal education and experience are grounded so heavily in cultural symbols, this kind of human capital also contains elements of cultural capital. Nontechnical social and symbolic assets constitute further forms of cultural capital 'that in legal practice include client relations and professional reputations' (1995, p.29). Cultural capital cannot be accumulated simply through formal study, but requires participation in complex forms of socialisation and 'initiation rites' (and it could be argued that this is the primary function of the traditional 'articles' and pupillage).[2] Exactly what will constitute 'cultural capital' in 'modern' or 'post-modern' contexts however is not fixed (Halford and Savage, 1995). Women's attempts to conform to a norm may be outflanked, especially where the yardstick is a concept like 'commitment'. In the words of one female respondent: 'you don't know what you have to do and they milk the situation for all it's worth, so partnership is dangled in front of you but you don't know how to achieve it, all you know is that you must show mega-commitment, so it makes you work very hard, especially since there's so much competition'.

Whilst credentialist strategies of exclusion have been countered by women's success in obtaining good results in their degrees and in the Legal Practice Course, and women entrants to the profession are employed in equal numbers to men (Skordaki, 1996), collectivist, gendered criteria of exclusion continue to operate at different points in their career paths. In addition to demonstrating professionalism through 'commitment', women's career trajectory must conform to the so-called 'golden pathway' (Davies and Rosser, 1987). Even then, the symbiotic relationship between the sexual and employment contracts means that only a limited number of women may be absorbed either on a long term basis, or into the higher strata of the profession. The participation of large numbers of women as permanent members of the professional workforce would require, as the data below will indicate, radical changes in professional culture, such as a challenge to fundamental patriarchal relations.

The Patriarchal Character of 'Commitment'

One of the principal ways in which it is recognised that commitment may be established is through working very long hours, and the vast majority of respondents, whether full or part-time, claimed to work regular and lengthy over-time.[3] One respondent wrote: 'some partners seem to literally spend all their time here - they really put the firm before anything else and I suppose you have to have that attitude to be equity partners, especially in certain departments; in fact of course assistants put in those hours as well; working in that way is viewed as a desirable ideal'.

Women in my sample challenged the economic rationalisation for long hours.[4] Many noted the fallacy of relating the quality of work done to the length of hours worked, and part-timers in particular argued that they were more efficient: 'with part-timers you tend to really put your back into it - you're enthusiastic to shift the stuff in the 2 days which you do'. A handful of managing partners also dismissed the orthodoxy. For instance, one argued that 'people who are longest in the office have the lowest measurable rates of performance - long hours can be used to mask a great deal'.

Others attacked the opposition to career breaks and part-time working and pointed to the damage done to business by frequent staff turnover, and the financial loss incurred by losing expensively trained staff. Perhaps most telling of all, were the criticisms of the orthodoxy on part-time partnerships. For example, one woman wrote: 'if you put in less time, get less share of the equity - no reason then why part-time partnership shouldn't be possible - of course it's not, because of the usual male prejudice'. The strength of this argument is revealed by the existence of only a handful of part-time female partners in the survey, one of whom worked in commercial law - precisely the specialism generally held to require specific attributes and a level of commitment which neither women nor those with caring responsibilities could possibly deliver. The specifically gendered character of opposition to part-time work was revealed by the comments of one managing partner who wrote that his practice would contemplate a part-time partnership but only in respect of 'early retirers or for health reasons. We don't feel that there is the same commitment from a 'family' part-timer'.

In addition to the function of long hours in simply excluding women with domestic commitments from the profession, the nature of the activities occupying the surplus hours is also functional to the patriarchal structure of the labour market. As Thornton found in Australia, the getting of business (or 'practice development' as it is referred to in the U.K.) is built around male networking (1996, p.181), and the culture of fraternity or 'mateship' (1996, p.173). One woman explained that it was the 'responsibility of all solicitors to go and get work - to cultivate clients - to do entertaining'. Furthermore, a managing partner specified a commitment to this sort of work as the primary criterion for partnership: 'you must get yourself known amongst accountants, bankers etc - meet with them socially ... there are clubs, associations which we join' (Epstein, 1981). One female respondent explicitly commented on this complete integration for the male of his social and work world: 'females in this firm tend not to generate the same fees as men because they tend to separate friendship and business - but men do tend to generate business from friends - it's an entirely different approach'.

The combination of the need to put in long hours in the office, a need which has greatly increased in commercial work as a result of globalisation and technological developments (Flood, 1996), and the requirements to adopt a complementary social life translates into a demand for near total availability and flexibility.

Correspondingly, it is clear that commitment as currently understood is generally incompatible with a lower level of availability: 'part-time partnerships should be possible but not here. You have to look at the clients we serve as well. They wouldn't contemplate part-time Partners because they work like that (i.e. long hours) too and they expect it from the solicitors. Most of the clients are men' (respondent in a commercial firm).

Long hours are, therefore, iconic: an essential element in the perpetuation of 'colleagueship', and hence of the 'boys' club'; a device to ensure conformity to this professional model of masculinity. Thus one woman commented: 'there is this macho 'I'm working all these hours and look what a clever boy I am' attitude'. A male solicitor who had deliberately changed from being a high-flyer in the corporate department of a large firm to doing a back seat research job remarked: 'I am regarded as a lesser being than I was before. If I were to cut my hours further (currently 8.30-5.30) then I really would be finished. I can only go so far in trying to step outside the culture; below a certain number of hours you are no longer a professional'.

The current conceptualisation of professional commitment is therefore integral to the construction and perpetuation of professional norms, and of male solidarity, and its most concrete manifestation is an absence of domestic commitments. In this sense, then, whilst a culture which persistently excludes good, expensively trained staff may be attacked on the grounds of making poor business sense, its derivation from the wider patriarchal culture to which most of its clients belong, will make it rational in another sense.

The Illusion of Choice

The current inflexibility of labour market conditions and their predication on traditional gender roles severely circumscribes the choices available to women in numerous ways, ultimately reducing them to whether or not to have children (Podmore and Spencer, 1987). As Arber and Ginn have noted: 'the persistence of male economic advantage in the public sphere is magnified in the family, reinforcing the ideology of women's subordination. There is a reciprocal relation between the labour market and the family, with women's economic disadvantage in the labour market influencing their domestic role in the family, which in turn reduces women's ability to participate to their full in the public sphere' (1995, p.40). For Brannen and Moss this is partly achieved by the complementary construction of gender identities in both the home and workplace (1991, p.6). Thus the workplace is constructed by patriarchy as an exclusive arena in which a choice has to be made between home and work; male solicitors then ascribe to women the desire to (ultimately) place their career second, whatever the evidence, and as a result consider them less commited. This is then tested by an environment which makes such an outcome virtually inevitable.

The research data cited above therefore indicates that there is in effect no choice open to women lawyers who wish to have children, because the (covert) definition of professional commitment is *the* fundamental contract term and it is the obverse of domestic commitment. Effectively, the measure of a woman's commitment to work is simultaneously a measurement of men's commitment to the home. Thus, Dixon and Seron's study of lawyers in New York found that women with children were considered to be 'unstable professionals', and revealed that parental status had 'a significantly different effect for men and women ... men's income goes up and women's income goes down with the presence of children' (1991). Consequently, the assumption of domestic commitments provides indisputable evidence of disloyalty or of a lack of commitment, vindicating previous comments on the pointlessness of training women in the first place.

The professional boundaries have been altered in as much as women can possess commitment to a limited degree if young and childless, in which case their availability is still of a kind distinct from their male counterpart, as it tends to become tinged with sexual availability. Many women, and especially those with commercial practices which required a lot of practice development with an overwhelmingly male corporate clientele, spoke of the pressure to 'look the part'; 'you have to be attractive in this firm'. Another spoke of the 'ambiguity' involved in many of the social interactions with male clients. In other words, a prominent aspect of the cultural capital of female solicitors at the early stage of their career will be their sexuality (Adkins, 1995). Later on, if, as women with children, they choose to continue to offer full professional commitment this is likely to be disallowed because it is incompatible with the sexual role stereotypes on which system is based, both conceptually and empirically. A woman returner with many years of legal practice outlined the various forms this attitude could take:

> There are Partners like * who've had wives who've devoted themselves to supporting their husband's career and who don't seem to envisage that women should do anything else, and then there's what was said to me by the senior Partner at * 'my view is that women should be at home with their children'... that attitude is still prevalent ... *'s attitude was more subtle, paternalist. In a discussion regarding my career aspirations ... I was told that because I had young children they were not happy with me doing the long hours required, and that they only wanted partners who could do very long hours.

Comments reported by other women are further illustrative of the point: 'I was told 'mothers should be at home with their children'; 'The attitude is that women should be pregnant and in the kitchen ...'; whilst the managing partner of one large commercial firm (a father of 3 young children who worked a 70 hour week) explained that one solicitor would not succeed because 'she was trying to do too much - she was trying to combine the roles of fee-earner, mother, wife'. Women's choices are constrained by men's view of their appropriateness, as well as a structure which makes only certain choices possible.

Conclusion

Historically, women solicitors have exhibited a belief in the impartiality of the legal labour market and have demanded equality of treatment rather than 'special favours'. To this end they have heavily invested in human capital. Their experience of legal practice, however, reveals that while their entry has wrought changes in the legal profession, the patriarchal discourse on professional work and sex roles has remained fundamentally unchanged.

In classical liberal discourse, the relationship between capital and labour is represented as resting on free contracts between rational, sovereign individuals; commitment and choice are essential components of this apparently neutral discourse. But commitment may be translated as loyalty to the employer, and in the legal labour market this tends to mean rigid conformity with a professional model which is based on an absolute exclusion of other commitments. On closer examination it can be found to indicate a way of life in which the public and private worlds are in fact almost entirely integrated for the male, in that commitments in the private world, social, and at times domestic, serve the public. Thus, one woman solicitor talked of the way 'business is done - for instance while drinking in bars, being part of the rotary club - probably even making deals in the gents loo'. This way of life entails, and indicates, total commitment as its understanding of domestic commitment is as another component in an integrated, complementary life style. Hence, another female solicitor spoke of the use of the wife in the forging of the successful career.

In comparison, the archetypal female career can rarely achieve such complementarity, but will generally be characterised by charges of a 'commitment deficit'. However, the construction of women's professional behaviour as indicative of a lack of commitment, and as representing an exercise of free choice rests on many highly contested positions. For instance, it accepts, the distinction between, and separation of, the labour market and the domestic relations which sustain participation in that market. Secondly, it assumes and naturalises a dominant domestic role for the woman, following childbirth, whatever her stated preferences. Thirdly, the employers' views of the qualifying conditions for labour market participation are treated uncritically. Finally, it is predicated on the neutrality of 'commitment' and 'choice', whilst in fact, as two of the key concepts which articulate the relationships between individuals and the labour market, they ineluctably construct the professional subject as male.

Notes

1. Similar findings were made by Brown, Curran and Cousins (1983) which, utilising the distinction between expressive and intrinsic rewards to test commitment, found both types of employment orientations equally present amongst men and women.
2. In this context it is interesting to note work which has pointed to the prevalence of 'intangible' discrimination: Laband and Lenz, in their work on North American lawyers, found that 'Male associates may be invited out to social functions by the partners more frequently than female associates. There may be a greater tendency for partners to interact with male associates on a first name basis, than they do with female associates. Not doubt the number of *mans* on which these forms of subtle discrimination may occur is very large' (1992, p.249).
3. Again, working extended hours is clearly a feature of lawyers' lives in many other jurisdictions; for instance, see Mossman (1994) on the situation in Canada; Seron and Ferris (1995) on the United States.
4. See Halford and Savage's discussion of professional masculinity and economic rationality (1995).

Bibliography

Adkins, L. (1995), *Gendered Work*, Open University Press, Milton Keynes.

Arber, S. and Ginn, J. (1995), 'The mirage of gender equality: occupational success in the labour market and within marriage', *British Journal of Sociology*, vol. 46, pp. 21-43.

Becker, G. (1981), *A Treatise on the Family*, Harvard University Press, Cambridge, Mass.

Bourdieu, P. (1977), *Outline of a Theory of Practice*, Cambridge University Press, Cambridge.

Bourdieu, P. (1984), *Distinction: a social critique of the Judgement of Taste*, Harvard University Press, Cambridge, Mass.

Brannen, J. and Moss, P. (1991), *Managing Mothers*, Unwin Hyman, London.

Brown, R., Curran, M. and Cousins, J. (1983), 'Changing Attitudes to Employment', *Department of Employment Research Paper*, No 40, H.M.S.O., London.

Burrage, M. (1996), 'From a gentleman's to a public profession: status and politics in the history of English solicitors', *International Journal of the Legal Profession*, vol. 3, pp. 45-81.

Caplow, S. and Scheindlin, S. (1990), 'Portrait of a Lady: the woman lawyer in the 1980s', *New York Law School Law Review*, vol. 35, pp. 391-446.

Cunningham, J. (1995), 'Women: should a groper get his hands on the Law Society', *The Guardian*, 10 July.

Davies, C. and Rosser, J. (1987), 'A male pathway unwilling to bend', *The Health Service Journal*, 5 February, pp. 158-9.

Dixon, J. and Seron, C. (1991), 'Lawyers in Love: Labor Market Segmentation and the effects of family status on the earnings of male and female lawyers' (unpublished manuscript).

Epstein, C. F. (1981), *Women in Law*, Basic Books, New York.

Epstein, C. F. (1991), 'Faulty Framework: consequences of the difference model for women in the law', *New York Law School Law Review*, vol. 35, pp. 309-336.

Flood, J. (1996), 'Megalawyering in the global order: the cultural, social and economic transformation of global legal practice', *International Journal of the Legal Profession*, vol. 3, pp. 169-214.

Galanter, M. (1983), 'Mega-Law and Mega-Lawyering in the Contemporary United States', in R. Dingwall and P. Lewis (eds.), *The Sociology of the Professions*, MacMillan Press, London.

Gilligan, C. (1982), *In a Different Voice: Psychological Theory and Women's Development*, Harvard University Press, Cambridge.

Hagan, J. and Kay, F. (1995), *Gender in Practice: A study of lawyers' lives*, Oxford University Press, New York.

Hakim, C. (1995), 'Five feminist myths about women's employment', *British Journal of Sociology*, vol. 45, pp. 429-456.

Halford, S. and Savage, M. (1993), 'Restructuring Organisations, Changing People: Gender and Restructuring in Banking and Local Government', *Work, Employment and Society*, vol. 9, pp. 97-122.

Halpern, D. (1994), *Entry into the Legal Professions*, The Law Society, London.

Hantrais, L. and Walters, P. (1994), 'Making it in and Making out: women in professional occupations in Britain and France', *Gender, Work and Organisation*, vol. 1, pp. 23-32.

Kaldenberg, D.O., Becker, B.W. and Zvonkovic, A. (1995), 'Work and Commitment among Young Professionals: A study of male and female dentists', *Human Relations*, vol. 48, pp. 1355-1377.

Kanter, R.M. (1977), 'Some effects of proportions on group life: skewed sex ratios and responses to token women', *American Journal of Sociology*, vol. 82, pp. 965-990.

Laband, D. and Lentz, B. (1992), 'Is there sex discrimination in the legal profession? Further evidence on Tangible and Intangible margins', *The Journal of Human Resources*, vol. XXVIII, pp. 230-258.

Lewis, V. (1997), *Trends in the Solicitors' Profession: Annual Statistical Report 1996*, The Law Society, London.

MacKinnon, C. (1987), *Feminism Unmodified: discourses on life and law*, Harvard University Press, London.

Marks, S. R. (1977), 'Multiple roles and role strain: some notes on human energy, time and commitment', *American Sociological Review*, vol. 42, pp. 921-936.

McConville, M., Hodgson, J., Bridges, L. and Pavlovic, A. (1994), *Standing Accused: The Organisation and Practices of Criminal Defence Lawyers in Britain*, Clarendon Press, Oxford.

Menkel-Meadow, C. (1989), 'Feminisation of the Legal Profession: The Comparative Sociology of Women Lawyers', in R. Abel and P. Lewis (eds.), *Lawyers in Society: Comparative Theories*, University of California Press, Berkeley.

Mossman, M.J. (1994), 'Lawyers and Family Life: New directions for the 1990s (Part One)', *Feminist Legal Studies*, vol. 2, pp.61-82.

Murray, G. (1987), 'Women Lawyers in New Zealand: Some questions about the politics of equality', *International Journal of the Sociology of Law*, vol.15, pp. 439-457.

New Ways to Work (1993), *Change at the Top; Working Flexibly at senior and managerial levels in organisations*, National Westminster Bank, London.

Pateman, C. (1988), *The Sexual Contract*, Polity Press, Oxford.

Podmore, D. and Spencer, A. (1982), 'The Law as a sex-typed profession', *Journal of Law and Society*, vol. 9 (1), pp. 21-36.

Seron, C. and Ferris, K. (1995), 'Negotiating Professionalism', *Work and Occupations*, vol. 22, pp. 22-48.

Sidaway, J. (1995), 'Gender and Status in the private practice firm', in *Removing the Barriers: Legal Services and the Legal Profession*, Proceedings of the Annual Research Conference of the Law Society, The Law Society, pp. 77-81.

Skordaki, E. (1996), 'Glass slippers and glass ceilings: women in the legal profession', *International Journal of the Legal Profession*, vol. 3, pp. 7-43.

Sommerlad, H. (1994a), 'The myth of feminisation: women and cultural change in the legal profession', *International Journal of the Legal Profession*, vol. 1, pp. 31-53.

Sommerlad, H. (1994b), 'Issues in the retention of women solicitors: a regional study', unpublished report prepared for the Law Society by Leeds Metropolitan University.

Sommerlad, H. (1995), 'Managerialism and the legal profession: a new professional paradigm', *International Journal of the Legal Profession*, vol. 2, p.159.

Sommerlad, H. and Allaker, J. (1991), 'Retrieve or retain: training for women returners to private practice', unpublished report prepared for The Law Society by Leeds Metropolitan University.

Sommerlad, H. and Sanderson, P. (forthcoming 1997), *Gender, Choice and Commitment: A study of women lawyers*, Trentham, Stoke.

Thornton, M. (1996), *Dissonance and Distrust: Women in the Legal Profession*, Oxford University Press, Melbourne.

Walby, S. (1990), *Theorising Patriarchy*, Basil Blackwell, Oxford.

Ward, S. (1995), 'Law Society chief strikes new blow in battle of sexes', *The Guardian*, 21 October.

Witz, A. (1992), *Professions and Patriarchy*, Routledge, London.

2. (Un)Sexy Bodies: The Making of Professional Legal Masculinities

RICHARD COLLIER

Introduction

This chapter is an attempt to understand the 'making of men' as legal 'professionals' - as practising lawyers and legal academics. The specific focus is the representation and reproduction of a range of categories of masculine (specifically heterosexual) subjectivities in this field. It is, in short, about the changing relationship between cultures of masculinity and the formation of men's 'professional' identities as 'lawyers'. Theoretically, it is concerned to explore what insights, if any, may be derived from recent scholarship on the relationship between identity, subjectivity and corporeality when seeking to re-conceptualise what has for some time, and from different perspectives, been identified to be the distinctly 'masculine' cultures of legal education and practice.

Far from conceptualising Woman as 'Other' to a masculine (legal) norm, therefore, this chapter seeks to unpack the nature of the 'norm' - the 'masculinism' of law - via an exploration of the ways in which sexed subject positions are held at particular moments and locations to be 'masculine'. I am concerned with the ways in which the 'taking up' (however insecurely or momentarily) of specific identities constituted as masculine play out in terms of, and depends upon, a systematic negation of men's corporeality. This project will involve disturbing and fragmenting a range of binary divisions (such as man/woman, hetero/homosexual, public/private) which continue to pervade representations of the masculinism of law and legal culture. Indeed, the chapter argues that the underlying conceptualisation of the relationship between masculinities, law and men's subjectivity within a body of scholarship concerned with women's position in the legal profession has itself been constituted in a way which has, ironically given its political intent, made it difficult to theorise how 'change' might be achieved in this area. In rendering social, accountable and contingent both the corporeality and behaviour of men - what men *do*, as opposed to the qualities of an abstracted signifier of their gender ('masculinity') - this chapter seeks to re-configure the relationship between the legal profession and men's 'identity', understood here as a social construction involving:

> ... a process of exclusion, negation and repression ... a process which, even if successful, results in an identity intrinsically unstable. This is bad news for masculinity one of whose self-conceptions is stability, and whose function is to maintain it socially and psychically (Dollimore, 1986, pp.6-7).

The legal profession has been depicted within a range of feminist scholarship as the apotheosis of a cultural field in which rationality, neutrality, competitiveness and authority are seen as distinctively masculine qualities. As such, the social and psychical consequences of this disavowal of the inherent instability of masculine identity are, for men and women, far reaching. In seeking to unsettle culturally encoded categories of masculinity, sex and gender this chapter is ultimately concerned to re-conceptualise the social practices of law as, I shall suggest, 'masculinising agencies'. In so doing it is my aim to 'name men as men' (Collinson and Hearn, 1994) in the legal profession.

A number of themes and issues organise the following discussion and the chapter is divided into three main parts. The first seeks to unpack the ways in which the male body has been conceptualised within a strand of feminist scholarship concerned to challenge the masculinism of legal culture. The second explores the iconography of men's legal 'professionalism' via an engagement with the masculine body 'at work' and the relationship between men, child care and conceptions of 'parenting' and 'career success'. The third and final section is an exploration of the ways in which shifting organisational/institutional, social, economic and cultural contexts are at present re-configuring the subject positions available to men in the legal profession. Conclusions address what some of the implications of this shift within the theoretical framework in which masculinity is conceptualised might be for seeking to understand and bring about change in gender relations in the legal profession.

Re-Framing the 'Problem' of 'Women and Law': Identity, Corporeality and the Sexed Male Body

That a correlation exists between the characteristics of 'masculinity' and the ethos, organisation and skills associated with law and legal practice has historically been central to feminist engagements with law, at the level of both theoretical jurisprudential scholarship and with regard to 'practical' interventions designed to undermine, and challenge, the 'masculinism of law' (Thornton, 1996a; Smart, 1995, 1989; O'Donovan, 1985). In each of the 'three phases' of feminist jurisprudence identified by Naffine (1990), for example, an engagement with masculinity is seen as inseparable from the critique of law. Be it in relation to liberal legal strategies promoting 'equality', 'radical' feminist articulations of the power of law and men as commensurate; through to recent postmodern encounters with legal discourse and the sociality of the legal subject, the terms 'masculinity', 'masculinism' and the 'masculine' have come to signify a range of features deemed to be inimical to women's full participation in legal culture. Notwithstanding the considerable changes in the gender profile of the legal profession which have taken place over the last twenty years, both in Britain and elsewhere, the picture which has emerged from a now extensive body of feminist research is, across jurisdictions, one of a profession in which discrimination and inequality in the employment of women at the levels of recruitment, promotion and career advancement is commonplace (Thornton, 1996a, 1994; McGlynn, 1996; McGlynn and Graham, 1995; Sommerlad, 1994; Laband and Lenz, 1992; Podmore and Spencer, 1982; Wynn Davies, 1996). It is also one in which sexual harassment is pervasive.[1]

To describe and recount the existence of such treatment - which is explicitly, it must be remembered, about behaviour on the part of men - takes the analysis so far. Certainly, at the present moment in Britain the issue of 'women and the law' is a high-profile and contested political issue.[2] However a body of recent feminist research has sought to build on and develop this (initial) focus on 'describing' the features of women's treatment in legal profession by moving towards, instead, a conceptualisation of the *social dynamics* whereby discrimination is reproduced and legitimated on a daily basis in the field of law; in, that is, the 'everyday' interactions of men and women, men and other men.[3] This has entailed recourse to a theoretical framework in which 'Women' have been depicted as Other to the (masculine) norms of law. From this perspective, far from assuming that transformative change will follow women's 'acceptance' into law school and legal practice, it is the gendered encoding of social, cultural and symbolic capital within the legal field which is seen as resulting in the 'masculinist' character of a legal culture which, intimately intertwined with its functional and facilitative role in advanced capitalism, 'prevent[s] women from being regarded as authoritative members of the jurisprudential community to the same extent as their male counterparts' (Thornton, 1996b, p.2; *c.f.* Menkel-Meadow, 1986).[4] Traditional theories of human capital, hierarchy and structural organisational analyses, it is argued, have systematically failed to address the dimension of sex, gender and power which is, in contrast, central to the emerging scholarship (Thornton, 1996b, p.21).

By locating the legal field in the broader context of social, economic and cultural processes whereby men's discrimination is both reproduced and legitimated; a different set of issues and questions have emerged from those which frame the liberal-legal equality model (the following list is by no means exclusive). First, the concept of a 'masculine career mode' has been identified as, alongside the social structuring of child care in terms of sexual division, locating men as 'unencumbered' whilst confining women to the 'double-shift (the 'women don't have wives model': on lawyering and 'family life' see further, Mossman, 1994). Secondly, the related 'fastracking' of men legal academics and lawyers and 'feminisation' of bureaucratic environments has been seen as ascribing to women 'caring' (for example, pastoral) roles which, whilst crucial to promulgating an appearance of a humanising ethos within the workplace, nonetheless works against women in terms of career advancement (Sommerlad, 1994). Thirdly, and drawing on a phenomenon well-documented within the sociology of masculinity, the existence of homosocial bonds and cultures have been identified as excluding women and militating against women's progression in legal organisations (Bell, 1995; Collier, 1991; Thornton, 1989; on homosociality generally; Collier, 1995, pp.271-3; Lipman-Blumen, 1976; Ramazanogolu, 1987; Rogers, 1988); and fourthly, and I would argue, crucially, central to women's marginality has been seen to be the pervasive sexualising of women's corporeality in the workplace, resulting in a negation of women's authority and status as legitimate legal 'knowers' in the public domain; like nature, women by virtue of their sexed specificity are 'natural, marked by fecundity and growth ... apparently uncontrolled and uncontrollable' (McDowell, 1995, p.80).

In each of the above four areas, of course, *something* is being said about masculinity, the behaviour of men, the 'structured relations of hierarchic heterosexuality' (Hearn, 1987, p.114). Something is also being said, I now wish to argue, about the sexed specificity of men's bodies. In revealing the *sociality* of this 'imaginary' masculine ideal as a discursive construct, the ostensibly 'natural' quality of the subject to which women are constituted as Other - the actions of the 'benchmark man', the 'man of law', the *men* who act in discriminatory ways - has itself been rendered problematic. If women's corporeality has been sexualised in the workplace, what does this mean for the bodies of men?

In order to take the analysis further and develop an understanding of how the complex relationship between sex, gender and power in the legal profession is reproduced and played out, it is necessary to re-configure the sexed specificity of men's subjectivities in this specific organisational and institutional context. Institutions do not merely reflect a dominant sexual ideology; they are, crucially, sites for the active *production* of gender divisions. Indeed, what is presently emerging from the growing literature on the gendering of organisations and bureaucracy (e.g. Davies, 1996; Collinson and Hearn, 1996, 1994; Adkins, 1995) is the complexity of the processes whereby practices have been historically constituted through reference to a 'masculinist' vision of 'professional' work; and, inter alia, with the implications of this sexing of professionalism for women and, increasingly, for men (Collinson and Hearn, 1996). Notwithstanding contradictions, ambiguities and tensions in the process of their constitution, both law school and law firm can thus be seen as domains for the 'making' of professional legal masculinities. As 'deeply gendered and heterosexual regimes, [which] construct relations of domination and subordination' (Mac an Ghaill, 1994, p.4) they function to constitute and regulate, to varying degrees of, a range of subject positions available to men.

Such an engagement with the sexed specificity of men's subjectivities in the legal field is not possible without an adequate conceptualisation of the ways in which the *bodies* of men are 'sexed' as masculine in specific contexts (Waldby, 1995). Without, that is, an understanding of men's corporeality. To focus on the 'fictive feminine' and the 'imagined masculine' as cultural constructs in this way (Thornton, 1996a) is not to argue that 'real' men and women's bodies do not exist. It does not follow that sexual difference has no meaning. Rather, it is to valorise, rather than negate the processes whereby the (sexed) bodies of women and men are constituted at particular moments and contexts as having differential access to 'knowledge' resulting from their embodied social locations in a gendered world (Grosz, 1994, 1990; Gatens, 1996). Positioning within a particular gendered scene of vision does not mean that all men will necessarily have that vision. However, it does mean that, as men, a particular (but non-reductive) relationship will be established with cultures and discourses of masculinities. In the case of the legal field, as is clear from feminist research, the *potential* situations of men and women as legal professionals are different because of the ways in which the existing distribution of social, cultural and symbolic capital is configured. As such, the constitution of professional and suitably masculine bodies and subjectivities can be seen as important factors in the production and maintenance of normative constructs of social, economic and cultural capital which have, in turn, served to marginalise and discriminate against women both in the legal profession and, of course, in other areas of employment. Discrimination does not just 'happen'. It is a significance attached to the (inter)actions of sexed individuals in specific contexts.

In the following two sections of this chapter I shall explore the contours of the 'sexing' of men via reference to a range of representations of men as legal professionals. I shall seek to answer the following questions. How do these subject positions make claims to authority? How - as distinctly 'masculine' identities - are they empowered? The gendering of cultural, symbolic and economic capital in the legal field is secured, I shall argue, via a two-fold process involving, first, a dissociation of men from child care (premised on the public/private dualism); and, secondly, a 'de-sexing' of men's corporeality in such a way that rationality, authority, the capacity to be objective and distant, are each evoked as 'key' masculine qualities. If there is a recurring theme in what follows it is, we shall see, not so much the hegemony of one form of masculinity as the contingency, fragility and instability of ideas of the 'normal' male heterosexual identity in the first place; and, related to this, the sociality of those binaries (Murphy, 1996) which have been and remain central to (but unspoken of in) the debates around the masculinism of law.

'Men in Suits': Authority and Gendered Representations of Legal Professionalism

> Lawyers are their clothes, their offices, their stationery ... There is no getting away from the link between how lawyers look and their character as professional advisers (David Stuart, of design company The Partners, quoted in Fennell, 1996).

> Sitting across from a man in a business suit, it is as if they did not have a body at all, just a face and a voice (Charles Reich, quoted in Reynaud, 1983, p.24).

The gender regimes of both law school and legal practice are microcosms of broader employment structures in which a particular (hetero) familial frame ascribes social meanings in such a way that terms like 'career', 'parenting' or 'child care' become entwined within a dualism of sexual difference. Indeed, in different ways both the legal practice and legal academy associate public, visible displays of 'availability' to work long hours with an individual's personal commitment to the institution and development of an appropriate professional attitude. In the case of the legal practice the primary reduction of lawyer's work to an economic nexus involving a commodification of time, captured in the dominant culture of 'billing', can be seen as emblematic of a career structure in which success is premised on 'visible commitment' and 'paying dues' in the form of working long hours, been 'seen' to 'be there' (Sommerlad, 1994). This is a career structure with which legal academics are becoming increasingly familiar (Wills, 1996). Nonetheless, it is possible to identify distinct and revealing differences in the respective masculine 'styles' of the legal academy and practice in terms of their economic, ideological and political locations within advanced capitalist economies. It is, in particular, via reference to the cultural norms of the post-war business and corporate world (Roper and Tosh, 1991; Mort, 1996) that the professional style of the practising lawyer has been constituted. Yet the sexed specificity of this style has, in contrast to the growing literature on the corporeality of women in the profession, remained largely unexplored (on managerialism and masculinities generally see Collinson and Hearn, 1996). What I shall term the resulting 'de-sexing' of men's bodies in legal practice has been dependent, however, on certain deeply problematic assumptions.

To clarify; feminist scholarship has explored at some length the representation and regulation of disciplinary controls exerted over women's dress in legal practice and law school and the multifarious dimensions to the processes whereby women are regulated within parameters which constitute 'being feminine' as, per se, a sexualised state (Thornton, 1996a, pp.224-5). This, however, begs a number of questions about the status of 'being masculine'. Consider the following. If it is argued that women's bodies inappropriately 'eroticise' a courtroom, that women are tolerated in a rational space as legal professionals only if they consciously 'suppress' the 'feminine' 'non-rational elements perceived to be corrosive of legality' (Thornton, 1996a, pp.226-7), does this then mean that the 'masculine' body somehow 'naturally' embodies rationality, legality and order? If overt messages of corporeality suggest a woman's presence is eroticising an otherwise rational public sphere, what does this say about men's bodies? Does this mean that a courtroom consisting solely of men is without, or beyond, the erotic? Such an argument would presume, first, that intra-male relations are asexual (thus revealing the presumptive heterosexism which frames understanding of men's social relations: Edwards, 1990); and, secondly, that as 'sexed' beings, men's eroticism is confined to the private, affective sphere (in keeping with the depiction of men's 'unencumbered' relation to child care discussed above).

It is not simply that such an apparently rigid hetero/homo dualism sits uneasily with the existence of pervasive and well-documented homosociality within the legal world (see above). It also begs the question of why the maintenance of these dualisms should appear so central to securing the stability of the normative masculine subject in the first place. With this in mind, and in seeking to relate men's 'professional' 'asexuality' to the mobilisation of forms of cultural and symbolic capital as a *gendered* phenomena, what might the 'return of the feminine' mean for a male subject which has been encoded - by virtue of being male - as an authoritative subject within the legal field?

There exists considerable variation among men lawyers in term of their dress, style and deportment. In law, the worlds of the corporate commercial multi-national (Galanter, 1983), the high street practice and the legal aid firm are so different they belie the idea that the legal profession is a homogenous entity (Hagan and Kay, 1995; Cain and Harrington, 1994; Cain, 1994, esp. pp.26-7; Sugarman, 1994). For example, the 'aggressive masculinity' identified as informing social practices in corporate City firms, epitomised by 'tough' negotiating styles and excessive 'macho' behaviour (McDowell, 1995), appears qualitatively different to workplace cultures of High Street legal practice. There is, moreover, a great diversity to men's bodies. Different shapes, ages, ethnicities, class background and physical abilities all mark the body in different ways. The body 'at work' may also not be what it seems: behind the suit may lie transgression, in the form of tattooing, body piercing, a subject 'passing' as one thing but 'really' being another (Bell and Valentine, 1995). It is, notwithstanding the above however, possible to identify a broadly hegemonic masculine style which corresponds, by and large, with Connell's description of professionalism as a historically constituted form of masculinity:

> emotionally flat, centred on a specialist skill, insistent on professional esteem and technically based dominance over other workers, and requiring for its highest (specialist) development the complete freedom from child care and domestic work. (Connell, 1987, p.181; *c.f.* on 'the professions, the control of emotions and construction of masculinity', Hearn, 1987, ch.8).

It is, generally, the style of the corporate and business world and its central icon is the business suit.

This 'smart' or 'distinguished' outfit is neither complicated nor very varied, encompassing a two or three piece suit in a (very) dark colour, black or dark coloured shoes, a pale shirt, white, and more often or not, dull socks and underwear (Reynaud, 1983, p.23).[5] Thornton (1996a, p.223) similarly depicts the man in the dark suit, plain shirt and unostentatious tie as ' ... most commonly equated with the image of impersonal authority'. He is the epitome of Connell's disembodied, rational worker. In the organisational context of the legal profession, in which the marketing of personal attributes are widely seen as part of the product of good effective lawyering (the ability of interact with corporate clients for example), the wearing of the business suit does more than 'impersonalise' men's appearance. It serves the crucial function of de-sexualising the male body, not in the sense of rendering men in suits beyond erotic attachment (far from it) but rather in terms of erasing the sexed specificity of the individual male body. Whereas women lawyers, like other business and professional women, 'are expected to look like women - that is, *sexed* - although the code requires that they do not look *sexual*' (Thornton, 1996a, pp.226-7), men do not look 'sexed' for what is here considered to be 'sexual' would deflect from the establishment of authority. By constituting the wearing of the business suit as cultural and symbolic capital, the women lawyer can only be 'a pale copy of her male counterpart in both appearance and style' (Thornton, 1996a, p.223).

Such a regulation of feminine and masculine forms of embodiment does not just serve to maintain a traditional gender ordering in the workplace therefore. It also constitutes men, as paradigmatic agents of legality, as:

> a neutral conduit of legal knowledge. To obtrude one's bodily persona detracts from the neutrality, the objectivity, and the universality of law. The male body is invisible in the business suit that disguises both primary and secondary characteristics. And this body is normative within the public sphere, it has come to represent neutrality and *dis*embodiment (Thornton, 1996a, p.216).

This is a male bodily persona constituted as an authoritative 'knowing' subject. The man who speaks with a suit takes up a position of authority. The occasional (socially licensed) 'dressing down' simply betrays the hegemony of this cultural norm, particularly when it is itself institutionalised (for example in the form of 'Casual Fridays'). Men are 'seen' in the context of the business world by virtue of wearing a suit. To dress otherwise is, in a sense, not to be 'seen'. At the individual level it denotes maturity, progression and acceptance into the institutional/organisational norm. A senior colleague in my own institution, a University where dress codes might seem (on the surface a least) more liberal and relaxed than within the profession, made quite explicit his conscious choice, as his academic career progressed, that it would be appropriate for him to change his dress from the casual wear (corduroys, jumper) of his 'youthful' days to the regular wearing of the business suit. This was, he stated, the only way to be 'taken seriously' by the other (men) in positions of authority in the University. He 'felt more powerful, more authoritative' and responded to others accordingly. It is not by chance that comic figures wear bright, ill-fitting or stylistically archaic suits.

I am not arguing here that the processes whereby professional codes are inculcated into the young legal initiate work on a tabula rasa. The point is that men have *already* absorbed the messages and, importantly, appear able and willing to discipline themselves in terms of appropriately masculine dress, voice and authoritative demeanour. The male legal recruit faces few of the disciplinary twists and turns faced by the women legal initiate (Thornton, 1996a; Seron and Ferris, 1995). Notwithstanding the complex codes of manly aesthetics and the pervasive cultural commodofication of the male body which has marked advanced capitalism (Mort, 1996), it continues to be taken for granted that, at least in the business and corporate domain, the body is of 'secondary' importance. The suit enables the man's body to 'blend in to uniformity and to use dress as the symbol of his power ... Masculine elegance provides a good example of the way man asserts himself through standardisation and through control over his body' (Reynaud, 1983, p.22).

The degree to which men seek, consciously or unconsciously, to efface that which is culturally coded as feminine, with all its connotations of dependency and passivity, may relate to the contingencies of life-history. Certainly, it would seem the emotional costs of the 'high pressure' stressful career in law play out differently within and between the sexes.[6] Political persuasion, sexuality, physique and social background might each render individual men more or less comfortable accommodating the style of the 'benchmark man'. A man's voice which comports with a feminine standard (and is thus associated with homosexuality), for example, may also diminish his authority (Thornton, 1996a, p.221). Others, by virtue of race, ethnicity, education, accent or class may never be in the privileged position to face such decisions in the first place, having already been excluded as 'players' in the legal field. However, and notwithstanding the fact that men are thus also clearly disciplined by the regulatory codes of legal professionalism, men have available to them cultures of resistance to the dominant cultural norms of masculinity in the form of a range of material and discursive spaces which have been constituted within a social frame which ascribes to men, as men, social power. For example, as Thornton so forcefully argues, while men may display character traits of various degrees of 'unattractiveness' (for example, aggression, poor personal hygiene, few social skills, overbearing arrogance) these failings 'will rarely constitute an impediment to their becoming authoritative knowers: the parameters of public conduct have always been broader for men than women' (1994, p.62). There is also, she suggests, some evidence that regional dialects may be acceptable in men at executive levels but not for women. There is, in short, no one 'masculinity' of law but, rather, a rich diversity of subject positions. What is necessary at this stage is to explore what these masculinities may *share*.

Beyond the Frame of (Hetero) 'Masculinity': Change, Identity and Subjectivity in the Legal Profession

The ways in which the differential constitution of masculinities in specific contexts is informed by notions of race and ethnicity, and mediated by structures of class, sexuality and physical ability, has been well-documented (Connell, 1995). Indeed, in relation to the legal field the iconography of a legal system has historically been bound up with trappings of nationhood, empire and authority, the question of how distinctive 'English' ethnicity and sense of 'Englishness' fits into the complex configuration of inter-ethnic interpersonal relations in the contemporary legal profession is, I believe, relatively unexplored (Mac an Ghaill, 1994, p.85). What becomes clear at this point is not simply that the 'masculine culture' of law is heterogeneous; that there are, in fact, a plurality of *masculinities* in the legal profession. In order to challenge the continued presence of cultures and practices which are inimical to women's acceptance it is necessary to address what these diverse subjectivities share; and that is, I would suggest, a social positioning which, by virtue of being a sexed man, is constructed as having at least the potential to make claims to the status of 'authoritative knower' within this particular social field. This is not, as I have argued above, to claim that men inherently or necessarily embody, display or manifest the particular values society deems 'masculine'. It is, in support of Fineman (1994), to advance a methodology based on *sexual difference*; not by way of arguing that women and men are 'essentially' (biologically, reductively) different, but rather by way of seeking to ground men and women's gendered existences in a constitutive analysis of law and legal institutions. This project involves, crucially, disturbing the sociality and contingency of a masculinity/femininity binary which is 'not necessarily congruent with the sexed bodies of men and women but contingent' (Thornton, 1996b, p.5). It is, in other words, with the social construction of discourses of femininity(ies) and masculinity(ies) that we are concerned. In 'naming' the sociality of men's subjectivities is itself problematic in this regard it is possible to re-configure and move beyond the model of 'women and the law'.

Subject positions coded as 'masculine' ascribe to men certain qualities and, in so doing, replicate familiar dualisms associated with the masculine/feminine divide. It may be argued that individual women in the legal profession can be equally as competitive and ruthless, ambitious, self-seeking and careerist, as generally 'unpleasant' as the men with whom they work. That, however, would be to miss the point about *the ways in which* that which is constituted as cultural, economic and symbolic capital in the legal field has been constructed historically within an over-arching cultural frame which systematically privileges the values deemed masculine over the feminine. It is from an *already* empowered subject position that the claims to authority, and the power to judge the validity of the knowledges of others, is taken up and assessed. Feminist agendas, for example, may be conceptualised by men, who may or may not be generally sympathetic to feminism within the terms of 'a managerialist pedagogical frame with its emphasis on technicist explanations and solutions' (Mac an Ghaill, 1994, p.8). 'Sex/Gender' research in the legal academy may be supported instrumentally as 'good' in terms of Research Assessment. Sexual harassment and (un)equal opportunities in the profession are 'problems' which can be 'solved'.[7] The relation of the 'problem' to the material and discursive reproduction of a masculinist frame is, however, negated as an issue.

Heterosexual(ising) Subjectivities

The subjective empowerment of the masculine is illustrated by a consideration of what subject positions, whether in the domain of legal practice or the academy, share. The professional 'asexuality' depicted above has been constituted within a heterosexual frame (or 'heterosexual matrix': Butler, 1990) which represents a normative (hetero)masculinity as benchmark. The ways in which readings of the differential empowerment of men's subjectivities are understood, however, is profoundly disturbed once this over-arching frame of heterosexism, of 'playing it straight' (Nayak and Kehily, 1996), is disturbed. In terms of hierarchic heterosexuality, who cooks, cleans and *takes care of* the law firm Senior Partner who works a ninety hour week? Who is the primary child carer? One of the fundamental decisions facing women in the legal profession has been the question of how to balance a 'career' and child care (Thornton, 1996a). How is it that men lawyers become 'unencumbered' from such decisions? Why are our primary responses to each of the masculine typologies *not* 'but where are the children?' but rather some *other* assessment of 'masculine' status (authoritative demeanour, status, cultural confidence)? Each of these questions is framed by, and only makes sense in terms of, the dominant dualisms of sexual difference and heterosexuality, exemplified perhaps by the ways in which workplace social relations are frequently coded as familial or, rather, as a simulacrum, a perversion, of the familial 'proper'.

Naming the 'Other': The Mutual Constitution of Heterosexualities - Masculinities

A range of subject positions available to men make claims, albeit in different ways, to quite traditional notions of masculine authority. If they are familiar, it is because they register with our taken-for-granted assumptions about men, masculinities and gender relations. The ways in which they do so are more complex, and are encoded more ambiguously, than simply by reference to the hegemonic 'benchmark' masculinism of the 'man in a suit'. There is, importantly, more to power relations amongst hetero-males than straightforward hierarchies based on age, money, status and so forth. Central to their encoding as culturally 'masculine' is a notion of normative *heterosexuality*. What analysis of the heterosexist assumptions which frame their constitution reveals are two key discursive moves which, together, construct a resultant normative (hetero)masculinity via the hierarchical mapping of sexual difference and negation, the disavowal of that which would appear as Other (the feminine, the homosexual).

First, normative (hetero) masculinity is constituted on a foundational disavowal, a denial of the feminine and femininity which secures the dualism of sexual difference. Men are not like women. From this stems the mapping of what 'being a man' is which, we have seen, is subject to historical and cultural variation. It is 'not being womanly', not being 'sexed' in a culture which equates the feminine with the sexual and the masculine with rationality, reason and authority. It is this difference which produces dominance. Any 'crisis' engendered for men by women's participation in the legal profession results from women's increased presence in a public space of work from which, it is clear, women are not retreating but are, significantly, establishing their own professional and frequently powerful networks (Benoit-Scott, 1996). To reframe the question of gender and/in the legal profession as other than a 'woman's problem' is to ask *why* it should be that, for so many men, actually 'being' (working) in a social situation with women is considered 'not normal' and (for the individual man) psychologically problematic. Far from being a 'crisis' of masculinity, men generally are no longer in workplace environments which shore up, defend and fortify a picture of masculine subjectivity which had in any case been constituted in key respects as always *outside* the world men share with women and children; that is, as beyond the terms of the heterosexual frame in which men's relation to women's corporeality in the workplace continues to be bifurcated as either surrogate-familial (wife, daughter, partner, mother), or as sexual and sexualising Other, as essentially (sexed) Woman as opposed to (desexed) Man.

Secondly, and somewhat less explored, is the related negation of the homosexual alongside the profound privileging of the homosocial cultures and organisation. The legal field is structured internally in terms of power relations, not only between men and women, but also *between men*. The cultures of masculinity which have surfaced in work on 'women and the law' highlight, though they do not tend to analyse, the complex relation which exists between male hetero - and homo-sexualities. It is the taboo on homosexuality which informs and mediates much of intra-male social relations. Through a rich diversity of male homosocial heterosexual interactions a dominant masculinity is reproduced as the 'norm' to which men are held accountable, notwithstanding the considerable variation within individual conceptualisations of masculine subjectivities which depart from that norm (Bird, 1996, p.120). Nonetheless, and crucially, non-hegemonic masculinities fail to influence structural arrangements significantly because their expression is, as Bird (1996) argues, either relegated to heterosocial settings or else suppressed entirely.

The reason both women and homosexuals transgress the erotic norms of hetero-masculine culture relates, I have argued, to the fact that the heterosexual bodies of men have themselves been understood as, a priori, outwith, beyond, the sexual: as de-sexed, *dis*-embodied neutral conduits of authoritative knowledge: as *un*sexy bodies.[8] The erotic ambiguities of homosociality are thus effaced. In this respect, and in the context of the legal profession, the saturation of City workplaces and practices with heterosexist imagery and behaviour frame a conformity to heterosexual social practices which 'demand ... of women a physically impossible performance' (McDowell, 1995, p.75). They also, however, demand of men a watchful eye. Presumptions of heterosexism derive meaning through reference to a dualism of difference central to the articulation, reproduction and management of notions of a normative (hetero) masculinity. This is, however, as fluid, fragile and vulnerable as it is seemingly pervasive and all-encompassing. The benefits for men of identification with the dominant masculinity ' ... derive from the social power it confers, the various attributions of mastery it solicits from others' (Waldby, 1995, p.271). In terms of the ways in which masculine subject positions are ascribed cultural and social capital the ostensibly more 'liberal' and relaxed disciplinary codes of the academy have, in fact, much more in common with the apparently more rigid regulatory practices of the business and corporate world than might at first seem to be the case.

Concluding Remarks

men in suits during heatwaves

men in suits being cologne cool in heatwaves
men in suits walking with precision during heatwaves
men in suits wearing distinguished ties in heatwaves
men in suits with tight collars in heatwaves...
sons of men in suits rolling forward towards those days when
they will become men in suits allowing nothing to get in the way:
undeterred by any kind of weather
(excerpt from Joanne Burns, 'Genetics')[9]

It has become almost commonplace within critical legal and feminist scholarship to state that the legal profession has historically been dominated by men of a particular social, economic and educational background. Indeed, it has become increasingly difficult for individuals, whether women or men, who are not from relatively wealthy, middle-class backgrounds to secure admission to a career in law (Halpern, 1994; Dyer, 1995; Howelllooks, 1996). In Britain the Universities of Oxford and Cambridge continue to dominate the upper echelons of the legal profession and the City. Many employers continue to be biased in favour of Oxbridge graduates (Ellis, 1994; Wright, 1994; MacLeod, 1994).[10]

Without downplaying the significance of such issues, what is much less common is any exploration of how these positions of empowerment and privilege bequeathed to men are secured, and generationally reproduced, through reference to gendered notions of cultural, symbolic and economic capital which traverse the legal field; through the ways in which bodies are encoded as, simultaneously, *professional* and *masculine*.[11] This has been my concern in this chapter. I have sought to address the absence of the 'bodies of men' from accounts of 'what men do' and engage with some of the ways in which, at the level of both individual psyche and social structure, a dualism of sexual difference has framed the ways in which the corporeality of men is variously conceptualised in terms of differential access to such capital.

This chapter has only begun an exploration of the demands which inform the construction of masculinities in one particular sub-section of the economy - the legal profession. I have argued that, in seeking to address and challenge the 'masculinism' of 'law', it is necessary to engage with the ways in which men's subjectivities remain predicated on a dualism between 'public' masculinities and 'private' domains (Hearn, 1992). Within both the bureaucratised academy and law firm, the discursive power of this public/private dualism has been fundamental to the mobilising of subjective commitments to institutional goals and values (working harder, putting 'work' first, 'getting on': see further Wills, 1996). What actually constitutes social, cultural and symbolic capital may vary between the discrete fields of the law school and law firm. However in each domain this 'capital' is a gendered, coded heterosexual phenomena. The legal profession has, like the 'public' world of work generally, been historically shaped in men's image and organised by institutions which have reflected the perspectives of men. In reproducing such social relations men are on a daily basis in their interactions with women and other men 'doing gender' (West and Zimmerman, 1987).

It is the archaic, still resonant but always negotiable masculine identity bequeathed men which is encapsulated by the ubiquitous concept of 'hegemonic' masculinity (Connell, 1987) and the emblematic status of the 'men in suits' model within the corporate-business world (Mort, 1996). Yet, I have argued, it is a *diversity* of men's subjectivies which is in fact threatened by women's entry into and success within the legal profession. Men are sharing environments with women that were once shared only with other men. In this process, different demands are being made on the multifarious heterosexual performances of men which are far more complex than simply variations on the hegemonic style of professional masculinity of the 'men in suits'. The fact that this should be seen as 'problematic', a 'woman's issue' or as the cause of a 'masculine crisis' is testimony to the rigidity of dominant cultural conceptions of 'masculine' and 'feminine' as sexed, hierarchical signifiers, each constituted via the dualism of sexual difference. Accordingly, strategies seeking to improve women's position in the legal field based on individual rights and entitlements will be of little use so long as the social edifice which valorises these notions of cultural capital remain in place. There is every indication that within the legal profession the difficulties of combining success with commitments beyond law firm life or law school are falling hardest on women, parents and those caring for others (Wills, 1996).

It is for this reason that, at the present moment, the debate around 'women and law' faces something of a paradox. For, at a time when there is a general acceptance of an ideology of gender 'equality' and 'equal rights' (few law firms and law schools would not claim to be equal opportunity employers), cultural re-configurations of men's power and privileges are taking place which seek, quite explicitly, to evoke, defend and celebrate traditional notions of sexual difference and, in particular, hetero-masculinity. So long as the sexed specificity of men is *effaced* within debates around gender, power and the legal profession it remains likely that the 'problem of men' will continue to be turned on its head and, in a neat discursive twist, the 'masculinism' of 'law' becomes, like so many other issues, a 'women's problem', a question of 'women in law'. Ultimately, transforming cultural practices within the legal academy or law firm means transforming broader cultures outside the profession (Garner, 1996, p.201). There is, for example, a clear lack of *political will* at the level of government to initiate meaningful change which might facilitate and encourage, for example, greater contact between men and children, either within or beyond the 'familial' context. To put it another way, there is every evidence that those men in positions of institutional and political power do not perceive the transformation of men's relationship with children (and, of course, as a necessary corollary with women and other men) as a pressing concern.[12] It cannot be assumed that this is a generational problem, nor that this might be explained solely in terms of the economic imperatives of advanced capitalism. Rather, the problem here relates to a (dominant) construct of a 'public' domain of paid employment as premised on the establishment of a reductive primarily economic relationship between men and children (Collier, 1995).

To conclude: I have argued that particular notions of masculinity are affirmed and valorised within the legal profession via a range of ideologies, discursive representations and material practices which, together and individually, systematically privilege those men with the capacity to claim social and cultural capital. Socio-economic background (education, the inheritance and/or financial support, the style and deportment promoted by private education, the 'right' accent and intonation) remain key gate-keepers into the legal field (Halpern, 1994). There are many masculine subjectivities and their relation, it is clear, is hierarchical. It 'pays' for men, for example, to be closely associated with certain cultural norms of legal 'professionalism' (instrumental rationality, ambition, competitiveness, aggression) rather than others, which might equally be seen to be components of 'good' lawyering (empathy, care, compassion). Nonetheless, and notwithstanding the fact that both women and men within the legal profession are subject to its disciplinary practices, the bureaucratic and epistemological scripts are profoundly different for men and women whose bodies are 'sexed' (that is, constituted as 'sexual') in different ways. A central argument of this chapter has been that the dominant construct of women as 'Other' (to be 'let in' to the masculine(ised) world of law) is dependent on, first, a denial of men's sexed corporeality and, secondly, and related, an evacuation of men from the domain of child care and, more generally, relations of 'dependency' (Fineman, 1995). It should not surprise that considerable ideological regulation goes into ensuring that men's *hetero* - sexual bodies do not surface as problematic entities.

This chapter has presented a multi-level analysis which has sought to incorporate an account of the 'masculinism' of 'law' at both the level of state discourses, the institution, social groups within the legal profession and the level of the individual. Further research might usefully explore the diversity of men's heterosexualities and the complex dynamics of men's resistances to and (re)negotiation of hegemonic norms. Certainly, more research is needed into the deeper structure and significance of everyday practices in the legal field, to the multifarious ways in which heterosexuality is performed and relates to understandings of 'lawyers work'. The multiple histories of the ways in which shifting commercial/business and (higher) educational cultures play out in terms of transforming the legal field is, for example, in terms of gender at least, similarly unexplored, notwithstanding the fact that cultural and economic life in the late twentieth century is significantly about the centrality of this commercial world (Mort, 1996, p.206).

One thing seems clear. Without the political will to address, let alone institute, questions of transformative social and economic structural change, it is likely that debates about men, women and the legal profession will continue to be a marginalised and peripheral issue, their inclusion on conference programmes and agendas, in journals and books marking a tokenistic deference to a climate of 'concern' about a problem which can be identified and experienced (there is something happening 'out there') but seldom analysed. In seeking to surface the sexed bodies of men within a 'situated knowledge' of law (Harvey and Haraway, 1995), to relate the personal and political in an account of the mutual constitution of heterosexuality and masculinity (Robinson, 1996, p.124), this chapter has sought to 'bring home' to the politics of the legal profession the question of what it means to speak of the 'maleness' of the legal field. For all recent, and welcome, attempts to place the gender order of the legal profession under scrutiny, at the end of the day an important question remains unanswered: how is it possible to talk about and address the 'masculinity' of 'law' when we remain so unclear and unsure as to what the term 'masculinity' actually means in the first place?

Acknowledgements

I am indebted to conversations with Simon Blyth, Alastair Bonnett, Clare

McGlynn, Anoop Nayak, Katherine O'Donovan and Margaret Thornton about issues discussed in this chapter and/or comments on earlier drafts of this paper.

Notes

1. In 1995 an unpublished Bar Council Working Party Report found that women Bar students were being regularly offered pupillages in return for sex. This reflected, it declared, an 'unacceptably high' level of 'misconduct' (*The Guardian*, 4 May 1995).
2. Notably during the period in which Martin Mears held office as elected President of the Law Society. During his tenure, in a series of highly publicised pronouncements on what he saw as the iniquities of the 'sex discrimination industry', Mear's was reported as describing women as 'the enemy'. 'Feminist zealots', he declared, 'thrive on grievances and use minorities as raw material for their whinge factories' (quoted in *The Guardian*, 22 April 1996; see further, Pembridge, 1996; M. Mears, letter to *The Independent*, 1 May 1996; 'Women Set To Oust Law Society Chief', *Mail on Sunday*, 28 April 1996.
3. Margaret Thornton's powerful book *Dissonance and Distrust: Women in the Legal Profession* (1996a) exemplifies this trend. On 'anti-feminism' in the academy generally see Clark *et. al.* (1996).
4. My use of cultural, social and symbolic capital is here drawing on the work of Bordieu (e.g. 1984, 1977). See further Jenkins (1992, p.85).
5. The young hero in John Grisham's novel *The Firm* is told to buy 'dark grey or navy wool suits, white or blue cotton button down shirt, medium starch, and silk ties'. On 'the suit theory' in the novels of Grisham generally, N. Walker, *The Guardian*, 3 May 1996.
6. See 'The Lawyer Lifestyle Survey', *The Lawyer*, 7 May 1996, which found lawyers generally were 'disillusioned with their jobs, highly stressed. Heavy workloads prevent over a quarter of fee-earners from taking their full holiday entitlement, a figure which increases to *a third of male lawyers across the board*' (my emphasis): *c.f.* Drummon and Dias, 1996. Also 'Career Pressure Driving Young Women To Suicide', *Sunday Times*, 10 August 1996. There is, interestingly, and as a response to the above, a trend amongst City law firms to offer staff in-house confidential counselling service as a means of combating stress, *The Lawyer*, 25 February 1997.
7. This is, on one level, evident in such developments as the introduction of in-house training as a solution to problems associated with men's behaviour in legal practice (specifically, sexual harassment), '...which could lead *his employer* into trouble: A recent payment should *alert law firms*' (Gibb, 1995: my emphasis).
8. This term is adapted from Grosz and Probyn (1995) use of the term 'sexy

bodies'.

9. In S. Lever (ed.), *The Oxford Book of Australian Women's Verse*, Oxford University Press, Oxford.
10. 'Oxford Retains Grip on the Judiciary', *The Guardian*, 18 May 1995.
11. It is to be remembered in relation to class, for example, that working-class bodies have historically looked different from middle-class bodies; 'leaner, shorter and less healthy' (Bourke, 1994, p.42). In the contemporary context bodies continue to be differentially constituted as aesthetic objects depending on contingencies of socio-economic, racial and ethnic positioning.
12. According to McGlynn and Graham (1995; para. 6), in a study of the largest one hundred solicitor's firms in Great Britain, just under a quarter of respondents (24 per cent) provide paid paternity leave for their staff. The maximum leave granted was five days paid leave; the lowest was two days. Interestingly, less than 1 per cent of male partners and assistant solicitors took paternity leave within the last twelve months. Elsewhere, attempts to develop 'family friendly' policies appear motivated primarily by economic self-interest: e.g., see 'Rich Man, New Man?', *The Independent*, 4 March 1997. The lack of political will is further evidenced in Britain's rejection of the European Working Time Directive limiting, with exceptions, the working week to forty-eight hours, albeit that the European Court has ruled that Britain must implement the directive.

Bibliography

Adkins, L. (1995), *Gendered Work*, Open University Press, Milton Keynes.

Bell, C.M. (1995), 'All I really need to know I learned in Kindergarten (playing soccer): A feminist parable of legal academia', *Yale Journal of Law and Feminism*, pp. 133-136.

Bell, D. and Valentine, G. (1995), 'The Sexed Self: Strategies of Performance, sites of resistance', in S. Pile and N. Thrift (eds.), *Mapping the Subject: Geographies of Cultural Transformation*, Routledge, London.

Benoit-Scott, D. (1996), 'Shattering the Instrumental-Expressive Myth: The Power of Women's Networks in Corporate Government Affairs', *Gender and Society*, vol. 10, pp. 232-247.

Bird, S. (1996), 'Welcome to the Men's Club: Homosociality and the Maintenance of Hegemonic Masculinity', *Gender and Society*, vol. 10, pp. 120-132.

Bordieu, P. (1977), *Outline of a Theory of Practice*, Cambridge University Press, Cambridge.

Bordieu, P. (1984), *Distinction: A Social Critique of the Judgement of Taste*, Harvard University Press, Cambridge, Mass.

Bourke, J. (1994), *Working-Class Cultures in Britain: 1890-1960: Gender, Class and Ethnicity*, Routledge, London.

Butler, J. (1990), *Gender Trouble: Feminism and the Subversion of Identity*, Routledge, London.

Butler, J. (1993), *Bodies That Matter: On the Discursive Limits of Sex*, Routledge, London.

Cain, M. (1994), 'The Symbol Traders', in M. Cain and C. Harrington (eds.) (1996), *Lawyers in a Postmodern World*, Open University Press, Milton Keynes.

Cain, M. and Harrington, C. (eds.) (1994), *Lawyers in a Postmodern World*, Open University Press, Milton Keynes.

Carpenter, M.W. (1996), 'Female Grotesques in Academia: Ageism, Anti-feminism and Feminists on the Faculty', in V. Clark, S.N. Garner, M. Higonnet and K. Katrak (eds.), *Anti-Feminism in the Academy*, Routledge, New York.

Clark, V., Garner, S.N., Higonnet, M. and Katrak, K. (eds.) (1996), *Anti-Feminism in the Academy*, Routledge, New York.

Collier, R. (1991), 'Masculinism, Law and Law Teaching', *International Journal of the Sociology of Law*, vol. 19, pp. 427-451.

Collier, R. (1995), *Masculinity, Law and the Family*, Routledge, London.

Collinson, D. and Hearn, J. (1994), 'Naming Men as Men: Implications for Work, Organisation and Management', *Gender Work and Organisation*, vol. 1, pp.2-32.

Collinson, D. and Hearn, J. (eds.) (1996), *Men As Managers, Managers As Men: Critical Perspectives on Men, Masculinities and Managements*, Sage, London.

Connell, R.E. (1987), *Gender and Power*, Polity Press, Cambridge.

Connell, R.W. (1995), *Masculinities*, Polity Press, Cambridge.

Cownie, F. and Bradney, A. (1996), *English Legal System in Context*, Butterworths, London.

Davies, C. (1996), 'The Sociology of the Professions and the Profession of Gender', *Sociology*, vol. 30, pp. 661-78.

Dobson, R. (1995), 'City gents?: Blokes Use Sexist Sliding Scale in the Office', *Independent on Sunday*, 9 July.

Dollimore, J. (1986), 'Homophobia and sexual difference', *Oxford Literary Review*, vol. 8, pp. 5-22.

Drummond, H. and Dias, E. (1996), 'What Makes a Happy Lawyer?', *New Law Journal*, vol. 146, pp. 23-24.

Dyer, C. (1995), 'No Room at the Inns', *The Guardian*, 9 May.

Edwards, T. (1990), 'Beyond sex and gender: masculinity, homosexuality and social theory', in J. Hearn and D. Morgan (eds.) (1990), *Men, Masculinities and Social Theory*, Unwin Hyman, London.

Ellis, W. (1994), *The Oxbridge Conspiracy*, Michael Joseph, London.

Fennell, E. (1996), 'A Message in the Image', *The Times*, 3 December.

Fineman, M. (1994), 'Feminist Legal Scholarship and Women's Gendered Lives', in M. Cain and C. Harrington (eds.), *Lawyers in a Postmodern World*, Open University Press, Buckingham.

Fineman, M. (1995), *The Neutered Mother, The Sexual Family and Other Twentieth Century Tragedies*, Routledge, New York.

Galanter, M. (1983), 'Mega-law and Mega-lawyering in the contemporary United States', in R. Dingwall and P. Lewis (eds.), *The Sociology of the Professions*, London, Macmillan Press.

Gallop, J. (1995), 'The Lecherous Professor: A Reading', *Differences: A Journal of Feminist Cultural Studies*, vol. 7, pp.1- 15.

Garner, S.N. (1996), 'Transforming Anti-Feminist Culture in the Academy', in V. Clark, S.N. Garner, M. Higonnet and K. Katrak (eds.), *Anti-Feminism in the Academy*, Routledge, New York.

Gatens, M. (1996), *Imaginary Bodies: Ethics, Power and Corporeality*, Routledge, London.

Gibb, F. (1995), 'Rising Cost of Harassment', *The Times*, 24 January.

Grosz, E. (1990), 'Contemporary Theories of Power and Subjectivity', in S. Gunew (ed.), *Feminist Knowledge: Critique and Construct*, Routledge, London.

Grosz, E. (1994), *Volatile Bodies: Towards a Corporeal Feminism*, St Leonards, Allen and Unwin, New South Wales.

Grosz, E. and Probyn, E. (eds.) (1995), *Sexy Bodies: The strange carnalities of feminism*, Routledge, London.

Hagan, J. and Kay, F. (1995), *Gender in Practice: A study of lawyers lives*, Oxford University Press, New York.

Halpern, D. (1994), *Entry into the Legal Professions*, The Law Society, London.

Harvey, D. and Haraway, D. (1995), 'Nature, Politics and Possibilities: A Debate and Discussion with David Harvey and Donna Haraway', *Environment and Planning D: Society and Space*, vol. 13, pp. 507-27.

Hearn, J. (1987), *The Gender of Oppression: Men, Masculinity and the Critique of Marxism*, Wheatsheaf, Buckingham, Brighton.

Hearn, J. (1992), *Men in the Public Eye*, Routledge, London.

Howelllooks, F. (1995), 'There's a crush at the bar: let's leave', *The Times*, 24 January.

Jardine, A. and Smith, P. (1987), *Men in Feminism*, Methuen, London.

Jenkins, R. (1992), *Pierre Bordieu*, Routledge, London.

Laband, D. and Lentz, B. (1992), 'Is there sex discrimination in the legal profession? Further evidence on tangible and intangible margins', *Journal of Human Resources*, vol. 28, pp. 230-258.

Lipman-Blumen, J. (1976), 'Towards a Homosocial Theory of Sex Roles: An Explanation of the Sex Segregation of Social Institutions', *Signs*, vol. 1, pp. 3-15.

McDowell, L. (1995), 'Body Work: Heterosexual Gender Performances in City Workplaces', in D. Bell and G. Valentine (eds.), *Mapping Desire*, Routledge, London.

McGlynn, C. (1996), 'Sex Discrimination at the Margins', *New Law Journal*, vol. 146, pp. 379-81.

McGlynn, C. and Graham, C. (1995), *Soliciting Equality: Equality and Opportunity in the Solicitors' Profession*, Young Women Lawyers, London.

Mac an Ghaill, M. (1994), *The Making of Men*, Open University Press, Buckingham.

MacLeod, D. (1994), 'Oxbridge Man Rules OK?', *The Guardian*, 27 September.

Menkel-Meadow, C. (1986), 'Feminisation of the legal profession: the comparative sociology of women lawyers', *Osgoode Hall Law Journal*, vol. 124, pp. 897-918.

Mort, F. (1996), *Cultures of Consumption: Masculinities and Social Space in late Twentieth Century Britain*, Routledge, London.

Mossman, M.J. (1994), 'Lawyers and Family Life: New Directions for the 1990s', *Feminist Legal Studies*, vol. 2, pp. 61-82.

Murphy, T. (1996), 'Bursting Binary Bubbles: Law, Literature and the sexed Body', in J. Morison and C. Bell (eds.), *Tall Stories? Reading Law and Literature*, Dartmouth, Aldershot.

Naffine, N. (1990), *Law and the Sexes: Explorations in Feminist Jurisprudence*, Unwin Hyman, Sydney.

Nayak, A. and Kehily, M.J. (1996), 'Playing it Straight: Masculinity, Homophobia and Schools', *Journal of Gender Studies*, vol. 5, pp. 211-230.

O'Donovan, K. (1985), *Sexual Divisions in Law*, Weidenfeld and Nicolson, London.

Pembridge, E. (1996), 'My Daft Learned Friend: Shut Up!', *The Independent*, 22 April.

Podmore, D. and Spencer A. (1982), 'Law as a sexed typed profession', *Journal of Law and Society*, vol. 9, pp. 21-36.

Ramazanogolu, C. (1987), 'Sex and Violence in Academic Life, or You Can Keep a Good Woman Down', in J. Hanmer and M. Maynards (eds.), *Women, Violence and Social Control*, Atlantic, Humanities Press International, Highlands, NJ.

Reynaud, E. (1983), *Holy Virility: The Social Construction of Masculinity*, Pluto, London.

Robinson, V. (1996), 'Heterosexuality and Masculinity: Theorising Male Power or the Wounded Male Psyche?', in D. Richardson (ed.), *Theorising Heterosexuality*, Open University Press, Buckingham.

Rogers, B. (1988), *Men Only*, Pandora, London.

Roper, M. and Tosh, J. (eds.) (1991), *Manful Assertions*, Routledge, London.

Seron, C. and Ferris, K. (1995), 'Negotiating Professionalism', *Work and Occupations*, vol. 22, pp. 22-48.

Smart, C. (1989), *Feminism and the Power of Law*, Routledge, London.

Smart, C. (1995), *Law, Crime and Sexuality: Essays in Feminism*, Sage, London.

Sommerlad, H. (1994), 'The myth of feminisation: women and cultural change in the legal profession', *International Journal of the Legal Profession*, vol. 1, pp. 31-53.

Sugarman, D. (1994), 'Blurred Boundaries: The Overlapping Worlds of Law, Business and Politics', in M. Cain and C. Harrington (eds.) (1996), *Lawyers in a Postmodern World*, Open University Press, Milton Keynes.

Thornton, M. (1989), 'Hegemonic Masculinity and the Academy', *International Journal of the Sociology of Law*, vol. 17, pp. 17-115.

Thornton, M. (1994), 'Discord in the Legal Academy: The Case of the Feminist Legal Scholar', *The Australian Feminist Law Journal*, vol. 3, pp. 53-71.

Thornton, M. (1996a), *Dissonance and Distrust: Women in the Legal Profession*, Oxford University Press, Oxford.

Thornton, M. (1996b), 'Authority and Corporeality: The Conundrum for Women in Law', paper presented at the Joint International Conference of the American Law and Society Association and the Research Committee on the Sociology of Law of the International Sociological Association, University of Strathclyde, Glasgow, 10-13 July 1996.

Waldby, C. (1995), 'Destruction: Boundary Erotics and Refigurations of the Heterosexual Male Body', in E. Grosz and E. Probyn (eds.) (1995), *Sexy Bodies: The strange carnalities of feminism*, Routledge, London.

West, C. and Zimmerman, D. (1987), 'Doing Gender', *Gender and Society*, vol. 1, pp. 125-51.

Wills, J. (1996), 'Laboring For Love?: A Comment on Academics and their Hours of Work', *Antipode*, vol. 28, pp. 292-303.

Wright, P. (1994), 'The Intellectuals Plot', *The Guardian*, 26 September.

Wynn-Davies, P. (1996), '2804 Men, 312 Women: that's progress, old boy', *The Independent*, 27 June.

PART II

INTERDISCIPLINARY AND THEORETICAL PERSPECTIVES

3. Fabled Explanations of Bias

KATHERINE O'DONOVAN

Introduction

> ... it is impossible to approach any human problem with a mind free from bias. The way in which questions are put, the points of view assumed, presuppose a relativity of interest; all characteristics imply values, and every objective description, so called, implies an ethical background. Rather than attempt to conceal principles more or less definitely implied, it is better to state them openly at the beginning (de Beauvoir, 1953, p.xxxii).

Simone de Beauvoir's words will strike a chord with those engaged in feminist legal scholarship. Yet whilst denouncing the possibility of individual freedom from bias, she simultaneously asserts that assumptions can be articulated. To advocate an ontology of consciousness of limitations and bias is to advocate honesty. But does this deal with patterns of thinking of which we are unaware? This chapter, using gender bias as an example, argues that stories may illuminate discussions of bias and help uncover our unconscious assumptions. Metaphor and fable may be able to persuade where argument does not (Ward, 1993). But, nevertheless, understandings through narrative may leave unconscious assumptions unexamined, as will be shown at the end of this chapter in a discussion of evidence as story.

The Language of Gender Bias

If a judge says of an eight year old victim of sexual assault that she was 'not entirely an angel herself,' or that 'if a woman upsets you, it's part of their function in life', or, of a rape victim that 'all she has to do is to keep her legs together' (Dalrymple, 1993), what words do academics use to criticise such utterances? The term 'gender bias' is current in Australia, Canada and the United States. There are problems in the use of this term: *definitional*, in the assumptions about the possibilities of neutrality it contains; *vagueness*, in its lack of specificity; *ontological,* in the sense that we are all situated and gendered selves, and are affected by our experiences; *epistemological,* in that some of what is under discussion contains assumptions about knowledge and truth; *psychological*, in that the unconscious remains inaccessible. The term has been called a 'sugar-coated concept', invented to spare the sensibilities of the judiciary (Schafran, 1989; Mahoney and Martin, 1987).

The Australian Law Reform Commission discussion paper on *Equality before the Law* (1993) uses *gender bias* as a key concept, defined as follows: 'Gender bias arises from stereotyped assumptions about the roles of women and men. When the bias disadvantages women, women as a group, are treated as, or believed to be, less entitled less valuable or less worthy than men' (1993, para.3.28). The paper uses the term in a systemic sense, as concerned with culture and social institutions. Examination of the discussion paper reveals that the agenda of bias covers topics such as the representation of women, violence, sexual harassment, undervaluation of women's work, enforced dependency and family responsibilities.

Gender bias is conceptually linked to discrimination, to a denial of human rights, to lack of equality. The paper marks the entry of the concept of gender bias into official knowledge, and possibly judicial notice. Preconceptions built on assumptions are condemned, as otherwise 'justice may be impaired'. But 'preconceptions and predispositions cannot be eliminated. They are an inevitable part of each person's makeup' (3.28). Bias is something more than preconceptions, 'a prejudice or special influence that sways the mind ... which distorts the final result' (3.28). A definition is sought which differentiates the 'inevitable part of each person's makeup' from 'what impairs justice', but that definition is not realised. The concept itself contains a number of assumptions which must be recognised if it is to retain its usefulness.

In an attempt to be more specific the Australian paper says gender bias 'can arise both as a predisposition and as a prejudgement. Courts may use stereotyped notions or assumptions about what is expected behaviour by women and men and what their roles are. This can happen consciously or unconsciously' (3.33). The paper states that law is gendered, 'that is, as being responsive principally to the needs and experiences of men and as operating principally from the perspective of men'. This is linked to personnel: lawmakers, judges, and lawyers. Law has 'an inherent gender bias' (3.37). The problem with this is its level of generality, which is in danger of turning what starts as a matter of concern about justice into a truism. Although the paper contains specific suggestions for judicial education programmes, the concept of gender bias requires elucidation. 'Changing judicial attitudes' is a phrase which is often used here; one aspect is changing ways of thinking. This cognitive issue is the concern of this chapter.

Courts and tribunals have rules against bias: no one is to be the judge of his own cause; a pecuniary conflict of interest must be declared, as must predisposition to one of the parties; statements by a judge before hearing a case, including 'attitudinal bias', may debar him, even if of a humanistic nature *(R v Commonwealth, ex parte Angliss Group*, 1969). The presumption that the judge can put aside personal feelings and be impartial is safeguarded by these rules. Thus is justice said to be seen to be done.

In Canada and the United States the literature on 'gender bias' is now fairly extensive (Resnik, 1988; Hackett, 1990; Grant and Smith, 1991; Western Judicial Education Centre, 1991; Brockman and Chunn, 1993). Schafran (1989) discusses three aspects: stereotyping the nature and roles of women and men, society's devaluation of women and what is perceived as women's work, and myths and misconceptions about the social and economic realities of women's and men's lives. Insofar as this is a problem of cognition, education in re-cognition is one answer. There are 'task forces' on gender bias in the courts of twenty-two American states, with a wide variety of tasks including collection of data and judicial education. Schafran admits that some judges merely want to know how to deal with matters of how to address women, how to raise matters of the dress code, how to cope with court interaction, but without going further to question substantive decisions. One significant aspect of the National Judicial Education Program in the United States is the evidence collected on different perceptions of bias and impartiality by women and men. This again suggests that one issue at stake is the problem of cognition.

The Canadian experience has been affected by the Charter of Rights and the protection it gives to rights and freedoms (Razack, 1991). The Canadian Government helped to promote understanding and observance of the Charter by funding the Women's Legal Education and Action fund, which has brought a number of test cases (*Andrews v Law Society of British Columbia*, 1989; *Brooks v Safeway Ltd.*, 1989; *R v Butler*, 1992). Further, the Canadian Bar Association has created a Task Force on Gender Equality. Brockman and Chunn (1993) give a fair sample of the Canadian form of analysis. It assumes that the law in its ideal form is free of bias, and that by various means, including the language of rights, this ideal can be achieved. My contention is that without a deepened analysis of 'bias', work in this area will remain caught between the formal legal approach of rules to prevent bias, and the social understanding that 'preconceptions and predispositions cannot be eliminated'. My suggestion is that stories, whether fictitious or experiential, can help deepen analysis through the development of imaginative empathy and identification. However we must be wary of reading our own assumptions and preconceptions into the narrative form.

Deconstructing Gender Bias

Thus far five aspects of difficulty with the current legal debate on gender bias have been identified. Definition and specificity have already been mentioned, and are discussed further in this section. Ontological, epistemological, and psychological aspects are discussed in later sections. If the word 'bias' is to be used it seems to imply that there is such a possibility as non-bias. Much of feminist and post-modernist writing is oriented towards disproving this proposition (Frug, 1992). Furthermore the legal discussion has been individualised, rather than seen as attitudinal to groups. The Australian text covers a wide variety of topics which have been staples of feminist writings on law since the seventies, including matrimonial property, violence, rape, anti-discrimination law and legal undervaluation of domestic labour. The paper's critique of law as neither neutral, objective or impartial is familiar. But the language reveals a lack of vocabulary with which to discuss the legal aspects of bias, particularly where it relates to the judicial function. In cases where judicial bias is unconscious, where there is reliance on 'common sense' or on 'what is natural and obvious', it is difficult to identify and displace bias. There follows a difficulty of naming. Nevertheless, judicial decisions have been 'sexed', that is, identified as gendered (Graycar, 1995).

'Misogyny' is a word that is sometimes used to discuss male fear or dislike of women, a word familiar in literary works. It has cultural connotations which fit better with the undercurrents under scrutiny than 'bias'. It is also useful in references to ontological aspects. We disqualify judges with a pecuniary interest from a case, but how can wife-beaters be disqualified from judging domestic violence? However, misogyny only covers one of many possibilities of bias. It is likely that the language of gender bias will re-pose many of the questions associated with attempts to make certain forms of discrimination illegal (Banton, 1994).

Cultural and representational factors cannot necessarily be confronted through law; nor can associations from infancy of a sub-cultural kind. The existing language of and literature on bias remains within a rationalist mode of discourse, unable to confront fully what critical legal scholars call 'the myth of neutrality' (Sachs and Wilson, 1978; Williams, 1989). Using conventional means of analysis - those very modes implicated in the criticisms - as a technique of explanation confuses rather than explicates. What is needed is work on how decision-makers understand the world from their own experiences, in other words, work on cognition. No doubt this is recognised in judicial education programmes. Attempts to broaden experiences using role play form part of such programmes. Whether members of the British judiciary find it easy to adopt the role of black working-class woman must be open to question. There are other ways to empathy. Entering into the experiences of another can also be achieved through reading, but for this to happen there has to be identification, or at least empathy, with that other. This is relevant not only to the judiciary, but to education generally (Wright, 1993).

The Cognitive Self

Recent critical writing has been interested in the body, particularly in its representational aspects (Butler, 1990, 1993). Of interest to this chapter is the positing of selves as embodied. This is not a concern with biology, or with an essential self, but rather with ourselves as embodied beings. The reaction of others to us is, in part, a reaction to the significance attached by culture to our bodies. Representations of persons in texts of law and literature, or visually and orally, affect these perceptions. This is why social constructionist theory has been painted on a broad canvas. Our bodies are signs to others which lead them to categorise us and place us. This must affect our experiences.

Feminist legal theory has focused on epistemology rather than ontology. The critique of the legal subject as embodying a particular kind of male subject has been directed towards theories of knowledge. MacKinnon's work (1983) on epistemology, despite the subsequent critique of its essentialism, has exposed the male norm as law's taken-for-granted subject. Naffine (1990, 1995) has refined this subject as a white, middle-class male. Grbich (1991) admits that a female subject is occasionally present, but as a 'projection of male imaginings'. Specific studies of areas of law such as abortion (Sheldon, 1993), sexual crimes (Duncan, 1994), employment law (O'Donovan, 1996), international law (Charlesworth, Chinkin and Wright, 1991), defences to homicide (Nicholson, 1995), have shown the absence of the female subject. Concepts in anti-discrimination law such as indirect discrimination, or disparate impact, recognise how law seems sometimes to require a particular type of body of its subject. But other examples have been analysed where representation according to gender enter into a seemingly neutral area of law, such as property (Green, 1995). Cognition has not yet been examined as a significant issue, although some attention has been given to language (Astor, 1995), legal method (Mossman, 1986, 1991), and law's insistence on categories (Finlay, 1989). The positioning of the decision-maker as one who knows has been analysed and criticised (Wilson, 1990), but a deep examination of the acquisition of knowledge - the cognitive aspect - has not been undertaken. This chapter does not claim such a deep analysis, but does intend to suggest some directions which might be pursued. As a starting point it attempts a deconstruction of statements about gendered epistemology in order to lead the reader to the issue of cognition. Some discussions of gendered knowledge in feminist jurisprudence fail to distinguish legal process, the content of legal rules, unconscious assumptions of the judiciary. We need a more complex model of 'bias' if we are to engage with issues about understanding and experience (Smart, 1990). What follows is an analytical sketch of how such models might be developed.

Partial Understanding

Where a woman conforms to a certain gendered feminine stereotype, i.e. acts appropriately in the eyes of the judge, she can use this to elicit differential treatment. After all it is well known that *women are helpless, docile and passive*. This partial knowledge can be turned to advantage in certain situations, but in others it may rebound. For example, cultural feminism claims special qualities for women of caring, nurturing and emotion. This partial knowledge can be deployed to undermine women's anti-discrimination claims, as happened in the American case of *EEOC v Sears Roebuck & Co* (1988). An action was brought alleging employment discrimination against women in commission sales positions in employment. The company claimed that sales workers required qualities of aggression, leadership, motivation, and extroversion. A feminist historian gave expert evidence that women have traditionally subordinated their paid labour activities to their domestic responsibilities. The EEOC countered with an expert, also a feminist historian, that women have successfully undertaken leadership roles in paid labour, when given the opportunity, as in wartime. The conflict of the experts enabled the employer to win the case.

Reflection on this case reveals that both experts accepted the construction of the sales worker offered by the employer, without query. Dichotomised images of femininity and masculinity were presented, with the feminised 'homemaker' contrasted with the masculinised 'exception'.

As Frug (1992) points out, both witnesses assumed an inherent, fixed content to sexual difference and failed to challenge the constructed dualisms.

False Claims to Understanding

Claims about 'common sense' may permit the introduction of gendered thinking or stereotypes. The following example of judicial discourse in a rape trial in Melbourne shows how persons in authority can purport to 'know' others: 'and often, despite criticism that has been lately directed at judges about violence and women (and) men acting violently to women during sexual intercourse, it does happen, in the experience of those who have been in the law as long as I have anyway, that no often subsequently means yes' (Judge Bland, 1993). The claim here concerns 'common knowledge'. This is knowledge which may have been acquired behind bicycle sheds, in the locker room, or a bar. It is not based on social scientific research. In depicting this as a false claim to understanding, I do not intend to imply that there is an essential truth about the behaviour of women in sexual situations, but rather that there is not. In other words, claims to know about the generalised behaviour of either gender may be false. At the very least, such statements should be based on validated empirical surveys.

The other issue posed by the words above is the claim based on 'the experience of the those who have been in the law as long as I have'. Experience has been advocated as relevant in feminist legal scholarship (Smart and Brophy, 1985). It can be presented as something women have and men lack, and vice versa, as particular to gender; or, as a female commonality of 'some widely repeated experiences' (Jackson, 1993, p.407). In the latter case this gives some content to the idea of non-essentialist 'women'. In the former it is a claim to authority. Because conventional legal method and legal discourse is essentialist, it is not surprising to find women countering one form of authority with another. But claims to authority have been traditionally made by those placed in positions of authority by systems such as the legal system.

Exclusion of Understandings

Individual understanding, based on personal experience, can be excluded by rules of evidence, or by refusal to admit testimony, or by admission of testimony only if it is 'expert'. The judge as *knower* can decide relevance and irrelevance. The idea of 'taking judicial notice' shows this power; for it is then that an official truth has been established. Cognition is within the power of the judge, as the device of 'taking judicial notice' shows. This requires a conscious act of cognition.

False Objectivity

The attack, first mounted by Catherine MacKinnon (1982), on the hidden masculinity of law's claim to 'neutrality' has become a truism of feminist theory. But this needs further examination for *how* it works. The danger is that the claim about hidden gender may be over-general and therefore discounted. A specific example is the insistence on 'expert opinion' as 'objective, scientific knowledge', where a woman makes a claim about her experiences, which deviates from the constructed norm; a claim which does not fit within existing categories. Women's accounts may be ignored or be deemed inexpert, irrational, unscientific, gossip. Whereas some male experience may be built into the body of the common law, for example in the narrow ambit of provocation as a defence to homicide, for a woman to claim to have her experiences inscribed often requires 'expert witnesses' (O'Donovan, 1993).

All or some of these aspects may be present in discussions of gender bias. A distinction between these aspects and those of differential standards can be summarised in the distinction between knowing and being. It must however be simultaneously acknowledged that our ways of thinking are affected by our genders and experiences.

My provisional conclusion is that gender can be brought into legal discourse in a myriad of ways. To a woman it may be a relevant consideration, or it may not. I don't think it is possible just to rule it in or out. However, if we understand how gender enters into legal discourse we may initiate debate on relevance. Feminist theorists are sometimes ambivalent on the relevance of gender. Current writing posits gender as a process (Butler, 1990, 1993) But it is also a form of differentiation, albeit relational. As Emily Jackson (1993) has argued, we need to move from categories to fluidity. But is this possible in a system of reasoning which relies on categorisation?

How Stories Can Help

In Gabriel Garcia Marquez's *Chronicle of a Death Foretold* (1983) the killing of a man is known in advance in a small town where the system of honour requires it. This death is outside the law. But it has an inevitability, as it is required by the honour system. In the legal system such a killing is unlawful, but the inhabitants understand what must happen. It is this understanding that I want to highlight. The honour system is part of the sex/gender order. When a woman is discovered on her wedding night not to be a virgin she is returned home to her parents by her bridegroom. It then falls to her brothers to kill the man alleged to be responsible for her seduction. A tragedy then unfolds.

the duty...

The brothers are reluctant to do the killing, but they see it as a duty. The narrative voice is given to a woman - Clothilde Armenta - the storekeeper. She urges the mayor to lock the brothers up, but he is satisfied with removing their knives saying: 'Now they haven't got anything to kill anybody with'. But Clothilde Armenta makes the duty aspect clear: 'That's not why. It's to spare those poor boys from the horrible duty that's fallen on them'. There is a communal understanding of what has to be done. Pablo, one of the brothers, is told by his future mother-in-law: 'Honour doesn't wait'. Later his fiancee and future wife said: 'I knew what they were up to, and I didn't only agree, I never would have married him if he hadn't done what a man should do'. But Clothilde Armenta did not agree, and tried to get the brothers drunk to prevent them. 'That day, I realised just how alone we women are in the world'. The other brother Pedro 'considered his duty fulfilled when the mayor disarmed them'. He was dragged off by Pablo 'almost by force in search of their sister's lost honour'. 'There's no way out of this', he told him, 'It's as if it had already happened'.

as to why the death was not prevented...

Those who could have done something but failed 'consoled themselves with the pretext that affairs of honour are sacred monopolies with access only for those who are part of the drama'. 'Honour is love', the narrator's mother says.

The brothers attempt to forestall their own act by telling all and sundry about their intentions, thinking of one, that 'he was the right person to stop the crime without bringing any shame on them'. But they are caught in a binary of duty and shame from which they cannot escape, and which mirrors the binary system of sex/gender. This is a system outside law; the understanding of which is reflected in the short prison sentences served by the brothers.

Introducing Marquez's story into this paper is intended to illustrate four themes: the co-existence of social orders and legal regulatory systems; the transmission of information informally between these orders; the gendering of these orders; how narrative may challenge, but also confirm our assumptions. We see how two systems, one social and one legal, exist side by side, and how information from one system is transmitted to another. There is a con- or parallel- text to the crime that has been committed. Thus in sentencing the brothers the court takes cognisance of the honour system. Notions of honour, shame and duty are gendered. It is inevitable that the search for a sister's lost honour falls on her brothers, and the reader is not led to question this. So the story helps us to understand not only how information and understanding may be acquired by law in the guise of 'common sense', or 'tradition', but also how the sex/gender system is understood and unquestioned.

Court Drama as Narrative

'Evelyn went to Sam's party. Everyone had a good time. Later Evelyn and Sam went to bed'. What gender has the reader ascribed to Evelyn and Sam? What sort of relationship is it assumed that Evelyn and Sam have?

Would someone from another culture, or sub-culture make those assumptions?

Psychologists working on the jury trial have undertaken cognitive experiments with subjects and concluded that the juror's explanation of legal evidence takes the form of a story (Pennington and Hastie, 1991). These researchers argue that people have knowledge about the kinds of information necessary to form a story, and that these expectations influence the cognitive processing of narrative, and the mental representation of a story. Linguistic analysis of texts such as letters from solicitors briefing barristers not only shows a narrative, but a narrative in a particular form in which the choice of words influences the point of view which is presented. This research, now accepted as orthodox by those working on the law of evidence, should lead us to ask questions about the narrative representation of a court trial by the judge to himself, which may affect decisions in civil cases without a jury, sentencing, awards of damages. In making this suggestion it is not necessary to make larger claims about 'a story that will claim to tell the truth in legal terms' (Kurzon, 1986, p.465).

Twining (1994) gives an example of a generalised assumption about sexual relationships between women and men which may have resulted in a miscarriage of justice and a hanging. Although not analysed by Twining in terms of gender, it is clear that gender is central to his theory of why a sentence of death on Edith Thompson was unjustly executed. The generalised assumption in question is that where a woman is older than her male lover she will dominate him. Thus Thompson, despite a lack of evidence linking her to the killing of her husband, was assumed to have instigated the crime and therefore to have entered into a conspiracy to murder (Twining, 1994, pp.290-293).

Conclusion

This chapter set out to examine writing about gender bias, particularly in relation to judicial education. It suggests that a deepened analysis, particularly of cognition, needs to be undertaken. Using narrative as a means of education and to increase empathy might be thought a promising means of education. Research shows that narrative plays a part in legal argument and judgment. It may therefore be possible to develop stories in legal and judicial education. However we should be careful not to overstate the importance of story-telling. And, as I have tried to show, stories in their representation of human actors may reinforce generalisations about gender, even whilst we are reading to empathise. Whether we shall ever get away from such differentiations and generalisations remains to be told.

Bibliography

Andrews v The Law Society of British Columbia [1989], 1 S.C.R. 143.

Astor, H. (1995), 'The Weight of Silence' in M. Thornton (ed.), *Public and Private: Feminist Legal Debates*, Oxford University Press, Melbourne.

Australian Law Reform Commission (1993), *Equality Before The Law*, Australian Government Publishing Service, Canberra.

Banton, M. (1994), *Discrimination*, Open University Press, Buckingham.

Bland, J. (1993), *The Age*, 7 May, p.1.

Brockman, J. and Chunn, D. (eds.) (1993), *Investigating Gender Bias: Law, Courts and the Legal Profession*, Thompson Educational Publishing, Toronto.

Brooks v Safeway Ltd. [1989], S.C.R. 1219.

Brophy, J. and Smart, C. (1985), *Women In Law*, Routledge, London.

Butler, J. (1990), *Gender Trouble*, Routledge, London and New York.

Butler, J. (1993), *Bodies That Matter*, Routledge, London and New York.

Charlesworth, H., Chinkin, C. and Wright, S. (1991), 'Feminist Approaches to International Law', *American Journal of International Law*, vol. 85, pp. 613-636.

Dalrymple, J. (1993), 'Judges in the Dock', *Sunday Times News Review*, 13 June.

De Beauvoir, S. (1953), *The Second Sex* (trans. H.M. Parshley), Penguin Books, London.

Duncan, S. (1994), 'Disrupting the Surface of Order and Innocence', *Feminist Legal Studies*, vol. 2, pp. 3-28.

EEOC v Sears Roebuck & Co. (1988), 628 Federal Supp. 1264 (Illinois, 1286), affirmed 839 Federal 2d. 302 (7th Circuit, 1988).

Finlay, L. M. (1989), 'Breaking Women's Silence in Law: the Dilemma of the Gendered Nature of Legal Reasoning', *Notre Dame Law Review*, vol. 64, pp. 886-910.

Frug, M. J. (1992), *Postmodern Legal Feminism*, Routledge, London.

Grant, I. and Smith, L. (1991), 'Gender Representation in the Canadian Judiciary', in *Appointing Judges: Philosophy, Politics and Practice*, Ontario Law Reform Commission, Ottawa.

Graycar, R. (1995), 'The Gender of Judgements' in M. Thornton (ed.), *Public and Private: Feminist Legal Debates*, Oxford University Press, Melbourne.

Grbich, J. (1991), 'The Body in Legal theory' in M. A. Fineman and N. S. Thomadsen (eds.), *At the Boundaries of Law: Feminism and Legal Theory*, Routledge, New York.

Green, K. (1995), 'Thinking Land Law Differently', *Feminist Legal Studies*, vol. 3, pp. 131-157.

Hackett, D. (1990), *Gender Equality*, Canadian Judicial Centre, Ottawa.

Jackson, E. (1993), 'Contradictions and Coherence in Feminist Responses to Law', *Journal of Law and Society*, vol. 20, pp. 398-414.

Kurzon, D. (1986), 'How Lawyers Tell Their Tales: Narrative Aspects of a Lawyer's Brief', *Poetics*, vol. 14, pp. 465-484.

MacKinnon, C. (1982), 'Feminism, Marxism and the State: An Agenda for Theory', *Signs*, vol. 7, pp. 515-540.

MacKinnon, C. (1983), 'Feminism, Marxism, Method and the State: Toward Feminist Jurisprudence', *Signs*, vol. 8, pp. 635-663.

Mahoney, K. and Martin, S. (eds.) (1987), *Equality and Judicial Neutrality*, Carswell, Toronto.

Marquez, G.G. (1983), *Chronicle of a Death Foretold* (trans. G. Rabassa), Picador, Pan books, London.

Mossman, M.J. (1986), 'Feminism and Legal Method: The Difference It Makes', *Australian Journal of Law and Society*, vol. 3, pp. 30-46.

Mossman, M.J. (1991), 'Feminism and Legal Method' in M.A. Fineman and N. Thomadsen (eds.), *At the Boundaries of Law: Feminism and Legal Theory*, Routledge, New York.

Naffine, N. (1990), *Law and the Sexes: Explorations in Feminist Jurisprudence*, Allen and Unwin, Sydney.

Naffine, N. (1995), 'Sexing the Subject of Law' in M. Thornton (ed.), *Public and Private: Feminist Legal Debates*, Oxford University Press, Melbourne.

Nicholson, D. (1995), 'Telling Tales: Gender Discrimination, Gender Construction and Battered Women Who Kill', *Feminist Law Review*, vol. 3, pp. 185-206.

O'Donovan, K. (1993), 'Law's Knowledge: the Judge, the Expert, the Battered Woman and Her Syndrome', *Journal of Law and Society*, vol. 20, pp. 427-437.

O'Donovan, K. (1996), 'Labour Law's Subject: A Hidden Agenda?', in Y. Kravaritou (ed.), *Le Sexe du Droit de Travail en Europe*, Kluwer, The Hague.

Pennington, N. and Hastie, R. (1991), 'A Cognitive Theory of Juror Decision Making: The Story Model', *Cardoza Law Review*, vol. 13, pp. 519-549.

R. v Commonwealth, ex parte Angliss Group (1969), 122 Commonwealth Law Reports 546.

Razack, S. (1991), *Canadian Feminism and the Law: the Women's Legal Education and Action Fund and the Pursuit of Equality*, Second Story Press, Toronto.

Resnik, J. (1988), 'On the Bias: Feminist Reconsiderations of the Aspirations for Our Judges', *Southern California Law Review*, vol. 61, pp. 1877-1955.

Sachs, A. and Wilson, J. H. (1978), *Sexism and the Law*, Martin Robertson, London.

Schafran, L. H. (1989), 'Gender Bias in the Courts: An Emerging Focus for Judicial Reform', *Arizona State Law Journal*, vol. 21, pp. 237-256.

Sheldon, S. (1993), 'Who is the Mother to Make the Judgement?: The Constructions of Women in English Abortion Law', *Feminist Legal Studies*, vol. 1, pp. 3-22.

Smart, C. (1990), 'Law's Truth: Women's Experience', in R. Graycar (ed.), *Dissenting Opinions*, The Federation Press, Annandale, NSW.

Smart, C. and Brophy, J. (1985), 'Locating Law' in J. Brophy and C. Smart (eds.), *Women In Law*, Routledge, London.

Twining, W. (1994), *Rethinking Evidence*, Blackwell, Oxford.

Ward, I. (1993), 'The Educative Ambition of Law and Literature', *Legal Studies*, vol. 13, pp. 323-340.

Western Judicial Education Centre (1991), *Judicial Education Program on Gender Equality*, Western Judicial Education Centre, Vancouver.

Williams J. C. (1989), 'Deconstructing Gender', *Michigan Law Review*, vol. 87, pp. 797-825.

Wilson, B. (1990), 'Will Women Judges Really Make a Difference?', *Osgoode Hall Law Journal*, vol. 28, pp. 507- 522.

Wright, S. (1993), 'Patriarchal Feminism and the Law of the father', *Feminist Legal Studies*, vol. 1, pp. 115-140.

4. When Mercy Seasons Justice: Shakespeare's Woman Lawyer

IAN WARD

Introduction

In this chapter, I want to use literature as a means to investigate some of the contemporary concerns which define feminist legal thought. In the first part of the essay, I will discuss briefly the uses of literature and literary theory in legal theory. In the second part, I will consider one particular text, *The Merchant of Venice*, and one particular character, Portia. Most immediately, I will re-examine Portia's role in the trial scene; a role which has been taken increasingly by certain feminist legal thinkers as symbolic of the situation of the woman in law. In the third part, I will attempt to destabilise this symbolism, introducing in the process a number of insights suggested by contemporary literary and Shakespearean criticism. In the final part of the essay, I will suggest the extent to which such a destabilisation reflects a comparable uncertainty in current feminist legal thinking.

Law, Literature and History

The interdisciplinary study of law and literature has emerged in recent years as one of the most exciting and challenging of jurisprudential ventures. Aside from its virtues as an educative medium, the study of law in its literary form invariably provides new insights and perspectives. It has become customary to refer to two complementary strategies. First, there is law *as* literature, which seeks to investigate the nature of law as a literary enterprise and a form of writing. Second, there is law *in* literature, which seeks to suggest the insights provided by the portrayal of law in literary form (Ward, 1995, pp.3-27). In this essay, I want to emphasise still further the interdisciplinary nature of this particular jurisprudential approach, by determining law and literature as an irreducibly historical exercise. Literature is history; a text is always historically situated. This essay is then, at once, an exercise in legal history, in legal theory, and in literary theory and criticism.

More particularly, I want to take one particular character in one particular situation in one particular piece of literature. That character is Portia in Shakespeare's *The Merchant of Venice*. In doing so, I am consciously adding a further perspective to our exercise, because it will also become an exercise in feminist theory, legal, historical, social and so on. The more that we investigate the particular instance of a textual situation, such as Portia's, the more we become conscious of what literary theorists term polyphony. Any textual situation, and textual characterisation, is irreducibly multi-textual. There is no one Portia. Rather, we will discover that there are lots of Portias.

The determination of interpretation in literature and literary criticism itself defies objectivity. The debate with regard to whether there is any such thing as an ascertainable authorial intention has been cast into doubt. According to French semiotician Roland Barthes, the author is 'dead' (Barthes, 1986). Reader-response theory suggests that all we can do is look to audiences. At an extreme, interpretation of any text is purely at the whim of its audience and their particular textual and social situation. In the light of such an extreme situation, Umberto Eco warns us against the twin dangers of overinterpretation and overintellectualism (Eco, 1992). There is a meaning to text, and it can be constructed within a particular text-audience relation. Such a conclusion is very much in line with the hermeneutical approach of such as Hans-Georg Gadamer. According to Gadamer, the interpretation of a text is the product of a three way collaboration, of author, of text, and of audience. The meaning of a text can be found within these three parameters (Gadamer, 1975; Gadamer, 1977).

It is not the purpose of this chapter to delve any deeper into the subtle, and as Eco suggests often rather too subtle, nuances of literary theory (Eco, 1992). However, it is, I think, important to bear in mind the controversy that surrounds any attempt to define objectively any particular text. When we come to re-engage with literary and legal theory in the final two parts of this chapter, such reservations will be cast into a clearer perspective, for their importance is not merely limited to Shakespeare's

Portia; they are of relevance to any woman and any projected feminist discourse.

There is one particular Portia that we cannot access, and that is Shakespeare's Portia. The 'death' of the author, even if not precisely extinctive, is sufficiently terminal to exclude that possibility. However, there are a number of textual facts which are common, in the hermeneutical sense, to any Portia. Perhaps these might be said to be constituents of a Shakespearian Portia, even if they depend for their constructive integrity upon the constitutive presence of an audience. Portia is a character, cast by Shakespeare as female, who plays a role in *The Merchant of Venice*. She lives outside Venice in a place called Belmont, where she waits for a husband to claim her by solving a riddle. When Bassanio solves that riddle, and Portia expresses her willingness to submit to him, Bassanio departs Belmont. Subsequently, Portia has to go to Venice in order to save the life of one of Bassanio's friends. In doing so, Portia adopts the particular appearance of a lawyer, and articulates a certain legal argument. This argument is sufficient to save Bassanio's friend. In the final part of the play, Portia tests Bassanio's integrity with regard to their relationship, and it is found wanting. Portia then demands a reaffirmation of Bassanio's love for her.

Given the particular attention of this essay, it is worth recounting the legal argument in greater detail. Shylock, a Jewish usurer, has contracted a bond with Antonio, a merchant. If the bond is not repaid as stipulated, then Shylock is entitled to take a 'piece of flesh' of his choosing. As the trial scene opens, Shylock is pursuing the technical forfeit, despite belated offers to repay the bonded sum. The Duke seems unable to stop Shylock. However, Portia, appearing in the guise of a young 'doctor of laws', and carrying an opinion of a reknowned lawyer, Bellario, provides him with the means. At first she appeals to Shylock to show mercy. Shylock refuses. Portia then, by a legal slight of hand, interprets the bond such that Shylock cannot take blood along with flesh. To do so, she suggests, would be itself a breach of Venetian law. Shylock recoils from committing such a crime. However, revenge is exacted against Shylock on the basis that, as an alien, he has already infringed the law by seeking to hazard the life of a Venetian citizen. His property is confiscated and he is forced to convert to Christianity.

Such, in the baldest sense, are the facts about the character of Portia. The rest is speculation, or as literary critics prefer to call it, constructive interpretation.

Jurisprudential Portias

In recent years, Portia has become something of an icon for feminist legal scholars. Supreme Court Justice Sandra Day O'Connor writes about women judges in the USA under the title 'Portia's Progress' (O'Connor, 1991). It is not a matter of providing any sort of commentary on Portia. It is Portia as icon and symbol that is important. The most recent jurisprudential sequestration of Portia is that of Carrie Menkel-Meadow. Indeed, Portia is an iconic centrepiece of her thesis. According to Menkel-Meadow, Portia is a 'symbol' for a particularly feminist legal perspective. In other words, she represents something essentially female (Menkel-Meadow, 1995, p.56). This is, of course, precisely the alignment which Gilligan assumed in her influential *In a Different Voice* (1982). In many ways, Gilligan's rather brief, almost tangential, reference to Portia can be seen as triggering this subsequent rash of Portia references, and thus laying the foundations for the Portia-myth which has followed (Gilligan, 1982, p.105). It is this myth which I want to address, partly because of its textual inaccuracy, but partly also because there is a value in deconstructing any such textual mythology, and it is a deconstruction which enjoys a particular resonance in contemporary feminist legal thought. I will discuss this resonance in the final part of the essay.

The Portia myth, like all myths, on closer examination can be seen to be something of a sham. Indeed, the implicit suggestion that Portia brings something essentially female to the legal situation is itself contradicted by Menkel-Meadow's own admission that Portia is in fact merely reinforcing the inherent wisdom of the patriarchal legal order by intepreting the law 'literally' (Menkel-Meadow, 1995, p.45). Simple alignments with regard to Portia's lawyering are impossible. There are simply too many contradictions and ambiguities. If anything, as I will suggest shortly, Portia can more plausibly be read as one of the most affirmatively patriarchal figures in Shakespeare.

It is, of course, true that Portia does play a prominent role in a particularly jurisprudential task. But, at the same time, there are a number of potential hazards in any easy ascription of anything which is somehow essentially feminine about Portia's lawyering. First, a simple affinity between Portia and mercy is now seriously doubted. Certainly, Portia appeals to Shylock to show mercy towards the unfortunate Antonio. But she does not, having failed in her pleas, seek recourse to a legal ethics which lies outside the ordinary common laws of Venice. In this she approves the Duke, who has 'ta'en pains to qualify' the law, but pointedly refuses to go outside it (4.1.7). Early interpretations of the scene suggested that Portia seeks recourse to a Chancery jurisdiction which lay outside the common law (Mackay, 1964; Knight, 1974). Such a misapprehension lingers amongst some literary commentators (Eagleton, 1986, pp.36-7; Hall, 1995, pp.55-8). It is fundamentally mistaken.

Historical revision has asserted the extent to which contemporary constitutional theory determined the chancery jurisdiction be means of the common law; not outside it. The monarchy was defined by the common law, and so was its prerogative (Burgess, 1996, pp.143-9, 157). Even Bacon, who so strenuously opposed Coke's elision of the common law and prerogative, accepted that the jurisdiction of the royal prerogative was determined by the common law, even if the substance of it was not (Burgess, 1996, pp.87-9). Moreover, both Bacon and Coke again agreed that, as Coke suggested, the 'Common Law itself is nothing else but reason' (Burgess, 1996, pp.166-9, 184). Rational determination of the sovereign prerogative was common ground in the constitutional discourse of Shakespeare's England.

This determination founds the trial scene in *The Merchant of Venice*. There is no recourse to an extra-juridical equity of mercy. Indeed quite the opposite is true. Portia reveals the justice inherent in the constitution of the common law, and in doing so reinforces a very particular position in the jurisprudence of the limited or mixed constitution. From the very outset, Shylock is convinced that he stands 'for the law' (4.1.142). However, such an understanding is premised on the Old Law, of the Old Testament. The New Law, the law of St. Thomas Aquinas and St. Augustine, in contrast, inheres qualities of mercy within its jurisprudence (Barber, 1972, pp.185-6; Colley, 1980, pp.185-7; Benston, 1979, p.378). The rule of law, in the Aristotelian-Thomist jurisprudence, derived its consistency from the common law of a commonwealth. According to the likes of Bracton and Fortescue, the common law of England was determined by the rationality of the New Law, and inhered mercy as a part of that immanent rationality. Justice was determined by reason and equity, but it was determined as part of the common law (Ward, 1995, pp.61-4; Beauregarde, 1988; Tucker, 1976, pp.100-1).

This is what Shylock and the Venetian court fail to understand. Shylock's rule of law is the law of the tyrant; outside the law of the community (4.1 38-9). It is law for law's sake (4.1.54-61). Shylock's law separates itself from the community, as does Shylock himself (Paster, 1985, p.196). Yet, it is no less insufficient than the primitive understanding of the common law seemingly enjoyed by such as Antonio and, more worryingly still, the Duke. As far as Antonio and his sovereign are concerned, the law simply serves the market. It no more serves the community than Shylock's law (3.2.26-31; Hamill, 1978, pp.237-9). Neither the Duke, nor his merchant courtiers, seem to understand the proper jurisprudential and constitutional nature of the common law. The constitution of the mixed monarchy, the monarchy determined by the common law, is a constitution determined by reason and justice. To be in accordance with justice, mercy and reason, Venetian law must be redetermined in terms of the theology and politics of mixed monarchy constitutionalism and the immanent rationalism of the common law prerogative.

What Portia articulates, therefore, is the inherent rationality of the common law. There is nothing radical about Portia's interpretation. Indeed, it emphasises the importance of the status quo, and the stability of the existing jurisprudence, as a very necessary constituent of the patriarchal political order. More precisely, what the Duke does not immediately appreciate is the situation of his common law prerogative. In terms of the prerogative, as Portia points out, it is the common law which determines the extent to which the offender's life 'lies in the mercy' of the Duke 'gainst all other voice' (4.1.351-2). In terms of constitutional jurisprudence, Shylock will be subject to precisely the same 'justice' as that which attends Antonio. He shall have 'merely justice and his bond' (4.1.311-12, 335).

Shylock's attempt to use the common law against the political economy of Venice is a political and constitutional challenge against the state, its sovereign and its ruling classes, and, to complete his defeat, he must be countered by the very law which is constituted by that political community. To seek recourse outside that common law would have been to diminish it, and to destabilise it in a way which would have seriously shocked Shakespeare's audience. If any one character in Shakespeare subjugates themselves to an established patriarchal constitutional order, it is Portia. Indeed, Portia's textual function is not to challenge patriarchy, but to reinforce it. Such was, of course, the function of all Shakespeare's great heroines, from Rosalind to Helena.

Aside from the strictly legal problems with regard to Portia's 'law', there are similar problems with regard to any easy assumption that Portia is a female lawyer, or one which at all illustrates any essential female qualities. First, the notion that she offers any particularly merciful voice is doubted by her unarguably vicious treatment of Shylock; a member of a minority group far more marginalised than that of wealthy aristocratic women. Second, the extent to which Portia is actually contributing anything herself to the legal proceedings is uncertain. She may, indeed, simply be the mouthpiece for another lawyer. There is no evidence that the actual letter from Bellario is fictional. If this is the case, then Portia is very much the mouthpiece of a patriarchal legal order, and patriarchal wisdom. Even if this is not the case, as I have already suggested, Portia is merely giving voice to the law; she is not creating any especially virtuous or equitable alternative. The precise law with which she condemns Shylock, against aliens who 'by direct, or indirect means' seek 'the life of any citizen', is already well established in Venetian common law (4.1.343-8).

On a broader note, moreover, there are plenty of other intelligent, perceptive and virtuous lawyers in Shakespeare. Despite Menkel-Meadow's assertion, ethical lawyering is not the preserve of women, and it cannot really be supported that Shakespeare reserved competent or even ethical lawyering purely for a female lawyer (Menkel-Meadow, 1995, p.50). The Lord Chief Justice in *2 Henry IV* is a far more competent common lawyer. Escalus is equally as effective in *Measure for Measure*. Ullyses in *Troilus and Cressida* enjoys a far more balanced appreciation of the Thomist jurisprudential tradition which underpinned the common law. Portia is certainly not special in any particular way, and it can fairly be suggested that the fact that it is she who emphasises the inherent justice and rationality in the essentially patriarchal legal system owes as much to textual chance and coincidence.

The situation is, of course, further confused by the fact that Portia disguises not only her person and identity, but her gender. Much has been made of this particular disguise. Menkel-Meadow suggests that Portia is a female lawyer, who shows herself to be 'as capable as any male lawyer' (Menkel-Meadow, 1995, p.46). But there was no such thing as a male or female lawyer. There were just lawyers, all of one gender; male. Portia, in *The Merchant of Venice*, is a women who dresses like a lawyer. She is not a woman who dresses like male lawyer.

It is common now to see legal apparel as inherently sexist, and to decry the need for women to appear in court wearing clothing usually worn by men. But it must be remembered that, in Shakespeare's day, lawyers wore a particular clothing appropriate to their essentially theatrical role; clothing that was not worn by men in any other situation. Indeed, to adopt the guise of a lawyer was as subversive as adopting the guise of a king or a minister of God. Today, as in Shakespeare's time, it is still unlawful to impersonate a monarch, a minister or an officer of the court. Only those called to bar can wear legal apparel in a court of law.

Portia dresses as a lawyer. To that extent she is subversive. But that is the limit of the subversion. She does not dress as a man. Indeed, it is striking the extent to which, unlike other Shakespearian heroines, such as Rosalind in *As You Like It*, or Olivia in *Twelfth Night*, Portia refuses to emphasise her femininity whilst dressed as a lawyer. Portia is clearly not affected by her change of appearance in the court. She only emphasises her change of gender identity in the events surrounding the court, and most particularly in the final ring scenes, when, as a 'fine bragging youth', she does indeed adopt the accepted language and performance of the theatrical transvestite (3.4.69).

It is quite clear that the Portia in court is not a male character, or indeed a female one. The legal Portia is, rather, a desexed Portia. The related matters of desexualisation and transvestism were of enormous importance in early modern England, and particularly in its theatrical culture. According to Catherine Belsay, the Renaissance theatre was obsessed by transvestism and its destabilising potential (Belsay, 1985, p.178; c.f. Greenblatt, 1988, pp.66-9). Terry Eagleton is keen to suggest that Portia is indeed transvestite, and by shifting her gender identity, is a destabilising figure (Eagleton, 1986, p.40).

However, the desexed character, in contrast, was consciously cast to stabilise a textual situation; to deny it the destabilising potential of transvestism. The precise sexual, or desexual, determination of Portia as a lawyer is thus of considerable importance to any suggestion that she might bring anything essentially female to the legal situation. Harold Goddard has suggested that, by transcending any gender determination, Portia as lawyer actually serves to reinforce the patriarchal order (Goddard, 1986, pp.30-3). Leonard Tennenhouse has similarly suggested that, by balancing her sexuality in the trial scene Portia succeeds in desexing herself, and thus depoliticising herself (Tennenhouse, 1986, pp.59-60).

This controversy which surrounds Portia's sexual identity, and its apparent shifts, is mirrored in a similar controversy which surrounds Elizabeth I. Elizabeth has long been championed by historians as a monarch who balanced essentially female attributes, of chastity and virtue, with distinctly male ones, of strength, constancy and integrity; the Elizabeth of the Tilbury speech in 1588, who declared herself to have the 'heart and stomach of a king, and a king of England too'. However, in more recent historical revision, this apparent balancing transvestism has been recast as more a kind of asexuality; something intrinsically harmonising and transcendent (Pye, 1990, p.33; Fletcher, 1995, pp.79-80;

Tennenhouse, 1986, pp.21,102-4). The similarities between Elizabeth in her public body, her constitutional role, and that of Portia in her public body, as a constitutional lawyer, are striking (Belsay, 1985, p.181).

If Portia is asexual, of course, then the notion that she brings anything essentially feminine to the legal situation must be dismissed. Indeed, the opposite is true; the lawyer is seen to be beyond any form of determinable, meaning consistent, gender ascription. The Shakespearean lawyer is defined by its lack of gender determination. If there is an ethical or political message here, it is not that women are subjugated by the law, but than everyone is subjugated, and it is a subjugation defined by the denial of gender identity. The patriarchal order is served by the jurisprudentially desexed.

Self-Fashioning Portias

So much for the jurisprudential Portias. The first thing which must be acknowledged is that this is only one Portia. In textual terms, moreover, it is probably the least important. In order to access a better appreciation of Portia, as a textual, as opposed to mythical, figure, it is important to note some of the other Portias. First, there are various literary Portias. Monica Hamill suggests that Portia is the classic portrayal of the poet-lawmaker, whilst, at the same time, at a deeper level, serving to effect a quasi-religious redemption of her lover, Bassanio (Hamill, 1978, pp.229-32). Bassanio, chronically unreliable and dishonest, seems to be in need of redemption. In fashioning this redemption, Portia has been placed in a series of proactive female characters in Shakespeare who justify their proaction by doing the work of God. Others include Isabella, Helena and Cressida.

Such a form of almost conditional submission has been perceived as being in line with the more aggressively proactive role of women in certain areas of protestant and puritan political and social theory. The more socially reformist variants of puritanism increasingly championed the virtue of women as creative contributors to community harmony (Fletcher, 1995, pp.5-13, 53). According to Lisa Jardine, the situation of women in early modern England was itself undergoing a 'cultural act of transference' (Jardine, 1996, p.131).

Moreover, it is popularly suggested that, in redeeming her lover, Portia is able to redeem the entire Venetian community. Venice is representative of a voracious market ethic, serviced by merchants who seem to exist in a state of perpetual financially induced anxiety. Portia is herself a commodity designed to attract a male investor on the marriage market, and her father's riddle is geared to ascertaining the most desirable of investors (Berger, 1981, pp.156-7). As Christopher Hill has recently emphasised, Shakespeare's England was one that was experiencing all the tensions which accompany a proto-capitalist state trying to get to grips with mercantile economics (Hill, 1996, pp.4-42, 273-338).

So, when Portia intervenes to enforce Venetian economic morality against Shylock, she is intervening in a intellectual debate regarding contemporary economic ethics which would have enjoyed considerable resonance amongst Shakespeare's audience. It is, of course, important that Portia comes from the country in order to provide the ethical, and financial, means to resuscitate the Venetian economy (Cohen, 1982, pp.776-7; Newman, 1987, pp.19-20; Hall, 1995, pp.53-4). The general economic crisis was seen by many to be inextricable from the complementary concern of court and country. The country was associated with something innately wholesome; the world of Arden, of Robin Hood, of Justice Shallow and simple good nature and integrity. A rather different world, it was perceived, than that of the city, and in particular, the city of London. Men of letters waxed lyrically about the contrast between the two. The country was quintessentially English; the city was not (Wrightson, 1982, pp.49-54). And so, when Portia comes from the country to the city, she comes from something identifiably English to something, which to many, was seen as being rather more alien.

It is of considerable importance, then, to see Portia as more than merely a lawyer, or even a disguised pseudo-lawyer. Portia is, at once, a woman, a wealthy woman, a woman whose wealth is founded on the land rather than in the markets or in usury or any other form of financial service, an unmarried woman, and a woman who enjoys a degree of proactive independence with regard to running her estates and fashioning her future situation within a patriarchal regime. All these characteristics, at least, contribute to the textual Portia, aside from our own added preconceptions with regard to her character, which we bring as a particularly contextually situated audience.

The legal Portia is only one such constituent, and then perhaps the most difficult to accommodate. This difficulty, as we have already noted, is described by her uncertain gender identity, her function in the court, the nature of the law which she articulates, the extent to which she stabilizes or destabilizes the existing legal order, and the extent to which that legal order is inherently patriarchal or asexual. Such confusion is only increased by the rapidity with which Portia assumes and then casts aside her legal persona. The legal is clearly only one Portia, and a decidedly uncertain one at that.

Portia is not a stable character. Indeed, contemporary deconstructive criticism suggests than none of Shakespeare's characters can be at all stable. The constitutive presence of the audience radically destabilises meaning. It has been suggested that the particular characteristic of Renaissance literature was the writing of texts by constitutive audiences. Stephen Greenblatt refers to Renaissance 'self-fashioning', as the tendency of Shakespeare and his contemporaries to emphasise the polyphonic quality of character. In other words, all the characters are actively constructed, and not merely performed, upon a stage (Greenblatt, 1980). This suggestion is repeated time and again in Shakespeare, most famously perhaps by Jacques in *As You Like It* and the Chorus in *Henry V*. The dominant Shakespearian characters can be defined by their theatrical determination.

This is, perhaps, most apparent of all amongst the major political and constitutional characters, Shakespeare's magistrates. The various characters often suggested to be Shakespeare's ideal godly magistrates, Henry V, Prospero, Duke Theseus in *A Midsummer Night's Dream*, all articulate an appreciation that the role of the magistrate is an acting role. To be a magistrate, at any level of government, was to be an actor. So, when Portia operates as a lawyer, she is an actor acting Portia acting a lawyer pretending to be a lawyer. In this instance, Portia is already assuming a multi-layered textuality; in part constituted by three competing identities. She is an actor, a woman, a lawyer. Yet in the trial scene, she is, of course, trying to destabilise all three characteristics. In such a situation, the audience is then asked to constitute their own Portia, using the textual situation of that scene, and all the other scenes of the play, together with their own textual and political situtation. The lawyering Portia cannot be perceived apart from the asexual Portia, the intensely feminine Portia, the wealthy Portia, the landed Portia, the assertive Portia, the submissive Portia and so on.

The early modern magistrate depended precisely upon this textual fluidity to effect government. Government, as Sidney emphasised, is not merely a matter of politics. *Arcadia* was written in order to 'sette downe the whole Arte of government'. Hobbes suggested that no sovereign was sovereign unless perceived as a 'visible power'. Sovereignty was a matter of spectacle; a fact no more apparent than in the coronation ceremony itself. To be able to dissimulate, to govern and to effect justice by means of theatrical feint, was not a matter of criticism amongst early modern political theorists. On the contrary it was thought to be an essential quality of good and godly magistracy. Machiavelli suggested that it defined the ideal prince.

According to Greenblatt, Henry V is Shakespeare's ideal magistrate, precisely because of his Machiavellian ability to elide identities (Greenblatt, 1985, pp.20-2; c.f. Holderness, 1992, pp.90-1). Early modern sovereigns themselves were only too aware that magistracy was a matter of art and performance. Elizabeth acknowledged that: 'We are princes set on stages in the sight and view of all the world' (Greenblatt, 1985, p.44). Elizabeth always dazzled. As John Hayward observed, like all great sovereigns, she was an actor first, who knew, above all, 'right well that in pompous ceremonies a secret of government doth much consist, for that the people are naturally both taken and held with exteriour shewes' (Pye, 1990, p.63).

Character in Shakespeare is, then, self-fashioned; the interactive process of text and audience. There is no determinative characterisation, just as there is no determinative interpretation of any particular text. This is precisely true of Portia and *The Merchant of Venice*. The stage provides a series of illusions, of government, of order, of law, of identity, of gender, and so on. Portia is constituted by precisely these illusions, and a multitude of others. There is no one Portia; merely infinite Portias. This infinity is forever preserved by the very nature of textuality and identity. Such self-fashioning, the appreciation of identity and interpretation as matters of inter-subjective determination, ensures fluidity of textual characterisation. It is this which serves to deconstruct the precise meaning of any text.

Portia and Feminist Legal Thinking

The suggestion that Portia is not quite what she seems, or at least what she seems to such as Menkel-Meadows or Gilligan, is one matter, and probably, in isolation, not a particularly important one. However, it might be illustrative of other more important potential hazards which accompany the establishment of any icons, feminist or otherwise. To establish an icon is to establish a model, usually an ideal. Moreover, though imprecise, and largely anecdotal in nature, it has become increasingly popular, following such as Gilligan, to suggest that women might lawyer or judge in a particularly female way. Yet the rather tentative, even aspirational, nature of such conclusions, both by academics such as Regina Graycar, and by judges such as Bertha Wilson, is itself perhaps instructive (Graycar, 1995; Wilson, 1990). Whilst suggesting that women might make a difference, and write a feminist jurisprudence, within the established patriarchal legal order, it is hard to be sure what that difference might be, or crucially, what it might look like.

Certainly, the Portia-myth is established in order to present some sort of model for women lawyers; perhaps a model of what they should aspire to; perhaps a model of what the essential female can add to law, the seasoning of justice with mercy; perhaps a model of what the woman lawyer has to endure with regard to the elision of identities. If these are the models, then the failure of Portia to conform to any particular image or icon is potentially destabilising. Maybe there are no precise models? Maybe there is no ideal woman lawyer? Maybe, feminism has nothing really important, or even interesting, to contribute to legal theory, either to women or to men? Such questions, and the doubts which reside behind them, immerses us in a pervasive contemporary concern in feminist legal thought. Is there anything particularly essential about a woman?

To a certain extent, radical feminism is premised on an essential woman. For some, such as Robin West, the essential woman is determined by biology (West, 1993, pp.179-249). For others, such as Catherine Mackinnon, the essential woman is a matter of ideological, even philosophical, principle, as well as political expediency (Mackinnon, 1989). For others the political expediency is what really matters. As Valerie Bryson emphasises, feminist politics needs to be able to identify woman as an interest subjugated by men. Too great a concern with the niceties of postmodern textuality will do nothing to help further the cause of the subjugated woman (Bryson, 1992, pp.228-9). Diana Majury makes the related observation that theory, as a strategy, must coincide with the more immediate political strategies of radical feminism. Women must define themselves in order to define their oppression, and the nature of their politics (Majury, 1991).

Political expediency is also cited by Patricia Williams (1987). Speaking as precisely the black woman feminist that is often presumed to be excluded by an essentialist model, Williams suggests that there is a virtue in striving to make political gains within the existing legal structure, if only because it is reasonable to assume that they are the only gains that are likely to be realised. This is not a matter of essentialism, of sameness or difference, but of political necessity. Women suffer within the political structure because of their gendered identity. To that extent there is a value in acknowledging an essential difference in order to erase its political effect (Williams, 1987).

Elizabeth Schneider reaches a very similar conclusion, in defending the attempt by women to access liberal rights. Such an attempt might be constructively to support a patriarchal system, but it can realise an improved condition for women in the real political situation. Again, like Williams, Schneider is prepared to countenance the description of an essentially different, and subjugated, woman in order to achieve strategic political gains (Schneider, 1991). Such a conclusion resonates with Gayatri Spivak's wider call for the writing of an essential woman as an exercise in 'strategic essentialism'; an idea translated into the jurisprudential sphere recently by Dianne Brooks (Brooks, 1994). Even an avowed anti-essentialist such as Deborah Rhode can support the idea of 'alternative visions', just so long as such visions are temporary and understood to be so (Rhode, 1990, p.635).

To this extent, then, there would seem to be a political need to establish something essentially different about women, and, thus, in establishing this essence, models of ideality must, to some degree, be described. Regardless of the textual niceties, Portia could be precisely such a model. But this leads us on to the next question, and it is *the* question, I would suggest, in contemporary legal feminism. Are such models really desirable? Or is it the case that the very multi-textuality which denies an objective Portia, also denies the possibility of a model woman lawyer? In other words, even if we accept, for reasons of political strategy, that a model woman lawyer could be invented, do we want such an invention? A lot, of course, then depends upon who the 'we' is, because if the 'we' is something less than everyone, or indeed, even every woman, then we have a potential problem. It is, of course, the problem which surrounds any attempt to invent an essential anything; not just 'what is being invented?' but 'who is doing the inventing?'.

It has become increasingly popular to attack the perceived essentialism of such as Catherine Mackinnon (c.f. Sandland, 1995). In political terms, Angela Harris has persuasively suggested that the establishment of any ideal woman is potentially exclusionary for those who fall outside. More precisely, she suggests that Mackinnon's essential woman is an uncomfortably white middle class one (Harris, 1991). Similar sentiments are expressed by Deborah Rhode. Adopting the anti-reification thesis of Critical Legal Scholars such as Peter Gabel, Rhode is keen to demystify and deconstruct any pretended ideal. Such deconstruction does not preclude the strategic use of such ideals, but it does deny the intellectual veracity of an accompanying essentialism (Rhode, 1990). Most recently, Eileen Fegan has referred to certain 'unsustainable essentialist notions of truth and feminity'. Ideology, Fegan rightly suggests, tends to create its own particular truth, and then deny its political and textual contingency. Essentialism is just another ideology (Fegan, 1995).

Political convenience, then, carries its price. The icon of the woman lawyer may have its uses, but it also carries a liability. In short, such an icon is not just descriptive, it is prescriptive. The process of description, as Shakespeare knew so well, is always an act of textual politics; an act of empowerment. To prescribe is to govern and to command. Intellectual doubts with regard to the veracity of writing the essential woman have been expressed, most forcefully perhaps, by Judith Butler. Developing Foucault's post-structuralist critique, Butler suggests that the prescription of identities is an innately political exercise. There is no 'common identity' for women; there is merely a prescribed cultural identity, a gender identity (Butler, 1990, pp.1-33).

In this sense, there is an acute danger in asserting anything essential about an individual, never mind any group of individuals. Such an assertion depends upon the stabilisation of identity against the contingencies of life and situation. Such a danger is always present in any particular area of social, legal or political theory, particularly when that theory is founded, to some degree, upon an identified interest group. Feminist theory is just one example. The same dangers apply to race theory, theories based on economic interests, theories based upon particular theologies and so on. Indeed, it might fairly be suggested that just about any theory or philosophy tends to be written for a particular audience, precisely because it is written by a particular author and audience. Any theory, just like any text, because it is a text, is constituted by and for a particular interest. In this sense, of course, there is little point in saying that feminist theory is inherently flawed because of the dangers of writing about the situation of one identifiable interest in society, women.

However, such a theory can be strengthened by a greater awareness of the presence of such dangers, and the irreducible nature of theory as text and as literature. The revelation of this danger is one of the most crucial insights that literature can lend to legal or political theory. It is certaintly not an unknown danger. As we have already noted it has been forcefully articulated by Judith Butler. Moreover, a number of feminist legal scholars have emphasised the textual nature of the feminist enterprise, and thus the instability of identities. One of the most persuasive is Drucilla

Cornell (1992). Cornell has developed a consciously textual feminism which she aligns with the deconstructive postmodernism of Lacan and, more particularly, Jacques Derrida. She concentrates on developing a postmodern ethics from textual deconstruction. The denial of objectified models or ideals respects the individuality of the subject. Such an approach is obviously resonant of Lyotard's famous denial of the metanarrative. Cornell's community is a fractured community which inheres multiple identities, and wherein power is dispersed in a radical plural manner. Intrinsic to such a polity is the acceptance of individual subjectivity. Women are not of a type, and neither are women lawyers. Furthermore, and perhaps most importantly, women must not be idealised. There is no ideal woman lawyer, no essential woman lawyer, and nor should there be (Cornell, 1992).

Cornell is not, of course, alone in aligning a textual feminism with a postmodern legal politics. Mary Joe Frug similarly stressed that gender questions were always at once questions of politics, of economics, of culture, of art and so on. Thus to pursue some particular identifiable woman is to pursue a certain preordained and objectified ideal; most importantly, someone else's ideal (Frug, 1992). Joan Williams has expressed similar sentiments (Williams, 1991). The textuality of feminism, like the textuality of law, cannot be avoided, and any attempt to deny it merely serves to undercut the potential for political change. As Fegan has concluded, politics must be understood as a textual exercise. The insights of postmodernism and deconstruction cannot be simply swept under the carpet (Fegan, 1995).

But neither, at the same time, must they be allowed to de-energise feminism. There is certainly no need for this to be the case. Postmodernism merely suggests the fluidity of ethics. It does not deny the possibility of a political ethics, providing such an ethics is appreciated to be textual as well as political. Such a conclusion is articulated by Carol Smart, who emphasises the importance of consciousness-raising, as a matter of both politics and textuality. As Smart concludes, the 'recognition that we live in postmodern times does not therefore mean that we have to abandon politics. But it does mean that we cannot make promises about what our politics will achieve'. Moreover, it is postmodernism's determination of contingent truth which permits the re-entry of 'ethics back into the discussion' (Smart, 1995, pp.171-8, 186-99, 211-20). Postmodernism reintroduces the creative space in which ethics can be nourished.

Ultimately, it is a matter of respect for the Other, as expressed in respect for the multi-textual identity of the Other. Echoing the American pragmatist, Richard Rorty, Cornell suggests that the postmodern community is one determined as a community of Others, where every constituent is Other. It will be, she suggests, a jurisprudential 'choreography of difference' (Cornell, 1985, pp.327-55, 375-8; Cornell, 1993, pp.168-9). Only a postmodern feminism can thus respect the essential difference of every woman, and it is only in such a way that the precise situation of the disadvantaged woman can be addressed in the particular.

Judith Butler gestures, albeit rather opaquely, towards a similar conclusion; identity as determined by the fluid and constitutive 'process of signification' as a discursive enterprise (Butler, 1990, pp.141-5). In turn, this essentially political-ethical solution resonates with Kathleen Bartlett's invocation of 'positionality'. Rather than merely accepting the textual indeterminacy suggested by postmodernism, as irreducibly destabilising in the political situation, Bartlett suggests that such a situation can be, at least partially, stabilised by the very act of acknowledging the contingency of truth (Bartlett, 1991, p.389).

Truth is 'situated and partial', and derived from all human relations across gender. Indeed, it is defined by such relations. Positionality, she continues, 'can reconcile the apparent contradiction within feminist thought between the need to recognize the diversity of people's lives and the value in trying to transcend that diversity'. Whilst, to 'understand human diversity... is also to understand human commonality' (Bartlett, 1991, pp.391-2). The essential woman, and indeed the essential man, is determined in the contingent political and textual situation, and is determined in relation to the Other. The resonance with Cornell, and with Rorty's postmodern liberalism, is obvious (Rorty, 1989). Bartlett's world of positionality is a world defined by its very contingency, and populated only by the Others who describe it or, to use Rorty's own metaphor, who generate its constituent conversation.

It is, in other words, a world of multi-textual Portias, where no woman is ever denuded to such an extent that she can be defined as a woman lawyer, or indeed, as a rich woman, or a white woman. Instead, each woman, like each man, is constituted by precisely the same infinity of textual indicators which deny the possibility of identifying an essential Portia. As we saw, there are numerous Portias; an infinity preserved by the textuality of character. Once it is appreciated that any woman, and any man, is textually created in precisely the same way, then we can appreciate that we are all actors engaged in the art of fashioning and refashioning identities. The presentation of a conference paper, the writing of an academic article, the writing of a shopping list, are all acts of dissimulation and self-fashioning; the adoption of a particular guise in order to effect a particular role. The writing of the woman lawyer, and the prescriptions which are thereby unavoidably made, must be understood as precisely such an exercise. Nothing could more obviously illustrate the textuality of identity. If Portia is a symbol of anything, it is of this textuality, and the extent to which it denies the possibility of any essential or idealised woman outside the boundaries of textuality itself.

Bibliography

Barber, C. (1959), *Shakespeare's Festive Comedy: A Study in Dramatic Form and its Relation to Social Custom*, Princeton University Press, Princeton.

Barlett, K. (1991), 'Feminist Legal Methods' in K. Barlett and R. Kennedy (eds.), *Feminist Legal Theory: Readings in Law and Gender*, Westview Press, Boulder.

Barthes, R. (1986), *The Rustle of Language*, Blackwell, Oxford.

Beauregarde, D. (1988), 'Sidney, Aristotle, and *The Merchant of Venice*: Shakespeare's Triadic Images of Liberality and Justice', *Shakespeare Studies*, vol. 20, pp.33-51.

Belsay, C. (1985), *The Subject of Tragedy: Identity and Difference in Renaissance Drama*, Methuen, London.

Benston, A. (1979), 'Portia, the Law, and the Tripartite Structure of *The Merchant of Venice*', *Shakespeare Quarterly*, vol. 30, pp. 367-85.

Berger, H. (1981), 'Marriage and Mercifixion in *The Merchant of Venice*: The Casket Scene Revisited', *Shakespeare Quarterly*, vol. 32, pp. 155-62.

Brooks, D. (1994), 'A Commentary on the Essence of Anti-Essentialism in Feminist Legal Theory', *Feminist Legal Studies*, vol. 2, pp. 115-32.

Bryson, V. (1992), *Feminist Political Theory: An Introduction*, Paragon Press, New York.

Burgess, G. (1996), *Absolutism and the Stuart Constitution*, Yale University Press, Newhaven.

Butler, J. (1990), *Gender Trouble: Feminism and the Subversion of Identity*, Routledge, London.

Cohen, W. (1982), '*The Merchant of Venice* and the Possibilities of Historical Criticism', *ELH*, vol. 49, pp. 765-89.

Colley, J. (1980), 'Launcelot, Jacob, and Esau: Old and New Law in *The Merchant of Venice*', *Yearbook of English Studies*, vol. 10, pp. 181-9.

Cornell, D. (1985), 'Toward a Modern/Postmodern Reconstruction of Ethics', *University of Pennsylvania Law Review*, vol. 133, pp. 291-380.

Cornell, D. (1992), *The Philosophy of the Limit*, Routledge, London.

Cornell, D. (1993), *Transformations*, Routledge, London.

Eagleton, T. (1986), *William Shakespeare*, Blackwell, Oxford.

Eco, U. (1992), *Interpretation and Overinterpretation*, Cambridge University Press, Cambridge.

Fegan, E. (1995), '"Ideology" After "Discourse": A Reconceptualization for Feminist Analyses of Law', *Journal of Law and Society*, vol. 23, pp. 173-97.

Fletcher, A. (1995), *Gender, Sex and Subjugation in England 1500-1800*, Yale University Press, Newhaven.

Frug, M. (1992), *Postmodern Legal Feminism*, Routledge, London.

Gadamer, H-G. (1975), *Truth and Method*, Sheed & Ward, London.

Gadamer, H-G. (1977), *Philosophical Hermeneutics*, University of California Press, Berkeley.

Gilligan, C. (1982), *In a Different Voice: Psychological Theory and Women's Development*, Harvard University Press, Cambridge, Mass.

Goddard, H. (1986), 'Portia's Failure' in H. Bloom (ed.), *The Merchant of Venice: Modern Critical Interpretations*, Chelsea House, London.

Graycar, R. (1995), 'The Gender of Judgments: An Introduction' in M. Thornton (ed.), *Public and Private: Feminist Legal Debates*, Oxford University Press, Oxford.

Greenblatt, S. (1980), *Renaissance Self-Fashioning: From More to Shakespeare*, University of Chicago Press, Chicago.

Greenblatt, S. (1985), 'Invisible Bullets: Renaissance Authority and its Subversion', in J. Dollimore and A. Sinfield (eds.), *Political Shakespeare: New Essays in Cultural Materialism*, Manchester University Press, Manchester.

Greenblatt, S. (1988), *Shakespearean Negotiations: The Circulation of Social Energy in Renaissance England*, University of California Press, Berkeley.

Hall, J. (1995), *Anxious Pleasures: Shakespearean Comedy and the Nation-State*, Associated University Presses, London.

Hamill, M. (1978), 'Poetry, Law, and the Pursuit of Perfection: Portia's Role in *The Merchant of Venice*', *Studies in English Literature 1500-1900*, vol. 18, pp. 229-43.

Harris, A. (1991), 'Race and Essentialism in Feminist Legal Theory' in K. Bartlett and R. Kennedy (eds.), *Feminist Legal Theory: Readings in Law and Gender*, Westview Press, Boulder.

Hill, C. (1996), *Liberty Against the Law*, Penguin, London.

Holderness, G. (1992), *Shakespeare Recycled: The Making of Historical Drama*, Harvester Wheatsheaf, Hemel Hempstead.

Jardine, L. (1996), *Reading Shakespeare Historically*, Routledge, London.

Knight, N. (1974), 'Equity, *The Merchant of Venice* and William Lambarde', *Shakespeare Survey*, vol. 27, pp. 93-104.

Mackay, M. (1964). '*The Merchant of Venice*: a Reflection of the Early Conflict Between Courts of Law and Courts of Equity', *Shakespeare Quarterly*, vol. 15, pp. 371-5.

Mackinnon, C. (1989), *Towards a Feminist Theory of State*, Harvard University Press, Cambridge, Mass.

Majury, D. (1991), 'Strategizing in Equality' in M. Fineman and N. Thomadsen (eds.), *At the Boundaries of Law: Feminism and Legal Theory*, Routledge, London.

Menkel-Meadow, C. (1985), 'Portia in a Different Voice: Speculations on a Women's Lawyering Process', in S. Parker and C. Sampford (eds.), *Legal Ethics and Legal Practice: Contemporary Issues*, Clarendon Press, Oxford.

Newman, K. (1987), 'Portia's Ring: Unruly Women and Structures of Exchange in *The Merchant of Venice*', *Shakespeare Quarterly*, vol. 38, pp. 19-33.

O'Connor, S. (1991), 'Portia's Progress', *New York University Law Review*, vol. 66, pp. 1546-58.

Paster, G. (1985), *The Idea of the City in the Age of Shakespeare*, University of Georgia Press, Athens.

Pye, C. (1990), *The Regal Phantasm: Shakespeare and the Politics of Spectacle*, Routledge, London.

Rhode, D. (1990), 'Feminist Critical Theories', *Stanford Law Review*, vol. 42, pp. 617-38.

Rorty, R. (1989), *Contingency, Irony, and Solidarity*, Cambridge University Press, Cambridge.

Sandland, R. (1995), 'Between "Truth" and "Difference": Poststructuralism, Law and the Power of Feminism', *Feminist Legal Studies*, vol. 3, pp. 3-47.

Schneider, E. (1991), 'The Dialectics of Rights and Politics: Perspectives from the Women's Movement' in M. Fineman and M. Thomadsen (eds.), *At the Boundaries of Law: Feminism and Legal Theory*, Routledge, London.

Smart, C. (1995), *Law, Crime and Sexuality: Essays in Feminism*, Sage, London.

Tennenhouse, L. (1986), *Power on Display: The Politics of Shakespeare's Genres*, Methuen, New York.

Tucker, E. (1976), 'The Letter of the Law in *The Merchant of Venice*', *Shakespeare Survey*, vol. 29, pp. 93-101.

Ward, I. (1995), *Law and Literature: Possibilities and Perspectives*, Cambridge University Press, Cambridge.

West, R. (1993), *Narrative, Authority and Law*, University of Michigan Press, Ann Arbor.

Williams, J. (1991), 'Dissolving the Sameness/Difference Debate: A Post-Modern Path Beyond Essentialism in Feminist and Critical Race Theory', *Duke Law Journal*, pp. 296-323.

Williams, P. (1987), 'Alchemical Notes: Reconstructing Ideals from Deconstructed Rights', *Harvard Civil Rights-Civil Liberties Review*, vol. 22, pp. 401-33.

Wilson, B. (1990), 'Will Women Judges Really Make a Difference?', *Osgoode Hall Law Journal*, vol. 28, pp. 507-22.
Wrightson, K. (1982), *English Society 1580-1680*, Routledge, London.

5. Rape Law: Harbouring an Implicit Relation between Law and Psychology

FIONA E. RAITT AND M. SUZANNE ZEEDYK

Introduction

This chapter argues that there is an implicit relation that exists between the disciplines of law and psychology. This relation is collusive and it serves to suppress women. The most effective way to illustrate this relation is to look at law and psychology in action, and this chapter will focus on the topic of rape law.

Traditionally, the connection between law and psychology has been one where clinical psychologists, mental health professionals and others are called as expert witnesses, to provide opinion testimony regarding an individual's mental state and behaviour. Recently, however, a new dimension to the law and psychology link has developed through the use of general psychological theory which takes group behaviour as its focus. This new dimension to expert testimony is known as social framework data, and is of particular value where the typical behavioural effects of an event are unexpected or unusual (Monahan and Walker, 1988). In social framework evidence the law draws on general psychological theory, presented through expert testimony, to interpret factual issues and to measure an individual's particular actions against that which might be expected based on results derived from group norms. This means that in a case of sexual harassment, for example, evidence may be led of sex-stereotyping and the typical effects on women of this activity. Similarly, in child sexual abuse cases evidence might be led of the typical reactions of a child who was being molested, as an aid to explaining the specific reactions of a child in the case in question. Some jurisdictions, including most states in the United States, New Zealand and Australia, now admit social framework data in areas such as these (Colman, 1991; Fiske *et.al.*, 1991; Loftus, 1991).

The rules of evidence in the United Kingdom, in both Scots and English law, are still relatively restrictive and in general discourage over-reliance on expert opinion, in the belief that it subverts the function of the judge or jury as trier of fact.[1] However, expert evidence testimony has always had a limited role to play in the British courtroom and psychological evidence is slowly gaining greater prominence. For example, in cases of battered women who kill their violent partners and who plead provocation or diminished responsibility, psychological evidence may be admissible in support of the claims regarding the defendant's mental state.[2] And in a recent civil case reported in the national press in November 1996, where an adult survivor of child abuse sued for damages against her alleged abuser, evidence in support of the defender was provided by experts who testified to the effects of repressed memories and their propensity to cloud the recall of adult survivors.[3]

It will be argued in this chapter that because of inherent biases shared by the two disciplines of law and psychology, neither the findings of fact, nor the content of opinion evidence in cases which come to trial or proof, are neutral or objective. Indeed, these biases frequently result in a particular disadvantage to women. The distinctive status accorded to the disciplines of law and psychology within the social sciences gives specific legitimacy to that disadvantage and deters much needed legal reform.

The Implicit Relation between Law and Psychology

In both traditional and developing realms for the use of psychological evidence, the relation between law and psychology is explicit. It is clear what the respective role of each is in the judicial process. By contrast, it is argued here that distinct from this explicit relation, and of even greater concern, is the implicit relation which also exists between law and psychology. We propose that three characteristics underpin this implicit relation: first, a bias towards the male norm and the subsequent pathologising of women's experience; secondly, a focus and dependence on objectivity; and, thirdly, an emphasis on individual explanations of behaviour. As law becomes more willing to take account of general psychological theory, the explicit link is strengthened, leading in turn to a consolidation of the underlying implicit relation. It is this implicit relation which poses a particular threat to women's autonomy.

The relation is implicit in that it is rarely acknowledged, far less articulated or addressed. It does however exert a powerful influence despite apparent regulation by the law. To take the example of clinical psychologists called as expert witnesses in court, the opinion evidence they give is subject to the constraints imposed by the rules of evidence and procedure.[4] To that extent the influence of psychology in the court is explicit, controlled and made overt. Ostensibly such rules are designed to enable fact finding to occur in a coherent and logical manner, the ultimate aim being determination of the 'truth' in the criminal trial or civil proof. However 'facts', 'logic' and 'truth' are all relative concepts and play a significant role in sustaining pre-determined notions of justice (Nicolson, 1994). It is in these relative concepts that the implicit relation flourishes.

The disciplines of law and psychology individually reflect and represent the dominant social order of patriarchy (Bohan, 1992; MacKinnon, 1987; Miller, 1976; Smart, 1989; Smart, 1995; Ussher, 1991). 'Knowledge' and 'truth' are defined according to patriarchal aims and objectives. At the intersection of law and psychology those patriarchal aims and objectives are reflected even more sharply and in a way that provides reciprocal authority and legitimacy to each discipline. This is most apparent in areas that directly affect women, such as domestic violence, rape, abortion, and memories of childhood sexual abuse. In exploring the area of rape, this chapter considers the use of a recently emerging form of psychological evidence - rape trauma syndrome evidence - to illustrate the extent to which the combined force of law and psychology is a potent instrument in the control of women.

The Characteristics of the Implicit Relation

The argument begins with an examination of the characteristics of the implicit relation. In the pursuit of knowledge, truth, fact and objectivity, law and psychology share a common goal - the declared determination to remain free from influence by contextual and societal factors. The modus operandi of each discipline, with the three key characteristics that underpin their implicit relation, sustains the continuance of this supposed detachment. Thus, the male norm and the measurement of women's behaviour against such a norm; the tenet of objectivity, integral to scientific methodology and legal fact-finding; and the tendency to analyse behaviour at the individual level, all coalesce to exclude external sociological circumstances.

The first characteristic is the requirement of both disciplines that human behaviour be measured against the male norm. In the classic conceptualisation of Simone de Beauvoir, woman is 'defined and differentiated with reference to man and not he with reference to her; she is the incidental, the inessential as opposed to the essential. He is the Subject, he is the Absolute - she is the Other' (de Beauvoir, 1988 p.16). The defence of provocation provides one classic legal example of this bias. This defence recognises retaliatory aggression resulting from 'a sudden and temporary loss of control'.[5] Limited in this fashion, the defence accommodates only male experience and behaviour. The more typical female response to violence, especially domestic violence with its cumulative effect, is that of a slow-burning fuse culminating in an explosive single act of violence. This reaction can appear to be planned and deliberate, as it often has to be if a woman is to defend herself successfully against a more powerful physical force (Nicolson, 1995; Edwards, 1996). But because such behaviour does not neatly fit male standards of provocation, battered women who kill their abusive partners are forced to plead pathological disorder - diminished responsibility - if they are to avoid conviction for murder. There is an inherent inequity, even iniquity, in women having to accept mental disability as the price of their act of self-defence.

Of course, such psychologically-based explanations have been provided by psychologists. The pathologising of women's experience has a long history in psychology and psychiatry (Chesler, 1994; Shields, 1975; Ussher, 1991). Women dominate in the statistics for mental illness (Ussher, 1991). Yet, if one considers the argument that mental illness is constructed rather than 'diagnosed', as argued by many feminist critics (Chesler, 1972 and 1994; Ussher, 1991), this situation is not surprising, for women's experience will always emerge as abnormal when judged by male norms. Thus, the explanations now being applied in the courtroom, which characterise women's common experience as pathological (e.g., rape trauma syndrome, battered woman's syndrome, false memory syndrome) are merely contemporary expressions of a historical pattern.

The second characteristic of the implicit relation, the tenet of objectivity, is also fundamental to both fields. Law places a high premium on objectivity, in that objectivity appears to offer an independent, impartial criterion by which behaviour can be measured and evaluated. This value is reflected in the law's attachment to concepts such as 'the reasonable man', central to so many aspects of legal discourse (O'Donovan, 1991; Kennedy, 1993). Psychology, too, takes as its primary aim the discovery of 'objective truths', using decontextualised empirical research methods. As Morawski has observed: 'Psychologists have set most of their deliberations over objectivity in institutionalised terms such as *methodological procedures*, or to a lesser extent, the *qualities of investigators*' (Morawski, 1994, pp.74-75, original emphasis). But 'objectivity' is not objective - it is in fact gendered. It is male 'objectivity'. As MacKinnon claims: 'the neutrality of objectivity and of maleness are coextensive linguistically, whereas women occupy the marked, the different, the forever female position' (MacKinnon, 1987, p.55). 'Male' and 'objectivity' become inseparable, each reflecting the other. If to be woman is to be 'other', no amount of effort will achieve for law, 'normality' or the purity of objectivity. Women are forced to succumb to standards established by and for the male. Her experiences are ultimately marginalised, distorted or absent altogether (Lees, 1996).

The final characteristic of the implicit relation between law and psychology is the respective tendencies of each to analyse behaviour at the individual level. Indeed, the definition of psychology is the study of individual processes (Banyard and Grayson, 1996). Law, for its part, assigns rights and duties to the individual person, assuming and requiring that she or he accepts sole control and responsibility for behaviour, thus artificially divorcing personal responsibility for actions from their external sociological influences (MacKinnon, 1987; Smart, 1995). External influences are excluded from consideration within the courtroom by labelling them 'irrelevant' and thus inadmissible under the rules of evidence. For example, a mother's neglect of her child may cause her to be regarded as unfit to have custody of her child even though an explanation of the neglect might be that the mother is being abused by a partner. The mother bears responsibility for her behaviour toward the child, and her partner's abuse of her is not considered relevant to her accountability. One of the greatest deficiencies with the individualistic approach is that it ignores systemic influences on behaviour and implies there is no need to look further afield for adequate explanation (Bohan, 1992). In the context of violence against women this leads to an unsatisfactory cul-de-sac. As Koss explains: 'the problem of violence against women cannot be understood let alone solved, by focusing exclusively on individual psychology. Only by changing the social and cultural institutions that have given rise to the problem can a lasting solution be achieved' (Koss, 1993, p.1055).

The Implicit Relation Illustrated in Rape Law

The effects of the implicit relation will now be illustrated through consideration of rape law. In particular, attention will be given to one relatively recent development in rape law - evidence of rape trauma syndrome, because it represents a singularly clear expression of the law and psychology relation.

The use of rape trauma syndrome evidence is well established in the United States but there is, as yet, no record of admissibility in the UK courts. However, the growing acknowledgement of battered woman syndrome and now false memory syndrome suggests it is likely to be only a matter of time before rape trauma syndrome, too, is introduced in the UK courts.

A syndrome is a group of concurrent symptoms of a disease. Rape trauma syndrome is the name given to a constellation of reactions which may be exhibited by a woman who has been raped. The name was coined by Burgess and Holmstrom in 1974 during a study documenting the reactions and behaviours of women who were admitted to a hospital casualty department alleging rape (Burgess and Holmstrom, 1974). The syndrome embraces a wide spectrum of behaviours ranging from numbness and impassivity to hysteria and uncontrollable weeping. These symptoms have been accorded the official status of a post traumatic stress disorder, otherwise known as PTSD, by the American Psychiatric Association and the syndrome was first classified as an anxiety disorder in the third edition of the Association's Diagnostic and Statistical Manual (DSM).[6] Syndrome evidence is generally given in court by a psychiatrist or psychologist or both.

The use of rape trauma syndrome evidence in the US courts was established in 1982 in the Kansas case of *State* v. *Marks*,[7] hailed as a landmark decision in its recognition of the reliability and admissibility of psychological testimony of the syndrome. By the mid 1980's there had been many rulings on admissibility of such evidence. While reviews of the case law at that point concluded it was premature to state definitively in what circumstances rape trauma syndrome evidence would be admitted, even then commentators were able to discern that syndrome evidence was likely to be admitted if the court was satisfied on various counts (Frazier and Borgida, 1985). These included how helpful the expert's evidence would be to the jury, how prejudicial it would be to the defendant and whether the expert's testimony unduly invaded the province of the jury as trier of the facts. By 1992, there had been a steady increase in the number of cases where it was sought to introduce expert syndrome evidence and in the appeals based on its improper admissibility in the trial court (Frazier and Borgida, 1992).

Typically, evidence of rape trauma syndrome as a form of PTSD is introduced during the prosecution of an alleged rapist for two main purposes: education and corroboration (Frazier and Borgida, 1985). With regard to education, the testimony is introduced to provide the jury with background information regarding the usual reactions to rape. This information is intended to enable jurors to make a more informed decision concerning the credibility and reliability of the victim's account. Thus, it functions as social framework data and can be particularly valuable as an antidote to the widespread mythology affecting jurors' perceptions about the crime of rape and the type of woman who is raped. The case law suggests that expert testimony is more likely to be admissible when confined to this role (Frazier and Borgida, 1992).

With regard to the second purpose, corroboration, the rationale is that if evidence is led confirming that a woman complainer exhibits symptoms of rape trauma syndrome, this helps to corroborate her allegations. Such testimony may be especially desirable where sexual intercourse is admitted but there is little to corroborate the complainant's assertion that she did not consent. The case law here tends to resist admitting expert testimony as unfairly prejudicial to the defendant (Frazier and Borgida, 1992).

The Implicit Relation: Rape Law and the Male Norm

Having reviewed the emergence of rape trauma syndrome, attention is now turned to the way in which the implicit relation increasingly functions within rape law. The first characteristic of the implicit relation is the assessment of women's behaviour against a male norm. Rape law exemplifies normative expectations of women's behaviour. An entire mythology has taken root and continues to influence attitudes of the police, lawyers, judges and juries. This mythology is a feature of normative expectations. As a mythology it dictates that 'nice women' do not get raped, that women put themselves at risk of attack by drinking in pubs, consuming excessive amounts of alcohol, wearing party clothes, wearing too much make-up, inviting men back to their houses or accompanying men to their homes. In fact any activity demonstrative of a free and independent lifestyle is suggestive of the sort of woman who puts herself at risk of rape. The notion that rape is a woman's fault is still extraordinarily prevalent; an idea that both shapes and drives the pre-eminence of consent as a defence to a rape charge (Edwards, 1996; Lees, 1996). As Soothill and others have shown, the press contains regular reports of judicial pronouncements reflecting a continuing attachment to such mythology (Soothill *et. al.*, 1990; Soothill and Soothill, 1993). For example, in 1993 Judge Smedley, in a case tried at the Old Bailey, declared that: '[e]xperience has shown that people who allege sexual offences, whether women, men, boys or girls, for some reason or no reason at all tell false stories' (Lees, 1996, p.111). This statement, made from the bench, contravenes evidence indicating that the rate of false complaints of rape is no different from other crimes (Temkin, 1987). In December 1995 *The Times* newspaper reported Judge David Griffiths in a case in Winchester Crown Court saying to the defendant that: 'had you made an apology and sent her a bunch of flowers, all this would have been ... forgiven'.[8] Attitudes of this sort romanticise the crime of rape and belittle a woman's experience of it.

Another aspect of mythology supporting male expectations was encapsulated in the English decision in the case of *D.P.P.* v. *Morgan*,[9] the ratio of which denies that rape can occur if a man held an 'honest' belief that a woman was consenting to intercourse. In the *Morgan* case each of the three men who had intercourse with Morgan's wife claimed they 'honestly believed' she was consenting despite her protests and struggles because Morgan had told them she would behave in that way as she liked 'kinky' sex. The defendants sustained this claim in the face of evidence that she had been seriously physically injured. On their appeal against conviction it was held that a defendant's belief must only be honest, though not necessarily reasonable. The convictions of the defendants in *Morgan* were upheld as it was considered their beliefs were not, in fact, honestly held.[10] This aspect of rape law has been criticised as reflecting the 'masculinist presumption of proprietorial right to sex' (Edwards, 1996, p.346). Despite some efforts to ameliorate this presumption, for example through the abolition in 1991 of the rule excepting rape within marriage from prosecution, scepticism remains that there has been a real sea-change in attitude. As Susan Estrich has noted, while some progress has been made, measured by the absence in current cases of references to 'Lord Hale, Professor Wigmore and the unchaste mentality', we should be wary as 'looks can be deceptive' (Estrich, 1987, p.57). Estrich argues that courts today remain suspicious of women victims and protective of male defendants in precisely the circumstances which their predecessors exhibited suspicion and masculine empathy in previous decades (1987).

Just as in traditional rape mythology, where a woman is judged by male expectations relating to her appearance, dress, drinking habits and sexual practices, so too in rape trauma syndrome evidence, women continue to be judged by normative expectations. The expectations are now those embodied in the criteria set out in the DSM. Thus, unless a woman conforms to these criteria, she may well not be seen as credible and the court will not believe she has been raped. There will be pressure on women complainers to exhibit the 'right' symptoms, in sufficient quantity and quality to merit the use of expert syndrome evidence as corroboration. This imposes a new normative standard, automatically discrediting any of a woman's reactions outside the range of expected ones. The expected response to rape becomes pathology.

If use of syndrome evidence in rape cases becomes standard practice, any prosecution case which omits to lead expert testimony of it will be targeted by defence counsel who will argue that the absence of syndrome evidence is indicative of a weak case. Women who fear they do not exhibit appropriate symptoms of rape trauma will be both discouraged from reporting crime and perhaps even reluctant to classify their experience as rape. This situation is as yet a prediction. However, it is easy to envisage rape trauma syndrome, which began as a clinical description designed as a therapeutic strategy to assist women's recovery, converted to a tool of oppression when operating within the legal system.

The normative standards surrounding rape law ignore the endemic nature of violence against women in this society. Sexual assault in its many forms, from rape to sexual harassment, from child abuse to obscene telephone calls, is a horribly familiar experience in many women's lives. To suggest that any reaction a woman has to rape is a psychiatric disorder is offensive, and it diverts attention from the failings in the investigative and trial processes. The frequency of rape can hardly be classified as abnormal by statistical standards, since published research discloses that rape is experienced by between 15 per cent and 27.5 per cent of women (Koss *et. al.*, 1987). If certain reactions to rape are considered abnormal it is only because they do not fit normative male expectations.

The Implicit Relation: Rape Law and Objectivity

The second characteristic of the implicit relation is objectivity. In rape law this characteristic is seen most clearly in the context of definitions. While the precise definition of rape may vary from jurisdiction to jurisdiction, the general requirement is penetration of the vagina by the penis without the woman's consent. In England and Wales the definition has recently been extended so that rape now includes penetration of the anus by the penis, but in Scotland the former, more limited, definition prevails.[11] None of the UK jurisdictions classify penetration by an instrument or weapon other than the male sexual organ as 'rape'. Insistence on such narrow and linear standards of rape create objective definitions of the act, but they ignore the possibility that a sexual assault by other than a penis might be of greater violence and could cause equal, or even greater, physical and emotional harm to a woman. In effect, a woman's subjective experience of the invasion of her body is discounted in the very definition of rape (Muehlenhard *et. al.*, 1992).

Penetration is, of course, present in both consensual and non-consensual sex. Therefore, the issue of consent becomes the pivotal aspect of the legal definition of rape. In order to prove rape, the law demands evidence that no consent was given, and a woman's verbal assertion that this was the case is rarely sufficient. In a culture where the act of penetration of the vagina by the penis is the very core of both consensual and non-consensual heterosexual sex, women are bound to be disadvantaged, since, as Catharine MacKinnon argues, '[t]he crime of rape focuses more centrally on what men define as sexuality than on women's experience of (their) sexual being' (MacKinnon, 1987, p.87). Acceptable proof of non-consent is to be found in tangible evidence: torn clothing, cuts, bruises and body fluids. If there is no obviously visible, 'objective', damage to a woman's clothes or body, her credibility and reliability will be doubted and negative inferences drawn (Temkin, 1993). It is this concentration on 'real' evidence, accompanied by negation of the complainer's emotional reaction, that is one of the most distressing aspects of the trial process for women. As Lees has reported, 'the majority of women found their experiences in court humiliating and distressing', with a common complaint being that 'they were not allowed to explain fully what had happened to them or how they *felt* during the rape' (Lees, 1996, p.31, original emphasis). Such evidence of feelings would of course be considered subjective, not objective, and therefore deemed irrelevant. Pressure to admit evidence on rape trauma syndrome has resulted from difficulties in obtaining such objective evidence. Researchers such as Frazier and Borgida argue that it can help to corroborate a woman's claims (1985, 1992). Inherent in this proposition is the notion that a 'diagnosis' of rape trauma syndrome is more objective than a woman's claims. It acquires that status by virtue of its classification as a scientific, medical phenomenon. To be scientific is to be objective. It is this quality of objectivity that increasingly draws courts to the use of scientific evidence. Thus, the evidential value of rape trauma syndrome is dependent on its scientific categorisation, as shown by the extent to which the issue of its scientific basis has dominated the debate about admitting rape trauma syndrome as evidence (Frazier and Borgida, 1992; Lauderdale, 1984). Yet, as we have already argued, objectivity is not neutral. Objectivity, within law, within science, and within psychology, is inherently gendered. It is male objectivity.

There is already a long list of what constitutes 'real rape'. Rape trauma syndrome all too easily becomes simply an addition to that catalogue, perhaps promoted due to its scientific aura. Women must now evaluate their psychological reaction, as well as their dress, language, and behaviour, to determine whether what happened to them was 'really rape'. There is much research to support the view that women are reluctant not only to report rape but may have difficulty in defining their experience as rape (Estrich, 1987; Lees, 1996). Despite published data which consistently reveals that women are more likely to be raped by someone they know, including their partner, the myth survives that rape is primarily a sex crime carried out by frenzied psychopaths. This demotes certain forms of rape such as acquaintance rape or marital rape to less than 'real' rape (Estrich, 1987; Koss *et. al.*, 1987; Kelly, 1988). The perpetuation of such mythology deters women from classifying an assault by their current or ex-partner as rape or from reporting it to the police. In this way, objectivity is used to affirm that coercive sex is behaviour located only outside personal relationships.

The Implicit Relation: Rape Law and Individualism

The third and final characteristic of the implicit relation is that of the focus on the individual. The legal system treats rape as the embodiment of an individual and private ordeal. As with so many forms of violence against women rape remains a very private matter, tending to occur behind closed doors. Eye-witnesses are rare. This, coupled with the problems raised by consent, compounds difficulties in producing sufficient evidence. Ironically, even where efforts are made to assist a woman once she is in the criminal justice system, such as clearing the court when she gives her evidence, these are detrimental. For in clearing the courts of all but those legal personnel deemed necessary to the trial, the complainant is left isolated in the courtroom and denied support from friends or family. Thus, the private, individual aspects of rape are elevated above those of the social context in which rape occurs and is recounted. It is clearly possible to try to explain rape in this manner, for that is precisely what law currently does. However, offering an explanation does not, of course, guarantee it is accurate or adequate.

Rape trauma syndrome also adopts an individualistic explanation, in its attention to the individual woman's experience. The 'pathology' is diagnosed and treated on an individual level. This focus stifles consideration of any wider societal aspects of rape (Bristow, 1984). The underlying assumption by both law and psychology is that consideration of such contextual factors is unnecessary for understanding the experience. Knowledge of the individual woman's experience and reaction is a sufficient analysis. This joint assumption sustains the implicit relation. By admitting psychological evidence on rape trauma syndrome, the law is confirming that an explanation at the level of the individual person is deemed to be helpful and appropriate. By serving as expert witnesses proffering opinions on rape trauma syndrome, psychology is affirming the propriety of law's choice. The scientific evidence suggests there is no need to look further in understanding rape.

Individual-level analysis is an inevitable consequence of defining experience according to a biological model. Psychologists and other 'scientific' or 'medical' personnel have used biological models to explain women's weakness and 'otherness' since the Victorian era. By positioning women as 'biologically labile, and madness as caused by biology', women are considered 'prey to all manner of disorders, both physical and psychological' (Ussher, 1991, p.248). The application of rape trauma syndrome evidence as a diagnostic tool reinforces the idea that biology handicaps the female. As such it has much potential for exploitation by the defence in a rape trial. After all, if science has affirmed women's susceptibilities to pathological syndromes, then the fact that a woman currently exhibits the relevant symptoms of rape trauma syndrome cannot be assumed to stem from this *particular* sexual assault. It might just as easily derive from past events unrelated to this incident. A woman's credibility and reliability can then be attacked in this trial and attention deflected from the alleged act of rape to an assessment of whether her biology, hormones or medical history renders her unfit as a witness. Nothing, then, has changed - the victim and not the rapist is still at the centre of legal attention.

Conclusion

The purpose of this chapter has been to draw attention to problematic aspects of the relation between the disciplines of law and psychology. It is our contention that there is an implicit relation at work which operates via three key characteristics: the male norm, objectivity and individualism. This implicit relation is well-placed to function as an instrument of control, due to the authority accorded by society to the 'objective, scientific' methods of psychology and the 'natural force' of the rule of law. Moreover, the hidden nature of the implicit relation between the two disciplines operates pervasively and invidiously. The result, whether deliberate or not, is a powerful collusion between law and psychology which works actively against the interests of women.

The example of rape was used to illustrate the implicit relation in practice. In so doing, the opportunity has been taken to appraise claims that rape trauma syndrome evidence offers a fresh and novel solution to deficiencies within rape law. In fact, evidence of this syndrome replicates many traditional deficiencies. In its educative capacity, it seeks to challenge old myths, but unfortunately creates new ones to replace them. In its corroborative capacity, it focuses on the victim's response and not the rapist's actions. Burdening the woman with responsibility for dismantling mythology and providing corroboration of her victimised state from psychological disorder is an indictment of the criminal justice system's willingness to investigate and prosecute sexual crime adequately or effectively. Expert testimony on women's mental state is no solution to the inadequacies of rape law. This is to offer bandaids, when only radical surgery will do.

Acknowledgements

The authors thank Audrey Harrow for her assistance in the preparation of this chapter.

Notes

1. The present law was laid down in *R.* v. *Turner* [1975] 1 All ER 70 where Lawton, L.J. declared that, 'Jurors do not need psychiatrists to tell them how ordinary folk who are not suffering from any mental illness are likely to react to the stresses and strains of life'.

2. *R*. v. *Thornton* [1992] 1 All ER 306; *R*. v. *Thornton* (No.2) [1996] 2 All ER 1023; *R*. v. *Ahluwalia* [1992] 4 All ER 889.
3. *The Daily Telegraph*, 30 November 1996.
4. There will obviously be jurisdictional variations but as a minimum, there will be a requirement to prove the expert's credentials and to satisfy the court as to the validity of the research relied upon, usually by reference to peer approval and publications.
5. *R*. v. *Ahluwalia* [1992] 4 All ER 889 at 895g.
6. American Psychiatric Association, *Diagnostic and Statistical Manual of Mental Disorders (DSM 111R*, Disorder Number 309.81). The current edition is the fourth edition and was published in 1994.
7. 1982 647 P. 2ed. 1292.
8. *The Times*, 19 December 1995.
9. [1975] AC 182.
10. In terms of section 1(2) of the Sexual Offences (Amendment) Act 1976 as amended by the Criminal Justice and Public Order Act 1994, the jury must now have regard to whether or not an accused who claims to have believed a woman was consenting to sex had reasonable grounds for so believing.
11. The extension to the law in England to include anal rape was in terms of section 142 of the Criminal Justice and Public Order Act 1994. Scotland does not recognise rape as other than penetration of the vagina. Anything other than this, such as forced anal or oral penetration, is indecent assault.

Bibliography

Banyard, P. and Grayson, A. (1996), *Introducing Psychological Research*, Macmillan Press, London.

Bohan, J.S. (1992), 'Prologue: Re-viewing psychology, re-placing women: An end searching for a means', in J.S. Bohan (ed.), *Seldom Seen, Rarely Heard: Women's Place in Psychology*, Westview Press, Oxford.

Bristow, A. (1984), '*State* v. *Marks*: An Analysis of Expert Testimony on Rape Trauma Syndrome', *Victimology: An International Journal*, vol. 9, pp. 273-281.

Burgess, A. and Holmstrom, L. (1974), 'Rape Trauma Syndrome', *American Journal of Psychiatry*, vol. 131, pp. 981-999.

Chesler, P. (1972), *Women and Madness*, Doubleday, New York.

Chesler, P. (1994), *Patriarchy - Notes of an Expert Witness*, Common Courage Press, Monroe.

Colman, A. (1991), 'Crowd Psychology in South African murder trials', *American Psychologist*, vol. 46, pp. 1071-1079.

de Beauvoir, S. (1988), *The Second Sex*, Pan Books, London.

Edwards, S.S.M. (1996), *Sex and Gender in the Legal Process*, Blackstone Press, London.

Estrich, S. (1987), *Real Rape*, Cambridge, Mass.

Fiske, S.T., Bersoff, D.N., Borgida, E., Deaux, K. and Heilman, M.E. (1991), 'Social Science Research on Trial: Use of Sex Stereotyping Research in Price Waterhouse v Hopkins', *American Psychologist*, vol. 46, pp. 1049-1060.

Frazier, P. and Borgida, E. (1985), 'Rape trauma syndrome evidence in court', *American Psychologist*, vol. 40, pp. 984-993.

Frazier, P. and Borgida, E. (1992), 'Rape Trauma Syndrome - A Review of Case Law and Psychological Research', *Law and Human Behaviour*, vol. 16, pp. 293-311.

Kelly, L. (1988), *Surviving Sexual Violence*, Polity Press, London.

Kennedy, H. (1993), *Eve was Framed*, Vintage Books, London.

Koss, M.P. (1993), 'Rape: Scope, impact, intervention and public policy response', *American Psychologist*, vol. 48, pp. 1062-1069.

Koss, M.P., Gidycz, A. and Wisniewski, N. (1987), 'The Scope of Rape: Incidence and Prevalence of Sexual Aggression and Victimization in a National Sample of Higher Education Students', *Journal of Consulting and Clinical Psychology*, vol. 55, pp. 162-170.

Lauderdale, H.J. (1984), 'The Admissibility of Expert Testimony on Rape Trauma Syndrome', *Journal of Criminal Law and Criminology*, vol. 75, pp. 1366-1416.

Lees, S. (1996), *Carnal Knowledge*, Hamish Hamilton, London.

Loftus, E.F. (1991), 'Resolving legal questions with psychological data', *American Psychologist*, vol. 47, pp. 1046-1048.

MacKinnon, C.A. (1987), *Feminism Unmodified: Discourses on Life and Law*, Harvard University Press, London.

Miller, J.B. (1976), *Toward a New Psychology of Women*, Beacon Press, USA.

Monahan, J. and Walker, L. (1988), 'Social science research in law: A new paradigm', *American Psychologist*, vol. 43, pp. 465-472.

Morawski, J.G. (1994), *Practising Feminisms, Reconstructing Psychology*, University of Michigan Press, USA.

Muehlenhard, C.L., *et. al.* (1992), 'Definitions of Rape: Scientific and Political Implications', *Journal of Social Issues*, vol. 48, pp. 22-44.

Nicolson, D. (1994), 'Truth, Reason and Justice: Epistemology and Politics in Evidence Discourse', *Modern Law Review*, vol. 57, pp. 726-744.

Nicolson, D. (1995), 'Telling Tales: Gender Discrimination, Gender Construction and Battered Women who Kill', *Feminist Legal Studies*, vol. 3, pp. 185-206.

O'Donovan, K. (1991), 'Defences for Battered Women Who Kill', *Journal of Law and Society*, vol. 18, pp. 219-240.

Shields, S.A. (1975), 'Functionalism, Darwinism, and the Psychology of Women: A Study in Social Myths', *American Psychologist*, vol. 30, pp. 739-754.

Smart, C. (1989), *Feminism and the Power of Law*, Routledge, London.

Smart, C. (1995), *Law, Crime, and Sexuality*, Butterworths, London.

Soothill, K. and Soothill, D. (1993), 'Prosecuting the Victim? A Study of the Reporting of Barristers Comments in Rape Cases', *Howard Journal*, vol. 32, pp. 12-24.

Soothill, K., Walby, S. and Bagguley, P. (1990), 'Judges, the Media and Rape', *Journal of Law and Society*, vol. 17, pp. 211-233.

Temkin, J. (1987), *Rape and the Legal Process*, Sweet & Maxwell, London.

Temkin, J. (1993), 'Sexual History Evidence: The Ravishment of Section 2', *Criminal Law Review*, vol. 1, pp. 3-20.

Ussher, J. (1991), *Women's Madness: Misogyny or Mental Illness?*, Harvester Wheatsheaf, Herts.

6. The Business of Equality

CLARE McGLYNN

Introduction

It is widely recognised that political debate has become increasingly dominated by the '3 E's of efficiency, effectiveness and economy' (Crawford, 1996, p.249; see also Tusa, 1997). This marketisation of our political culture has profound implications, with cost-benefit analyses being applied to all policies, 'including human life itself' (Willets, 1997, p.9).[1] Few areas remain sacrosanct and, in recent years, the test of market viability has been applied to equal opportunity employment policies and sex discrimination legislation. Governmental action in this area has been guided by the perceived need to 'strike a fair balance between the rights of employees and the obligations on employers, consistent with the objective of improving the flexibility of the UK labour market' (Department of Employment, 1994, p.138); and writers with a similar economic aim in mind have suggested that anti-discrimination legislation should be repealed *in toto* in order to improve the efficiency of the market and ensure profit maximisation (Posner, 1987, 1989; Epstein, 1992; Quest, 1992).

Advocates of sex equality[2] have responded to this marketisation of political rhetoric by seeking to justify existing, and develop further, equal opportunity employment practices in economic terms: the development of the 'business case' for sex equality. The business case takes the existing legislative framework as a given, and calls for the effective implementation of such legislation, together with the voluntary adoption of equal opportunity employment practices, on the grounds that these measures will promote economic efficiency and profit maximisation. Thus, whereas sex equality was once seen as an end in itself, it is now put forward as a means by which to achieve an alternative end, namely improved economic performance.

The development and adoption of such a strategy is understandable;

many feminists have argued that reform must be sought within the existing political framework (Wolf, 1993),[3] and adopting the rhetoric of markets is doing just that. In doing so, the business case provides armour with which to defend sex equality measures in economic terms, premised on the belief that the moral or ethical case for equality has been won, and that it is the perceived costs of introducing equal opportunity policies which acts as a barrier to change (Humphries and Rubery, 1995, p.1).

Notwithstanding the possibility that the business case has invigorated debate, and encouraged the adoption of fairer employment practices amongst those employers hitherto hostile to equal opportunities, the wholesale adoption of market rhetoric to justify sex equality has profound implications. At the level of policy debate, the acceptance of economics as the trump card means that were it possible to show that a particular policy or legislative proposal did not contribute towards economic prosperity, there would be little justification for pursuing such a course of action. Normatively, a concentration on the economics of sex equality renders invisible the moral and ethical reasons why a society should seek sex equality.

This chapter will attempt to draw together some of the common themes of the business case, as articulated in present political debates. In doing so, what is offered is no more than a first attempt to outline some of the underlying premises of the business case and a preliminary consideration of some of its shortcomings. In doing so, the intention is not to reject the business case as a political strategy, but to engender a deeper understanding of the limitations and implications of pursuing such an economically-based strategy.

The Business Case for Sex Equality

The business case for sex equality is not an overarching economic theory, but a collection of themes, ideas and arguments (for a wide discussion see Humphries and Rubery, 1995). Nonetheless, there would appear to be three principal elements to the business case as presently advocated which will each be considered in turn, but uniting these elements is an emphasis on voluntarism. The business case advocates the adoption *by employers* of equal opportunity employment policies, and in doing so reduces both the perceived need for governmental and legislative action, and any responsibility on the part of government. It is this particular, voluntarist, manifestation of the business case which is its principal failing. The business case relies on persuasion and exhortation as the means by which to improve the position of women in the workplace. Sex equality becomes dependent on the voluntary actions of employers, obviating governmental responsibility. This 'privatisation of sex equality policy' (Forbes, 1996, p.145) is at the core of the business case.

In focusing on the voluntary actions of employers, the business case merely seeks to convince individual employers of the particular arguments being advanced. Accordingly, its impact at a sectoral level, or in terms of society as a whole, is limited. For example, although an economic or business case could be made as to why high unemployment amongst single mothers is wasteful of resources, the business case itself does not provide any specific remedy to such a problem. An improvement in the employment prospects of women may be aided by repeated exhortations that they are capable of performing work to the same standard as men (and it might even be suggested that of course women will work for less pay than men), but the unemployment is only likely to be alleviated by governmental action and/or legal requirements imposed on employers. Similarly, one of the principal reasons why women's pay remains on average less than men's is due to occupational segregation, with women employed in occupations which are less valued and less well remunerated (Rubery, 1992). Again, the business case, by focusing on individual employers, can have little impact on occupational sex segregation. Indeed, lower remuneration for women will improve profit maximisation, leaving little room for a business case justification for equal pay (but see *infra*). Finally, in advocating voluntary, as opposed to governmental, action, the message being made is weakened. If it was generally accepted that, for example, the adoption of equal opportunity employment practices improve economic performance, then it would be incumbent upon government to legislate, in so far as possible, accordingly. One of the reasons why such governmental action is not taken is the reason why the strategy was developed in the first place, the reluctance of government to be seen to 'interfere' in business decisions, whether contrary to equality of opportunity or not. As well as reducing the impact of the business case, this refusal to take action may in fact hinder economic performance. If there are no minimum employment standards imposed on companies by legislation, employees will move to those companies which do offer the desired policies. In doing so, the delivery of such policies becomes prohibitively expensive for those employers, and it is only by imposing obligations on all employers can any costs incurred be evenly spread (Balls, 1996).

The reliance of the business case on voluntary actions may in part explain its widespread support. The business case has the backing of government, the Equal Opportunities Commission, the Confederation of British Industry, the Social Justice Commission and the Institute of Personnel and Development. Further, the business case forms the basis for the campaign organisation Opportunity 2000, formed in 1991, Opportunity 2000 is a campaign which seeks to improve the quality and quantity of women's employment at all levels by promoting the business case for equality (Opportunity 2000, 1996). As its fifth year review confirms: 'Right from the start, Opportunity 2000 has emphasised that the rationale for joining the campaign is not rooted in a moral or social imperative but in hard commercial facts' (Opportunity 2000, 1996). Opportunity 2000 was launched with governmental support, with the Prime Minister John Major referring to it as the 'boldest corporate equal opportunities initiative we have yet seen' (The Guardian, 27.10.92), perhaps because the voluntarist aim of it tied in closely with the Conservative Government's overarching political philosophy of reducing the role of the state (Forbes, 1996; Willets, 1997). The success of the campaign can be seen in the support it receives from government, the EOC, Confederation of British Industry and from its membership as a whole which employs 25 per cent of UK employees.

Together, these various organisations and institutions represent a critical mass of political weight in support of the business case for sex equality. This is significant both in terms of the lack of political space for alternative strategies, and as a reflection of the extent to which this strategy is being adopted despite evident limitations with this approach. It is to an explanation of the business case, and an examination of its limitations that the next sections will turn.

Productive and Worker Efficiency

The first element of the business case contends that the implementation, and effective enforcement, at firm level, of equal opportunity policies will improve employee morale to an extent that is positively reflected in the productivity of the firm. Hence, the Confederation of British Industry has argued that 'effective equal opportunities policies and practices provide business with the facility to ... increase morale at work', leading to 'sustained competitiveness' (Confederation of British Industry, 1996, p.4, 6). Similarly, the Chairwoman of the Equal Opportunities Commission

(EOC) commended the EOC's new Code of Practice on Equal Pay to employers by reasoning that '[t]here is a strong business case for employers to follow an equal pay policy' (Equal Opportunities Review, 1996, p.2). The economic benefits that would accrue to an employer following the Code of Practice were said to include 'improved staff morale and motivation, reduced staff turnover and improved productivity' (Equal Opportunities Review, 1996, p.2).

This argument has a long pedigree in the field of labour standards generally. For example, Deakin and Wilkinson have argued that 'the adoption of an effective system of labour regulation is an essential pre-condition to ... economic competitiveness' (1996, p.8). The foundation for this argument is that undervalued labour has negative influences on productive and worker efficiency at firm level, and on consumption and growth in the economy as a whole (Deakin and Wilkinson, 1996, pp.8-13). This view also informs many social policy proposals emanating from the European Community which seek to improve economic performance by improving co-operation between workers and management (Wise and Gibb, 1993; Holland, 1993; McGlynn, 1995).

In so far as this aspect of the business case suggests that employee morale would be increased with the effective adoption and implementation of equal opportunity policies, it presupposes two conditions. First, it is dependent on the existence of women workers in the particular enterprise. If there are no, or few, women employees, this element of the business case can have little impact. Thus, it provides no basis for seeking the integration of women employees into hitherto male-dominated occupations which might otherwise be considered an appropriate aim of sex equality policy. In addition, the focus on the individual employer inhibits comparisons between undertakings and occupations. Accordingly, this aspect of the business case can have little to no effect on the systemic sex segregation of the workforce as a whole, such segregation being the primary cause of the continuing pay inequality between women and men (Rubery, 1992).

This element of the business case is also premised on the assumption that morale would be improved with the effective adoption of equal opportunity policies. The end goal to be achieved is high morale, leading to improved productivity, and equal opportunity policies are one means by which this is to be achieved. The difficulty with this approach is that were it to be established that the introduction of equal opportunities policies reduced morale amongst, for example, a predominantly male workforce, the rationale for the policies would be lost and the end goal of improved morale would dictate the non-implementation of the policies. Equality, therefore, is trumped by the business imperative of improved performance.

Consequently, although this first element of the business case rests on established foundations regarding a means by which the efficiency and productivity of a workforce may be improved, via the introduction and maintenance of social standards, the argument only supports equal opportunities policies in certain contexts. This is because the end result being sought is not sex equality, but productive and worker efficiency.

Capitalising on Investment

The second element of the business case emphasises the fact that it makes financial sense for employers to capitalise on any investment made in their employees. In the particular equal opportunity context, this imperative translates into the need to retain skilled women employees, and to utilise their skills to the appropriate standard, i.e. by promotion where appropriate. Making the best use of resources is axiomatic in most areas of business, but, it has been argued, '[w]omen are a high profile example of a bad use of resources' (Janet Gaymer, quoted in Langdon-Down, 1997).

Capitalising on investment in human resources can take a number of forms. The Social Justice Commission has argued, for example, that giving women employees seeking maternity leave benefits over and above the statutory minimum can '*save* employers money by improving recruitment and retention rates and by reducing skills shortages' (original emphasis) (Social Justice Commission, 1994, p.189). A further example relates to employers' estimated costs of recruiting replacements for women who do not return to work from maternity leave. A number of employers have estimated that such recruitment expenses far outweigh the costs of providing help with childcare responsibilities, or in developing suitable part-time or job-share working practices, or in changing the culture of the organisation to make it more amenable to workers with family responsibilities (Confederation of British Industry, 1996, p.15-18; Social Justice Commission, 1994, p.188-191; McGlynn, 1996, p.816; Langdon-Down, 1997). Finally, of those organisations which are members of Opportunity 2000, the main reason given for joining was to ensure a 'return on investment' in staff resources (Opportunity 2000, 1996, p.5).

This strand of the business case relies on an elementary business proposition; that profits are derived from capitalising on investment. However, its particular orientation towards women's employment opportunities is significant. In contrast to the argument considered above, that the implementation and enforcement of equal opportunity policies may improve productive efficiency, improvements which are peculiarly difficult to quantify, it is possible to quantify monetary gains made where considering measures which have been implemented to retain women employees. For example, Boots plc. found that it increased its profits by £1 million by reducing the turnover of its staff (Langdon-Down, 1997). Accordingly, it may be that this element of the business case is more likely to produce gains and be accepted than the first.

Nonetheless, as with the debate regarding productive and worker efficiency, the focus of this element of the business case is not on the justice of the case for promoting and retaining women where their performance demands it, nor on granting maternity benefits over and above the statutory minimum in order that women do not bear the financial burden of pregnancy and childcaring. On the contrary, the focal point is profit maximisation; with the clear implication that where profit maximisation does not dictate fair employment practices, such policies cannot be justified. In addition, this argument is conditional on women comprising a substantial part of any workforce, as only then will the utilisation of female resources have a financial implication. Consequently, where an employer does not, nor wishes to, employ women, perhaps because they are perceived as being more costly (as articulated in a recent survey of members of the Institute of Directors (1994)), the business case provides no rationale for employing women, nor does it provide any basis for condemning such discriminatory behaviour (albeit that such a decision may constitute unlawful sex discrimination). Indeed, it may be that the profit maximisation argument provides a justification for men-only employment practices, or provides a rationale for paying a predominantly female workforce lower pay than would be given to a predominantly male workforce. The business case provides no normative basis for resisting such arguments.

Avoiding Sex Discrimination Claims

The third aspect of the business case is directed at frightening employers into adopting and enforcing equal opportunities policies in order to obviate expensive sex discrimination claims. This element of the argument has had a particular resonance since the ceiling on damages payable for successful discrimination actions has been lifted, making employers' liability unlimited (McColgan, 1994). Thus, whereas employers might once have been able to factor in the costs of claims being brought against the company, as against the potential economic benefit of the actions proposed, to a greater extent, this option is no longer available. Although the median for sex discrimination claims in 1994-5 was £5,700 (Equal Opportunities Review, 1996b), the publicity surrounding a number of high profile cases has portrayed a different picture to the public. In particular, considerable publicity surrounded the awards given to a number of ex-servicewomen who had been dismissed from the armed forces on the grounds of pregnancy, the highest of which was £350,000, albeit that the average was around £11,000 (Arnull, 1995). In addition, where an award of £140,000 was made to a woman director who was dismissed after bringing an equal pay claim, the headlines broadcast the message: 'Female director wins £140,000 in equality case' (The Independent, 1996). Similarly, the award of £200,000 to a female firefighter who had suffered sexual harassment was reported in much of the press with the emphasis being placed on the cost of being discriminatory (McGrory, 1997; Pearson, 1997; Veash, 1997). Allied to the fear of substantial damages claims, this element of the business case also focuses on the cost of lost management time involved in managing and possibly defending a discrimination action, and firms fear the potentially adverse effects on the organisation of negative publicity.

This aspect of the business case is perhaps the least satisfactory basis for sex equality. It is purely defensive: employers seeking to protect themselves against unwanted costs, as opposed to seeking improvements in staff morale or retention. Nor is the emphasis on the wrong of discrimination, but on the adverse costs of not complying with legal obligations. This may have the effect of diluting the rhetorical force of the legislative regime designed to eliminate discrimination in that the emphasis moves away from the morality and fairness of sex equality to the need to reduce business costs, with the effect that the legislative regime is simply seen as adding another layer of regulation to employers' businesses.

Whereas arguments regarding the improvement of staff morale and capitalising on staff resources would be applicable, albeit to a lesser extent, were the existing sex discrimination legislation to be repealed, the final argument regarding compensation for discrimination is solely reliant on the existing law. There is therefore a clear paradox in that the business case is said to be without 'moral' foundation (Opportunity 2000, 1996), and based on pure economic pragmatics, yet it rests solely on laws adopted as a result of social policy arguments regarding women's status in society. This is exemplified by the fact that the business case would not have provided a justification for removing the limit on compensation claims for discrimination. Indeed, it would have provided ample grounds for resisting such a change on the basis that it imposes greater costs on businesses, and that the rationale of the business case is to improve competitiveness and profits. Thus, the business case is a defender of the status quo; indeed it may provide a basis for resisting reforms which may improve the position of women in the workforce on the grounds that such measures might restrict profit maximisation.

This latter point is exemplified with regard to proposed reforms from the European Community to amend the burden of proof in sex discrimination cases.[4] The UK Government has objected to the proposed directive on the grounds that 'it would impose a huge and unnecessary burden on employers' (Ian Lang, President of the Board of Trade, quoted in Grey, 1996). In so far as the proposal might impose costs on employers, the business case would advocate a rejection of the proposal. Yet, were this proposal to become law, it would then be used by the proponents of the business case as a basis for the business case: i.e. that equal opportunity policies must be adopted and enforced, otherwise large awards for damages for sex discrimination may be payable by the company, claims which are now more likely to be successful as a result of this change in the law.

To the extent that the business case is not reformist, but is protective of the status quo, it provides few grounds basis on which to resist the dismantling of sex discrimination law and equal opportunity policies. Thus, not only does the business case provide little basis for the future development of the law, its ability to defend the existing legal structure is limited.

Future Implications of the Business Case

It is this inability to provide either a basis for the development of the law or a defence of the existing legal structure which will be considered in this section. As was noted above, one of the concerns with the business case is that debate is solely focused on economic considerations. The adoption of equal opportunities legislation and employment practices are seen as the means by which to achieve the end of profit maximisation: equality is the means by which to achieve the end of improved economic performance. The effect of this is to open up for argument the question of whether or not equal opportunity policies do in fact improve economic performance.

One basis on which the existing sex discrimination legislation can be defended in economic terms is that a legislative prohibition on sex discrimination can affect the employment market by 'inducing it not to act in an arbitrary and ultimately inefficient fashion' (Fenwick and Hervey, 1995, p.444). In so doing, such legislation 'disallows the individual biases of employers to feed into the market, and may therefore promote genuine competition based on individual merit, thereby preventing the unwarranted under - or over - advantaging of certain groups' (Fenwick and Hervey, 1995, pp.444-445). There are two alternative bases for this proposition: either that without legislation such biases would continue to the detriment of the economic performance of those enterprises engaging in such behaviour and the economy as a whole; or that although the market may eliminate such biases in time, in that those enterprises making rational choices will be more successful than those not, legislation can speed up this process. In either sense, anti-discrimination legislation 'may be thought of as a tool to perfect the market response to employer discrimination' (Donohue, 1986, p.1431).

The principal concern with this approach to the justification of sex discrimination legislation is that it is inherently limiting. The focus remains economic and therefore if a provision of discrimination legislation, or an interpretation thereof, does not fit the aim of perfecting the market, then it is not sustainable under this justification. As has been shown in the context of European Community sex equality law, the market imperative limits the extent to which legislation can be used to effect substantive equality for women (Fenwick and Hervey, 1995; Fredman, 1992).

Nonetheless, at least the argument regarding the 'perfecting' of the market is based on the existence, and maintenance, of the legislative framework. The ability of the legislative framework to contribute to any appreciable extent to economic betterment is hotly contested. Richard Posner, amongst others, has argued on a number of occasions that sex discrimination legislation should be repealed on the grounds that it does not in fact improve the position of women (Posner, 1987, 1989; Epstein, 1992).[5] Posner's argument is that 'sex discrimination law has not increased, and it may even have reduced, the aggregate welfare of women'

(Posner, 1989, p.1312). He reaches this conclusion by suggesting that it would be economically more efficient to allow employers to pay women less and discriminate against them in terms of employment opportunities. If this were allowed, Posner argues that the aggregate welfare of all women would increase by reason of the fact that the wages of men would increase and Posner contends that 'women derive a benefit from an increase in the income of a husband or other male relative' (Posner, 1989, p.1316). In addition, Posner suggests that the administrative costs of policing sex discrimination laws may be sufficiently high to outweigh any alternative potential benefits which the legislation might bring. Posner does recognise that there may be reasons other than economic ones why women wish to work, but economics trumps: 'the price tag for an increase in women's self-esteem, if known, might be thought to be too high by society' (Posner, 1989, p.1335).[6]

The clear focus with Posner is on wealth as opposed to equality; a societal not individual focus. Accordingly, there are grounds not only on which the economic basis of his arguments can be challenged (Donohue, 1986, 1987, 1989), but also on the basis of whether in fact wealth, as opposed to individual equality, is to be preferred. However, in advancing sex equality in economic terms, the strategy is too accepting of the economic questions, and leaves no space for other priorities. Thus, Posner's analysis, notwithstanding is obvious flaws, has been echoed in the UK. It has been argued that the interference in 'free market' caused by anti-discrimination legislation is 'insidious' in that it interferes with freedom of contract (Paul, 1992), and that 'current equal opportunities legislation is causing society to produce less wealth than it would do in the absence of such legislation' (Conway, 1992, p.57). Indeed, for Quest, who condemns anti-discrimination and equal pay legislation as 'abrogations of freedom and private property', and claims that such 'interventions into the free market do not enhance justice; they undermine it' (1992, p.2), the foundation of Opportunity 2000, despite its economic, amoral, message, merely demonstrates the success of the 'feminist message about work' (1992, p.1).

Notwithstanding the fact that the wholesale repeal of equality legislation is perhaps unlikely, and indeed impossible for so long as the UK remains a member of the European Union, the conduct of a debate regarding the utility of sex discrimination in economic terms opens up this question. Even if in wholesale repeal is unlikely, the argument has a powerful force because '[r]hetoric is not just shaped by, but shapes, reality' (Radin, 1987, p.1870). The actual conduct of such a debate reduces the impact and weakens the case for sex equality legislation. It marks out the terrain of the economic debate regarding sex discrimination legislation, demonstrating that despite the fact that in its present political formation the business case takes for granted the existence of sex discrimination legislation; in moving the debate onto economic terrain, the arguments for total repeal are given a forum where they might once have been dismissed as fanciful. In other words, emphasising the economics of sex equality legitimates the articulation of views hitherto ignored.

Conclusions

It has been argued that, in response to the increasing marketisation of political culture, the principal strategy being employed to eliminate discrimination against women in the workforce is the articulation of a business case for equality. A number of limitations with this strategy have been considered, particularly its defence of the status quo, its concentration on voluntary action, its subrogation of equality to a means by which to achieve the end of improved economic performance, and its inability to deal with some of the pressing causes of discrimination against women, particularly occupational segregation. Underpinning these concerns is the fact that conducting a debate regarding women's equality on economic terms does not, and cannot, do justice to either the extent of discrimination against women, or to the motivations for discrimination, or to the reasons why society should seek to ensure equality for women. In effect, 'support for equal opportunities becomes associated with a set of values unrelated to equality, difference, justice or diversity' (Forbes, 1996, p.161). As Radin argues, 'a world in which human interactions are conceived as market trades is different from one in which they are not' (1987, p.1870), with the effect that considering issues such as equality solely in terms of whether or not it promotes economic efficiency, alters our understanding of the issue and 'transform[s] the texture of the human world' (1987, p.1884).

However, notwithstanding such criticisms, gains can be made with the promotion of the business case for equality. Not least is the fact that the strategy is managing to persuade employers that equality in the workplace is not a 'woman's issue' but a legitimate and serious business concern (Freely, 1996). In addition, there is some evidence that member firms of Opportunity 2000 offer more extensive equal opportunity employment practices than employers in general (Opportunity 2000, 1996; McGlynn, 1997). However, in pursuing this strategy, it is imperative that those seeking to eliminate discrimination against women, as opposed to those simply seeking to improve profit maximisation, recognise the inherent limitations in pursuing an economically-based strategy, be aware of the long term implications of the approach, and seek a variety of ways in which to improve the lives of women.

Acknowledgements

I should like to thank all those who participated in the Newcastle Law School Staff Seminar and the SLSA 1997 conference at which I presented earlier versions of this work. I would also like to thank Ian Ward for his helpful comments on an earlier draft of this chapter, and Nina Hall and Richard Mullender for their thoughts on some of the ideas advanced.

Notes

1. David Willets M.P. is seen as one of the intellectuals of the Conservative Party and his views may therefore be taken as representative of the mainstream of the Conservative Party.
2. The term 'sex equality' is adopted despite its limitations (Lacey, 1987; Fredman, 1992) as it is the term commonly used in political debate and is the professed aim of the present sex discrimination legislative regime (Home Office, 1974).
3. Naomi Wolf takes the title of her book *Fire with Fire* from the proverb, 'fight fire with fire' (1993, p.viii).
4. Com (96) 340 *final*.
5. To a certain extent, there is always a danger in creating a caricature of the law and economics movement, and Posner in particular. It is therefore conceded that in some ways Posner, in more recent work, has acknowledged the need to take account of the role of ethics in economic analysis (Duxbury, 1995). Nonetheless, it is maintained that there is still value in presenting his arguments, if only to identify the most extreme outcome of this strand of economic analysis.
6. Although Posner is concerned with US sex discrimination laws, his analysis can apply equally to the UK's legislative provisions on sex discrimination which are in many respects similar.

Bibliography

Arnull, A. (1995), 'EC Law and the Dismissal of Pregnant Servicewomen', *Industrial Law Journal*, vol. 24, pp. 215-234.

Balls, E. (1996), 'New Man faces up to parental leave dilemma', *The Guardian*, 19 February.

Confederation of British Industry (1996), *A Winning Strategy - The business case for equal opportunities*, Confederation of British Industry, London.

Conway, D. (1992), 'Do Women Benefit from Equal Opportunities Legislation?' in C. Quest (ed.), *Equal Opportunities: A Feminist Fallacy*, Institute of Economic Affairs, London.

Crawford, A. (1996), 'The Spirit of Community: Rights, Responsibilities, and the Communitarian Agenda', *Journal of Law and Society*, vol. 23, pp. 247-262.

Deakin, S. and Wilkinson, F. (1996), *Labour Standards - Essential to Economic and Social Progress*, Institute of Employment Rights, London.

Department of Employment (1994), *United Nations Fourth World Conference on Women - Beijing 1995 - Report of the UK of Great Britain and Northern Ireland*, Department of Employment, London.

Donohue, J. (1986), 'Is Title VII Efficient?', *University of Pennsylvania Law Review*, vol. 134, pp. 1411-1431.

Donohue, J. (1987), 'Further Thoughts on Employment Discrimination Legislation: A Reply to Judge Posner', *University of Pennsylvania Law Review*, vol. 136, pp. 523-551.

Donohue, J. (1989), 'Prohibiting Sex Discrimination in the Workplace: An Economic Perspective', *University of Chicago Law Review*, vol. 56, pp. 1337-1369.

Duxbury, N. (1995), *Patterns of American Jurisprudence*, Clarendon Press, Oxford.

Epstein, R. (1992), *Forbidden Grounds - The Case Against Employment Discrimination Laws*, Harvard University Press, Cambridge, Mass.

Equal Opportunities Review (1996a), 'Pay is an equal opportunity issue', *Equal Opportunities Review*, vol. 70, p. 2.

Equal Opportunities Review (1996b), 'Tribunal Statistics 1993-5', *Equal Opportunities Review*, vol. 69, p.26.

Fenwick, H. and Hervey, T. (1995), 'Sex Equality in the Single Market: New Directions for the European Court of Justice', *Common Market Law Review*, vol. 32, pp. 443-470.

Forbes, I. (1996), 'The Privatisation of Sex Equality Policy', in J. Lovenduski and P. Norris (eds.), *Women in Politics*, Oxford University Press, Oxford.

Fredman, S. (1992), 'European Community Discrimination Law: A Critique', *Industrial Law Journal*, vol. 21, pp. 119-134.

Freely, M. (1996), 'Five alive', *The Guardian*, 2 December.

Gibb, R. and Wise, M. (1993), *Single Market to Social Europe*, Longmans, London.

Grey, S. (1996), 'Europe turns heat on employers to target "sexism" in the workplace', *The Sunday Times*, 29 December.

Hervey, T. and Fenwick, H. (1995), 'Sex Equality in the Single Market: New Directions for the European Court of Justice', *Common Market Law Review*, vol. 32, pp. 443-470.

Holland, S. (1993), *The European Imperative*, Spokesman, London.

Home Office (1974), *Equality for Women*, H.M.S.O. (Cmnd. 5724), London.

Humphries, J. and Rubery, J. (eds.) (1995), *The Economics of Equal Opportunities*, Equal Opportunities Commission, Manchester.

The Independent (1996), 'Female Director wins £140,000 in equality case', 26 March.

Institute of Directors (1994), *Women at Work - The Business Woman's Perspective*, Institute of Directors, London.

Institute of Personnel and Development (1997), *A Vision for the Development of Equal Opportunities - Managing Diversity*, Institute of Personnel and Development, London.

Lacey, N. (1987), 'Legislation Against Sex Discrimination: Questions from a Feminist Perspective', *Journal of Law and Society*, vol. 14, pp. 411-421.

Langdon-Down, G. (1997), 'More women equals money', *The Independent*, 23 April.

McColgan, A. (1994), 'Remedies for Discrimination', *Industrial Law Journal*, vol. 23, pp. 226-229.

McGlynn, C. (1995), 'European Works Councils: Towards Industrial Democracy?', *Industrial Law Journal*, vol. 24, pp. 78-84.

McGlynn, C. (1996), 'A Different Voice?', *New Law Journal*, vol. 146, pp. 816-817.

McGlynn, C. (1997), 'Where men still rule', *The Times*, 22 April.

McGrory, D. (1997), '£200,000 for firewoman bullied by colleagues', *The Times*, 18 March.

Opportunity 2000 (1996), *Fifth Year Review*, Opportunity 2000, London.

Paul, E. F. (1992), 'Fetal Protection, Women's Rights and Freedom of Contract', in C. Quest (ed.), *Equal Opportunities: A Feminist Fallacy*, Institute of Economic Affairs, London.

Pearson, R. (1997), 'Harassment sounds alarm bells', *The Lawyer*, 8 April.

Posner, R. (1987), 'The Efficiency and Efficacy of Title VII', *University of Pennsylvania Law Review*, vol. 136, pp. 513-521.

Posner, R. (1989), 'An Economic Analysis of Sex Discrimination Laws', *University of Chicago Law Review*, vol. 56, pp. 1311-1335.

Quest, C. (ed.) (1992), *Equal Opportunities: A Feminist Fallacy*, Institute of Economic Affairs, London.

Radin, M. (1987), 'Market-Inalienability', *Harvard Law Review*, vol. 100, pp. 1849-1937.

Rubery, J. (1992), *The Economics of Equal Value*, Equal Opportunities Commission, Manchester.

Rubery, J. and Humphries, J. (eds.) (1995), *The Economics of Equal Opportunities*, Equal Opportunities Commission, Manchester.

Social Justice Commission (1994), *Social Justice - Strategies for National Renewal*, Vintage, London.

Tusa, J. (1997), 'The price of the separation from the Good Society', *The Independent*, 30 January.

Veash, N. (1997), 'Firefighter who was harassed wins £200,000', *The Independent*, 18 March.

Wilkinson, F. and Deakin, S. (1996), *Labour Standards - Essential to Economic and Social Progress*, Institute of Employment Rights, London.

Willets, D. (1997), *Why Vote Conservative?*, Penguin Books, London.

Wise, M. and Gibb, R. (1993), *Single Market to Social Europe*, Longmans, London.

Wolf, N. (1993), *Fire with Fire*, Chatto & Windus, London.

PART III

INTERNATIONAL, EUROPEAN AND COMPARATIVE PERSPECTIVES

7. Contextualising International Women's Rights: Canadian Feminism, Race and Culture

DAVID S. BERRY

Introduction

Feminists are subtly challenging and changing our understanding of international law. They are highly critical of its structure and content, and yet offer practical suggestions about ways of re-vitalising it to take into account women's perspectives and concerns. In doing so, these feminists are providing international law with new insights and giving it an increased momentum.

One problem which feminists have highlighted is that of clashes between cultures and international human rights, or more specifically, traditional cultures and international *women's* rights. I will examine this issue by looking at the conflicts between the rights of aboriginal women, aboriginal communities and the wider Canadian state. The first part of this article will highlight some of the basic problems involved in using international law for feminist strategies. The second part will set out three potential feminist remedies to these problems, and the third part will illustrate these issues by examining the *Lovelace* and *Native Women's Association of Canada (NWAC)* cases. In the final part, I will apply an international feminist analysis to these cases and their underlying conflicts, and in doing so will argue that there are several potential bridges between what appear to be two incommensurable divides.

International Law as Failing Feminism

International law fails to address the concerns of women at several different levels. At the first and most general level, international law fails women simply by not considering them a subject of scrutiny. This is not exceptional, as it is rare for international law directly to deal with *any* category of persons, and instead it almost uniformly concerns itself with the behaviour of states and actions attributable to states. But international law aggravates this problem by also refusing to address the specific needs of women, *as women,* by excluding their concerns from its scrutiny. This happens because most of the issues related to women are matters which fall within the state's sovereign domain. Thus, as succinctly put by Karen Knop: '[i]n an international society peopled by States, women are analytically invisible because they belong to the State's sphere of personal autonomy' (1993, p.295).

This 'invisibility' can be best illustrated at the international level by looking critically at the various distinctions between what is considered 'public' and 'private' by the law. Feminist theories have identified already several kinds of 'public/private' dichotomies underlying much of the national law of states, with the 'public' domain viewed as 'naturally' subject to legal scrutiny, and the 'private' domain not (i.e., domestic work, marital violence) (Engle, 1993; Mahoney, 1996; Romany, 1994; Sullivan, 1995). At the international level feminists have shown that this is compounded by yet another 'public/private' split through which the law creates a further area in which it will not interfere - the 'private' sphere of a state's domestic jurisdiction. All matters within this area are things 'in which the international community has no recognised legal interest' (Charlesworth, Chinkin and Wright 1991, p.625). Thus women's concerns can be doubly-private, unchallengeable as outside domestic law and also outside international law.

Further, the 'public/private' distinction can work against women at a deeper level in international law, because the 'private' sphere is not only unregulated but also accorded less weight or value. Activities in the 'public' sphere are assigned a higher normative force or value than 'private' or 'women's' sphere activities, and hence the latter are not only unregulated by international law but also *denigrated* in its eyes (Charlesworth, Chinkin and Wright, 1991). Thus, at a practical level, the types of work done by women in societies tend to be less valued, less regulated, and provided with less support in comparison to the types of work done by men.

The second problem with international law can be characterised generally as one of enforceability. Even when women's issues are raised by states in the international *fora* and binding treaties are created to govern state behaviour, these treaties are flouted consistently by their signatories. One of the most striking instances of this kind of practice is the treatment of the *Convention on the Elimination of All Forms of Discrimination Against Women* (CEDAW) (adopted 18 Dec. 1979, 1249 U.N.T.S. 13, in force 3 Sept. 1981), by the international community. CEDAW generated significant controversy because its signatories attached the greatest number of reservations to their acceptance of its terms, and some of these reservations appear to defeat the purpose of it (Clark, 1991; Funder, 1993; Mayer, 1995; Mahoney, 1996). Such reservations are prohibited both by Article 28(2) of CEDAW itself, and by the general law of treaties (Clark, 1991).

The third and final problem that feminists have found with international law has to do with the notion of 'rights' that it employs. Feminists point out that the *use* of human rights law and rights-rhetoric are both problematic for a variety of reasons, from the way they oversimplify complex power relations, to their tendency to come in competing or contesting pairs, to the way that they may be used by powerful elements in a society to block progressive changes (Smart, 1989; Charlesworth, 1994; Fudge, 1989). These critics have then added a specifically feminist component to their analysis by arguing that international human rights law, like its domestic cousin, relies upon a specifically *male* vision of rights (Engle, 1992a). The 'male' orientation of rights can be identified by the way that the formal possession of a right, rather than a woman's actual ability to use it, is considered sufficient, and by the implicit use of a 'male comparator test' to determine the meaning of a right. At a deeper level, this 'male' bias is revealed by the fact that the form and content of rights are predicated on their masculine origins (i.e., made by men for needs perceived by men) (Brown, 1993; Charlesworth, 1994).

Having considered some of the problems, the next section will examine three different feminist remedies.

Feminist Remedies

Doctrinalist [1]

The doctrinalist approach is the simplest of the three, as it seeks to make international law responsive to feminist concerns simply by more stringently applying existing tools. Feminists using this approach attempt to stretch the existing legal framework to cover new issues and thus tend to work by analogy, fitting practices that discriminate against women under existing international legal structures, usually under human rights law (Engle,

1992a).

To give a concrete example of their technique, doctrinalists who attempt to prevent a practice that is not explicitly prohibited under international law, such as clitoridectomy, would look for as many binding international legal instruments that could be construed to prevent this practice, and then argue for the offending state to comply with them (Engle, 1992a). At a more sophisticated level, doctrinalists might have to characterise the practice in a strategic manner in order to gain domestic support for the change. This would involve developing a specific line of argument against clitoridectomy as involving violations of an already-protected and *domestically accepted* human right, such as the right to health, or the rights of the child (Engle, 1992b; Lewis, 1995; Funder, 1993).

The doctrinalist approach has the advantage of using the existing tools without threatening any of the basic assumptions of international legal practice. Also, it may be more pragmatic as it focuses on particular, discrete problems, without concerning itself with overall goals or the problems of mediating between competing feminist strategies. But it is problematic because it falls prey to some of the weaknesses of international law mentioned earlier. Thus, doctrinalist arguments will be limited by notions of formal equality, the 'public/private' split, traditional notions of state sovereignty, and the latter's shielding of cultural practices. A more fundamental weakness, however, is that by using *analogous* legal doctrines to challenge otherwise unregulated practices, doctrinalists may be unable to address the practice and its causes directly. Thus, for example, by turning clitoridectomy into a health problem rather than attacking the practice *per se*, feminists may end up merely changing the nature of the practice instead of actually discouraging it. This result has occurred in urban parts of the Sudan, where clitoridectomies are now performed through the health care system (albeit under more sterile conditions) (Engle, 1992b).

Institutionalist

Institutionalists differ from doctrinalists in that they do not rely on particular rights strategies to promote feminist interests; instead they see the problem as lying more in the nature of the institutions and structures of international law, which are seen to be deficient and biased (Engle, 1992a). Nevertheless, institutionalists do not abandon or reject these structures, and instead promote feminist changes by working within them. Thus they tend to advocate such things as stronger enforcement mechanisms, higher priority for women's issues and greater representation of women within international institutions (Engle, 1992b). Also, since a main focus of the institutionalist approach is to challenge the 'male' nature of the international legal system, they argue for such things as 'affirmative' measures in the hiring and appointment policies of international institutions including the United Nations, the World Court and the World Bank.

A problem with the institutionalist approach, however, is that by working within and using only the existing structures, institutionalists become unable to *see beyond* them. Thus, if the international structures *themselves* are patriarchal (either intrinsically or through their long-standing associations), any 'corrections' to these structures may prove ineffective (Engle, 1992a). Equally, shifting powers from a mainstream, established institution to a newer, specialised one may not break the hierarchy, as the newer one often will work in the same environment and under the same constraints (Engle, 1992a). Worse, such 'tinkerings' may provide an air of legitimacy to these structures, and institutionalists may end up further entrenching and reinforcing them.

A second handicap lies in their limited vision of the nature of discrimination against women, with the institutionalist focus resting mainly on a 'male/female' power dynamic. Under this view, international institutions are set up and run on the basis of 'male' or patriarchal models, and therefore should be changed to include 'female' values (Engle, 1992a). As part of an overall strategy, this viewpoint is very powerful, but, as with any simple dichotomy, when *only* this framework is used it can be limiting. When a 'male/female' power dynamic becomes the sole focus, it tends to produce simplified visions of what is 'male' and what is 'female', and thus essentialises women's values and women's views. In doing so, institutionalists may cut off or suppress divergent feminist voices, ones that do not agree with the particular institutional strategy being proposed or the vision of women's needs in an area (Engle, 1992a and b).

Expanded Integrationist

The expanded integrationist critique of international law goes further than the previous two, as it calls for more pervasive and far reaching changes to the way we see and use international law. The term 'expanded integrationist', as I will use it, is really an umbrella term. Although for the sake of simplicity I will call it an 'approach', it might more accurately be described as a series of approaches or a set of strategies. It is 'expanded', and thus differs most significantly from the earlier approaches in two ways: first, it does not limit itself to one particular international category for action, such as human rights law, and secondly, and perhaps most importantly, it does not pre-suppose the adequacy of existing international law or institutions to address women's issues. In fact, it may reject using international law at all.

Thus the expanded integrationist approach requires what analytically can be separated into two tiers of strategy. At the first, 'expanded' tier, an assessment must be made about the *usefulness of existing international law* for the particular feminist concern. When looking at the concrete problem to be addressed, a strategic choice must be made about whether or not to use international human rights law (or law generally), or instead to rely upon other, non-legal approaches; further, this choice must be re-negotiated each time a new problem is approached by the feminist group. Factors that will help in making this determination include: first, sceptically considering the effectiveness of the existing international institutions and human rights (Kingdom, 1996); secondly, surveying the experiences of women around the globe regarding particular approaches and strategies; and, thirdly, carefully contextualising the particular feminist issue (as in some parts of the globe different approaches may be more effective or appropriate (Tabak, 1990)). As a result, this first, expanded tier will require a positive assessment about the capabilities of international law for the particular concern. If an overwhelmingly negative assessment is made, then the expanded integrationist approach - and an international *legal* strategy generally - should be abandoned.

At the second, 'integrationist', tier we apply international law. But no specific legal technique need be prioritised here, and integrationists may decide to use several (even competing), strategies *simultaneously*. This is productive because different feminist techniques will work better in different spheres of society or different countries, and may each reveal a different form of discrimination (Mahoney, 1996; Tabak, 1990). Again, a concrete illustration may be made with the example of clitoridectomy. As neither the doctrinalist nor institutionalist approaches are sufficient to address this issue (even if applied together), the expanded integrationist approach will *add* to them by suggesting changes that, for example, force the human rights system *as a whole* to accommodate women's rights. Instead of fitting women *under* human rights, feminists could attempt to make specifically *women's* concerns into rights (i.e. 'women's rights') (Mahoney, 1996; Cook, 1994b). This involves more than the simple inclusion of women under an existing right (the doctrinalist approach), and instead means such things as: first, formulating *new* rights that are specific to women's concerns; secondly, applying rights in areas of human life currently considered 'private'; and, thirdly, re-thinking rights arguments from a women's viewpoint (Engle, 1992b). An example of the latter kind of formulation of a women's right would be a right to be free from 'genital mutilation' (Engle, 1992b, p. 1519). Additionally, an expanded integrationist approach could work through extra-legal or non-human-rights orientated processes (Lewis, 1995), or work through grassroots organising, such as encouraging groups in one country to use practical knowledge gained by feminist movements in other countries to help institute local advances (Toro, 1995).

Although an expanded integrationist approach might at first seem impossible to apply (i.e. it is questionable whether any single group could gain such a broad overview of an area, or unite about which strategies to use for an issue), I would argue that in fact feminists around the world may be using it already. Perhaps 'expanded integrationist' only gives a new name to the general viewpoint that allows feminists globally to see competing strategies as fitting within an eclectic, but nonetheless *overall* framework.

In the next two parts, I will examine the *Lovelace* and *NWAC* cases to see how this expanded integrationist approach might prove helpful within a particular national context.

Contextualising the Conflict

The following cases illustrate the dichotomy seen to exist between aboriginal self-governance and human rights. Each case prioritises one side of this dichotomy, but I will argue that both fail to address the deeper issues involved, namely, identity and culture.

The Lovelace Decision

Sandra Lovelace brought her case before the Human Rights Committee against Canada under the *Optional Protocol to the International Covenant on Civil and Political Rights* (adopted 16 Dec. 1966, 999 U.N.T.S. 302, in force 23 Mar. 1976, reprinted in 6 I.L.M. 383 (1967), hereafter '*Optional*

Protocol'). The facts of the case are summarised succinctly by the Committee as follows (para. 1):

> [Sandra Lovelace] ... is a 32-year-old woman, living in Canada. She was born and registered as a 'Maliseet Indian' but has lost her rights and status as an Indian, in accordance with Section 12 (1) (*b*) of the Indian Act, after having married a non-Indian ... Pointing out that an Indian man who marries a non-Indian woman does not lose his Indian status, she claims that the act is discriminatory on the grounds of sex and contrary to articles 2 (1), 3, 23 (1) and (4), 26 and 27 of the Covenant.

In the Committee's final view, the operation of the impugned section violated Lovelace's rights under article 27 of the *International Covenant on Civil and Political Rights* (adopted 16 Dec. 1966, 999 U.N.T.S. 171, 1057 U.N.T.S. 407, in force 23 Mar. 1976 (except art. 41), and 28 Mar. 1979 (art. 41), reprinted in 6 I.L.M. 368 (1967), hereafter '*Covenant*') (para. 19).

The first cautionary point about this case is that it shows that proceedings under the *Optional Protocol* are neither speedy nor simple, as it took three and a half years for the Committee's final views, and another four years for Canada to comply with its obligations (paras 1-8 and 19; Bayefsky, 1982; Moss, 1990). Part of the reason for this delay, as well as for the ready finding of admissibility by the Committee, may have been Canada's early admission that 'many of the provisions of the ... Indian Act, including section 12 (1) (*b*), require serious reconsideration and reform' (para. 5). In light of this admission, the most interesting substantive issues involved first, the nature of Canada's justifications for the section, and second, which articles of the *Covenant* could be found to be violated by the section. Regarding the former, Canada justified the section with arguments including: (a) that the *Indian Act* was designed to protect its Indian minority in accordance with article 27 of the *Covenant*, (b) its definition of an 'Indian' was necessary to preserve their special privileges, and (c) because the Indian communities themselves were divided on the issue of equal rights, therefore that 'no quick and immediate legislative action could be expected' on the part of Canada (para. 5).

These 'justifications' highlight the dilemma regarding which section of the *Covenant* might be infringed, as the first explicitly invokes Canada's duties to minorities under the *Covenant* in its own defence. Surprisingly, and mainly due to a procedural hurdle, the most obvious infringement - discrimination on the basis of sex - was removed from the Committee's consideration. This was because the *Indian Act* section was applied to

Lovelace *before* the *Covenant* came into force in Canada and therefore, according to the Committee, neither 'her loss of Indian status nor its effects could at that time amount to a violation of the Covenant' (para. 10). Thus the Committee was restricted to looking only at violations of Lovelace's rights that had 'continuing effects,' and therefore focused upon possible violations of article 27, the article protecting each minority's right to enjoy its own culture, religion or language. The Committee found that article 27 was violated because the workings of the *Indian Act* provision excluded Lovelace from her reserve and thus prevented her from effectively enjoying her minority rights.

The irony then, is that the Human Rights Committee ended up deciding the case based upon the provision most strongly argued by Canada to *support* its own behaviour. Also of note is that fact that the Committee's decision protected Lovelace's rights to enjoy her *culture* rather than her individual rights, as a woman. As will be seen, this contrasts with the discussion in the following case.

The Native Women's Association of Canada Case (NWAC)

The *NWAC* case revolved around a series of negotiations about the entrenchment of an inherent right to aboriginal self-government under the Canadian Constitution (Constitution Act, 1982, being Schedule B to the Canada Act 1982 (U.K.), 1982, c. 11). The case arose because only four national aboriginal groups were funded a total of $10 million by the federal government and only they were invited to participate in the constitutional discussions. NWAC was neither directly funded by the government as part of this process nor invited to the discussions, although it did receive some of these funds indirectly from two of the four groups, as well as a contribution from the government for a separate matter. Nonetheless, in total NWAC only received about 5 per cent of the funding (S.C.C., 230-31). NWAC requested funding and rights of participation equal to that of the four other aboriginal groups, but after being denied both took its case to the Federal Court, seeking an order of prohibition against the government to prevent any further disbursement of the federal funding to the four groups until NWAC's requests were granted. The gist of NWAC's argument was that the other four groups could not adequately represent the views of aboriginal women, and that therefore NWAC should be included directly in the negotiations. At the Trial Division level NWAC lost its case, on appeal it won (although only obtaining a declaration), and then at the Supreme Court of Canada level it lost again.

At the Court of Appeal NWAC's case was most clearly vindicated as Mahoney J.A. held that NWAC's freedom of expression rights were violated (C.A., 120-21). The judgement is problematic, however, because of Justice Mahoney's dismissive treatment of NWAC's argument about violation of equality rights. When discussing the meaning of equality under the Canadian Charter of Rights and Freedoms (Part 1 of the Constitution Act, 1982), Mahoney J.A. tersely stated that the rights protected were 'guaranteed to individuals, not to collectives,' and that since any loss of equality to the individual appellants only could occur *after* the creation of aboriginal self-governments, this could not be considered 'a present denial of a right under s. 15 [the equality provision]' (C.A., 117).

The irony of the requirement for a 'present denial' of equality rights in the context of the future creation of potentially unchallengeable aboriginal governments must not be missed. As pointed out by Ms. Stacey-Moore in her affidavit before the trial judge, without Charter protection aboriginal women would be defenceless against discriminatory Band Council or other self-government body actions, because federal and provincial human rights statutes do not apply to the Indian Act (reproduced C.A., 112). Thus, under a Charter-immune form of aboriginal self-government, the 'present denial' test effectively would remove any infringement of equality rights from all Canadian human rights scrutiny. This is a startling conclusion and stands out in comparison to the broad, substantive conceptions the Court of Appeal used when dealing with infringement of freedom of expression rights. When looking at the latter, Mahoney J.A. held that by funding the other four groups and excluding NWAC, the federal government had placed the 'male-dominated' view in a preferred position, and thus had restricted the freedom of expression of aboriginal women contrary to the Charter (C.A., 119-21 and 127). Because of political developments during the case, however, the Court limited its remedy to a declaration that the government had violated the freedom of expression rights of aboriginal women (C.A. 126-7).

The Supreme Court of Canada's decision involved a more subtle argument. Justice Sopinka, writing for the majority, agreed in part with the Federal Court of Appeal regarding its freedom of expression analysis, but broke away by asking whether there is a *positive* duty on the part of the government to fund NWAC. The Supreme Court of Canada answered this question in the negative and held that the government was not required to implement positive action (S.C.C., 243-5). The Court acknowledged that once a government decides to provide assistance to one party it may not do so in a discriminatory fashion or contrary to the Charter, but in the present case the government was held not to have done so because, first, it was not required to take into account all views on the subject, and secondly, in the Court's view the four groups chosen in fact were representative (S.C.C., 245-7). This latter point is one regarding the *actual* ability of the four challenged groups to represent the views of aboriginal women, and the judgment deals with it at great length. This is interesting because it raises questions about whether the Court in effect made a new finding of fact at the highest level of appeal (or, more accurately, *removed* a finding of fact by holding that there was insufficient evidence to support it) (S.C.C., 249-50).

Thus the final stage of the *NWAC* case represented an interesting complement to the Court of Appeal decision, as the Supreme Court of Canada used *formal* arguments to show that in most cases the government was not required to implement positive measures to allow exercise of a right of freedom of expression, and yet at the same time used *substantive* arguments to put the actual position of NWAC as a representative body in context. The effect of the final judgement in the *NWAC* case therefore, is to leave the federal government's hands free to implement a form of aboriginal self-government that would not be subject to the Canadian Charter or any other national human rights instruments (whether directly or through 'opt-out' provisions).

The Possibilities of an Integrated Solution

These two cases presented such difficulties for the Canadian government and courts because of the deeper issues that they raise about conflicting notions of identity. Both the *Lovelace* and *NWAC* cases involved struggles for definition and control of the identity of Canadian aboriginal peoples, with the former raising questions about *who* is aboriginal (**'Indian', as under** the *Indian Act*), and the latter those about *what it means* to be aboriginal.

Applying the Expanded Integrationist Approach

Let us apply an expanded integrationist approach to the issues raised by these cases. In doing so we must first step back and ask whether law is the appropriate tool to address this problem in the Canadian context. Factors discouraging its use include the divisive nature of a legal confrontation on all aboriginal peoples involved, and the Canadian government's potential to use this division as an excuse for inaction (as indicated by Canada's submissions in *Lovelace*, above); factors encouraging its use include fears raised by the possibility of a Charter-immune, and therefore human rights-immune, form of aboriginal government (as illustrated in the *NWAC* affidavit, above), as well as the previous lack of political success for aboriginal women's groups.

Assuming a positive answer, the next step involves looking at particular legal strategies to help resolve the conflict. The best use of the doctrinalist strategy would be to move outside of the Charter context, which proved so limiting in the *NWAC* case. In any event, if a Charter-immune government is created, then the only doctrinal strategy remaining would be to appeal to international human rights law, as in the *Lovelace* case. An institutionalist strategy could help by working to include more aboriginal women in positions of authority in Canadian, aboriginal and international organisations; but this only would be part of a longer term strategy. Additional strategies that could be invoked under the expanded integrationist umbrella include applying the 'public/private' critique. This would reveal as that because the demands of culture and tradition fall within the 'private sphere' they are most often visited upon women, and therefore these demands infringe women's human rights to a greater extent than those of men (Rao, 1995). Also, grassroots strategies could be used to raise consciousness about the problems of culture as well as to share ideas globally about possible solutions.

Nonetheless, since not all culture will be a tool of patriarchy (Coomaraswamy, 1994), the real question may not be so much one about survival of culture *per se,* as about survival of certain cultural *practices*. Thus the key issues become first, whether we can distinguish between helpful and harmful cultural practices with respect to women, and secondly, whether such distinctions can avoid the problems associated with Western cultural imperialism.

Reinterpreting 'Culture' and 'Human Rights'

Because of the problems involved in finding a culturally 'neutral' vantage point from which to judge these practices, perhaps a better strategy would be to move *outside* of the legal sphere and re-examine the meanings of 'culture' and 'human rights'. Even though this involves moving beyond the expanded integrationist approach, I would argue that *only through using such a multi-faceted and sceptical technique* are we forced to reconsider such basic notions.

The first crucial step is to understand that culture itself is not static, and that instead it is constantly changed and enriched by forces inside and outside its domain (Rao, 1995; Funder, 1993). Jeremy Webber (1993) expresses this notion of the fluidity of culture with the metaphor of a conversation, which changes in form and content over time, but still maintains a basic level of continuity. Webber's understanding of the centrality of *continuity* to culture, and his rejection of frozen notions of constancy, help us both to appreciate its flexible nature and also to decide which particular cultural practices should be preserved, enforced or even selected for re-introduction. Although this does not allow us to see culture as completely fluid, it becomes far less restricted by tradition.

The power of this kind of approach to culture is that it opens the dialogue to voices of cultural 'outsiders.' Such an external, or 'cross-cultural' dialogue is important because it allows women to influence practices in both local and foreign cultures by globally transplanting progressive cultural practices and norms (An-Na'im, 1994). By 'conversing' in this way we also encourage an opening up of cultures, and can understand that cultural conflict may be not only inevitable, but welcome.

International human rights law can play a discursive role as well, because its *rights* have a variety of levels of meaning, and these create their own form of conversation. Rather than being static, international human rights law may yield a rich mixture of rules, standards, contesting principles and ideals. At a slightly more abstract level than their simple enumeration of rules, human rights also create *standards* towards which states can strive (Funder, 1993). This gives rise to the further, *aspirational,* role of rights, where they can be seen as articulating the profound ideals that underlie and give them meaning, such as 'human dignity' (Mayer, 1995; Donnelly, 1989). Because they have this content, rights continually raise basic questions about implementation and interpretation - questions involving competing values, ethical and political choices, and differing conceptions of the good. By raising these kinds of questions, human rights become sites of conflict, where different visions of human dignity play out in a variety of ways.

Thus, in sum, both culture and human rights may be seen as existing in a dialectic relation, each checking and inspiring the other at several different levels. If the ultimate purpose of both human rights and traditional cultures can be expressed as 'human dignity,' then this may be the mechanism with which to balance their different visions.

Conclusions

Despite the many failings of international law it nonetheless shows clear potential to be used by feminists to bring a broader, more far-reaching analysis into play. I have suggested that an approach such as the expanded integrationist one is particularly useful because of its multi-faceted nature and ability to carefully contextualise problems. In both the *Lovelace* and *NWAC* cases we saw the failings of international and domestic legal strategies for solving competing claims between women's rights and traditional culture. By looking at these cases from an international perspective we could see their underlying problems more clearly and address them in a nuanced and flexible manner. We also were encouraged to seek alternative solutions to what would otherwise seem intractable dilemmas, and in this way were able to use the tools and experiences of international legal feminists to sceptically and continually contest such notions as 'culture' and 'human rights'. In being able to do so, and re-articulate these debates in ways sensitive to women, feminist theory at the international level offers the most exciting critique of law, rights and culture available today.

Acknowledgements

I would like to thank the following for their help and enthusiasm with respect to this chapter: Stephen Neff, Emilios Christodoulidis, Karen Knop, Patrick Macklem, Linda Bauld, Edward Berry, Elizabeth Kingdom, Clare McGlynn, Anne Griffiths and Rebecca Cook.

Note

1. The labels 'doctrinalist', 'institutionalist', and 'integrationist' are borrowed from the work of Engle (1992a and b) and Lewis (1995). However, the first two will be used here in a slightly different manner, and the latter term in such a substantially different manner that I have re-named it '*expanded* integrationist' in order to avoid confusion.

Bibliography

An-Na'im, A. A. (1994), 'State Responsibility Under International Human Rights Law to Change Religious and Customary Laws' in R. Cook (ed.) (1994a).

Bayefsky, A. F. (1982), 'The Human Rights Committee and the Case of Sandra Lovelace', *Canadian Yearbook of International Law*, vol. 20, pp. 244-65.

Brown, B. (1993), 'Feminism' in R. Bellamy (ed.), *Theories and Concepts of Politics: An Introduction*, Manchester University Press, Manchester.

Case of Sandra Lovelace, Communication No. 24/1977, United Nations Human Rights Committee, decision of 30 July 1981 (13th session). Reproduced in: United Nations (1985), *Human Rights Committee: Selected Decisions Under the Optional Protocol (Second to Sixteenth Sessions)*, United Nations, New York.

Charlesworth, H. (1994), 'What Are "Women's International Human Rights"?' in R. Cook (ed.) (1994a).

Charlesworth, H., Chinkin, C. and Wright, S. (1991), 'Feminist Approaches to International Law' *American Journal of International Law*, vol. 85, pp. 613-45.

Clark, B. (1991), 'The Vienna Convention Reservations Regime and the Convention on Discrimination Against Women', *American Journal of International Law*, vol. 85, pp. 281-321.

Convention on the Elimination of All Forms of Discrimination Against Women (1986), reprinted in *International Legal Materials*, vol. 19, p. 33.

Cook, R. J. (ed.) (1994a), *Human Rights of Women: National and International Perspectives*, University of Pennsylvania Press, Philadelphia.

Cook, R. J. (1994b), 'State Accountability Under the Convention on the Elimination of All Forms of Discrimination Against Women' in Cook (1994a).

Coomaraswamy, R. (1994), 'To Bellow Like a Cow: Women, Ethnicity, and the Discourse of Rights', in R. Cook (ed.) (1994a).

Donnelly, J. (1989), *Universal Human Rights in Theory and Practice*, Cornell University Press, London.

Engle, K. (1992a), 'International Human Rights and Feminism: When Discourses Meet', *Michigan Journal of International Law*, vol. 13, pp. 517-610.

Engle, K. (1992b), 'Female Subjects of Public International Law: Human Rights and the Exotic Other Female', *New England Law Review*, vol. 26, pp.1509-26.

Engle, K. (1993), 'After the Collapse of the Public/Private Distinction: Strategizing Women's Rights', in D.G. Dallmeyer (ed.), *Reconceiving Reality: Women and International Law*, The American Society of International Law, Washington, D.C.

Fudge, J. (1989), 'The Effect of Entrenching a Bill of Rights upon Political Discourse: Feminist Demands and Sexual Violence in Canada', *International Journal of the Sociology of Law*, vol. 17, pp. 445-63.

Funder, A. (1993), '*De Minimis Non Curat Lex*: The Clitoris, Culture and the Law', *Transnational Law and Contemporary Problems*, vol. 3, pp. 417-67.

Kingdom, E. (1996), 'Transforming Rights: Feminist Political Heuristics', *Res Publica*, vol. 2, pp. 63-75.

Knop, K. (1993), 'Re/Statements: Feminism and State Sovereignty in International Law', *Transnational Law and Contemporary Problems*, vol. 3, pp. 293-344.

Lewis, H. (1995), 'Between *Irua* and "Female Genital Mutilation": Feminist Human Rights Discourse and the Cultural Divide', *Harvard Human Rights Journal*, vol. 8, pp. 1-55.

Mahoney, K. (1996), 'Theoretical Perspectives on Women's Human Rights and Strategies for their Implementation', *Brooklyn Journal of International Law*, vol. 21, pp. 799-856.

Mayer, A. E. (1995), 'Cultural Particularism as a Bar to Women's Rights: Reflections on the Middle Eastern Experience', in J. Peters and A. Wolper (eds.) (1995).

Moss, W. (1990), 'Indigenous Self-Government in Canada and Sexual Equality Under the *Indian Act*: Resolving Conflicts Between Collective and Individual Rights', *Queen's Law Journal*, vol. 15, pp. 279-305.

Native Women's Association of Canada et al. v. The Queen; Inuit Tapirisat of Canada et al., Interveners (1994), 119 D.L.R. (4th) 224 (S.C.C.), appeal from a judgement of the Federal Court of Appeal (1992), 95 D.L.R. (4th) 106.

Peters, J. and Wolper, A. (eds.) (1995), *Women's Rights, Human Rights: International Feminist Perspectives*, Routledge, New York.

Rao, A. (1995), 'The Politics of Gender and Culture in International Human Rights Discourse' in J. Peters and A. Wolper (eds.) (1995).

Romany, C. (1994), 'State Responsibility Goes Private: A Feminist Critique of the Public/Private Distinction in International Human Rights Law' in R. Cook (ed.) (1994a).

Smart, C. (1989), *Feminism and the Power of Law*, Routledge, London.

Sullivan, D. (1995), 'The Public/Private Distinction in International Human Rights Law' in J. Peters and A. Wolper (eds.) (1995).

Tabak, F. (1990), 'Obstacles to Implementing Equal Rights in Third World Countries', in A.-J. Arnaud and E. Kingdom (eds.), *Women's Rights and the Rights of Man*, Aberdeen University Press, Aberdeen.

Toro, M. S. (1995), 'Popularizing Women's Human Rights at the Local Level: A Grassroots Methodology for Setting the International Agenda' in J. Peters and A. Wolper (eds.) (1995).

Webber, J. (1993), 'Individuality, Equality and Difference: Justifications for a Parallel System of Aboriginal Justice' in *Aboriginal Peoples and the Justice System*, Royal Commission on Aboriginal Peoples, Ottawa.

8. Women and Water Law: from Theory to Practice

ELIZABETH A. KIRK AND JENNY A. TOOZE

Introduction

The aim of this chapter is to consider the extent to which the International Law Commission's Draft Articles on the Non-navigational Use of International Watercourses[1] might lead to discrimination between uses and users. Rather than meeting their main purpose - ensuring the equitable and reasonable use of resources - the ICL Draft Articles lead to bias in their allocation of use of resources. To demonstrate this, we shall focus on one distinct group of users - women[2]- on one particular use - agricultural irrigation - and concentrate on a limited geographical area - less developed States.

We shall focus on women because they form an easily identifiable group and because they form the greatest portion of the world's poor and powerless (Harrison, 1991; World Bank OD 4.15, 1991; Dreze and Sen 1989).[3] In addition, it has been noted that the principles being formulated in this area by the international community are not gender neutral, that water management between different sectors and uses is gender specific, but that this gender specificity is generally ignored when implementing water projects (van Wijk, *et al.*, 1996). For example, at the national level the smallest unit considered is the household; yet within households men, women and children play different roles, have varying access to resources and areas in which they can make decisions (van Wijk, *et al.*, 1996; World Bank Policy Paper, 1994).[4] These divisions are, however, often ignored in implementing projects. Van Wijk *et al.,* also note that, when projects are being introduced, women are often excluded from the decision making process, either directly, or as a result of local customs.[5] In addition, although education and training projects have often been gender specific, the wrong gender in the specific community in question is often targeted for education and training (Momsen, 1991; van Wijk *et al.*, 1996; MRC Report, 1996).

Irrigation was chosen as a further focusing criterion for the simple reason that it proved easier to find information on impacts resulting from improved irrigation than on impacts from other uses.

Finally, in an attempt to make the project manageable, we decided to focus mainly on the impacts in less developed States, largely because the impacts of development and use of rivers on society in general would be more obvious in these States. Our theory ought, however, to be equally applicable in all countries, although the specific impacts from individual projects may vary.

To demonstrate our thesis we shall first of all expand upon our theory and illustrate its links with certain feminist theories. We shall then look at the law as expressed in the ILC Draft Articles and at some of the mechanisms used to implement it and at their effects in practice. Throughout we shall refer to illustrations from practice as appropriate.[6]

The Theory

The theory is that the law is incapable of doing what it purports to do: ensuring that rivers are used in an equitable and reasonable manner. This is due to the fact that, when combined with the mechanisms used to implement it, the law largely promotes certain types of uses (those in the public sphere) and ignores others (those in the private sphere). In so doing it automatically promotes the interests of the dominant sector in society, which does not necessarily equate with ensuring an equitable or reasonable use of the river.

Our theory is closely aligned with some feminist legal theories. One of the key arguments of feminist theorists is that seemingly gender-neutral laws in fact discriminate against women (Conaghan, 1986). It seems that feminist theorists would argue that the dominant economic and political group in any society is generally, largely comprised of males and that the law protects the position of the dominant group within society at the expense of women (MacKinnon, 1983; World Bank Policy Paper, 1994). It also appears that the laws being discussed here, despite appearing to be neutral, often enhance the position of the dominant/wealthiest sector of society at the expense of others.[7] This is a direct result of the fact that the laws, combined with the mechanisms used to implement them, render certain uses invisible, so discounting their contributions to society and the impacts of projects on them. Those uses rendered invisible tend not to be the uses enjoyed by the dominant sectors of society; the result being that the law automatically leads to a bias in favour of certain users and their interests.

Another of the basic tenets of many feminist theories - the public/private distinction in law - is also relevant to our thesis. That is, that activities deemed to fall within the private realm are not subject to regulation whereas those that fall within the public realm are (Charlesworth, 1992; Walker, 1994). Traditionally, the law was thought to have no place regulating matters that take place in the home (Wright, 1992), the feminist critique being that it ignores situations which ought to be regulated and so leads to, amongst other things, discrimination and bias.[8] Similarly with our thesis, certain uses and interests are either undervalued or ignored which leads to bias in deciding which uses should be made of international rivers.[9]

Our focus on women is not, however, intended to suggest that they represent a homogenous group,[10] nor that all women face the same impacts from projects involving international rivers. For example, Biswas and Habr noted that, in the Bhima irrigation project in India, improved irrigation facilities had very positive impacts on women. As a result of the improvements, families were able to settle in one place and increase their incomes. The increase in incomes meant that, for the first time, girls received an education where previously only boys had been educated. In contrast, improvements in irrigation in a Kenyan project led to a measurable increase in malaria-bearing mosquitoes with adverse health consequences for the community (Biswas and Habr, 1993).

In line with this rejection of homogeneity, we have kept one eye to the criticism raised by Mohanty and other Third World Feminists that when Western women look at issues pertaining to Third World women, they effectively colonise them by comparing the situations they find the Third World women to be in with the positions in which they, the Western women, find themselves (Mohanty, 1991; MRC Report, 1996).[11] Thus the Western women, according to Mohanty, become the subjects of the discourse. We have no intention of comparing one with another in this chapter, nor of hypothesising on the needs of various women. Rather we merely draw out some of the impacts of projects which are rendered invisible, by the mechanisms employed to decide which projects should proceed.

We should also stress that the impacts highlighted in the examples discussed *infra* do not simply affect women. Our examples illustrate the intersection of gender with other factors such as class which have led us to agree with the anti-essentialist approach[12] of some feminist legal theorists and to reject a polarised debate.[13] For example, two projects studied illustrate that relative lack of wealth can lead to adverse effects from a water project. A survey carried out following completion of the Kano State irrigation project in Nigeria[14] showed an increase in urban migration. It also showed that the families who migrated tended to be the poorest in the region: those with the smallest holdings and least fertile land were those most affected by the flooding caused by the dams (Main, 1990).[15] In addition, in a particular irrigation project in Vietnam, it was thought that the project would, by controlling flooding, guarantee production of a second rice crop. Production did not, however, double as expected, rather, the increase amounted to a meagre 20 per cent.[16] Again, it was the poorer classes who failed to reap the benefits of the projects, this time because they could not afford fertiliser to replace the nutritional value of the silt previously deposited by the floods (Hitchcox, 1992).

The Law

In brief, the obligations found in the ILC Draft Articles are: to use the waters of the river in an equitable and reasonable manner;[17] to inform others of proposed activities which may affect them;[18] to consult;[19] to negotiate in good faith where those others object to the proposed activities with a view to finding a mutually acceptable solution which ought, to be based on the idea of equitable utilisation.[20] This should mean that each gains an equitable (note that does not mean an equal) benefit from the resource. Tied to these obligations is the obligation to exercise due diligence to ensure that activities within one's territory do not cause significant harm to the territory or interests of another State.[21] The obligation not to cause significant harm is, however, subsumed by the obligation to negotiate in good faith with those likely to be affected. This means a significant harm may be allowed if, in the circumstances, it leads to an equitable utilisation of the river.[22]

We shall focus largely on the notion of 'equitable and reasonable use' and how it is intended to be and how it is implemented in practice, as it is the main principle in this area. [23]

Equitable and Reasonable Use

This, the most fundamental of obligations, also provides the most basic and fundamental of problems. The term equitable and reasonable is necessarily fluid. More importantly, its practical implementation is determined primarily by the States concerned, failing which by appointed arbiters, or by a court (failing which development may well be foregone). While this fluidity is clearly very important - it allows each situation to be analysed according to its own relevant facts - leaving the determination to States means they have the freedom to emphasise or ignore relevant factors as they choose. This means they can accord importance to whichever factors they feel relevant: possibly leading to bias.[24] If it is true that States are patriarchal institutions which exclude women from elite positions (Charlesworth *et al.*, 1991), and if our thesis is correct that the laws operating in this area largely promote the uses enjoyed by, and interests of, the most powerful groups within society, then this freedom to determine which uses should be accorded the greatest importance will *automatically* lead to discrimination against less powerful groups in society and so against women.

State freedom to determine which factors are relevant to specific cases is diminished to a certain extent by the requirement to follow Article 6 when determining what is reasonable and equitable. Article 6 outlines some of the factors States ought to take into account and covers such things as geography, social and economic needs and existing and potential uses of the water.[25] The list is relatively comprehensive, but not exhaustive. Its terms are quite neutral and it does not exclude any uses, merely lists the sorts of things States ought to take into account. But this does lead to a number of problems. First, because it is not possible to dictate for all situations, no uses or impacts are accorded any sort of priority or primacy. It is up to the States in each case to determine the relative importance of each factor. Secondly, it is also possible for the parties concerned to decide to offset the harm to one use through compensation, or by allowing other disputed uses. Finally, and perhaps most importantly, it is left to the States to determine exactly which uses, interests and impacts to include. All of these problems increase the possibility of discrimination and bias in favour of the interests and uses enjoyed by the more powerful sectors of society, at the expense of the interests and uses of others. So, for example, projects like the Kano State project which led to increased urbanisation of the rural population, particularly the rural poor,[26] may have been judged to be highly beneficial overall, if the impacts of urbanisation are ignored or under valued. If, however, proper account were taken of the effects of urbanisation on the poor, such projects may be judged either a complete failure, or perhaps just less beneficial.

The Gendered Implementation of 'Equitable and Reasonable Use'

The importance of Article 6 of the ILC Draft Articles, however, lies more in the fact that when determining such things as social and economic worth, the value of a given use is generally its economic value,[27] traditionally determined by applying methods such as the Keynsian method of measuring national income (Rogers, 1989).[28] This system concentrates on estimates of Gross National Product (GNP) and excludes 'informal and non-cash output ... the sectors in which women are particularly concentrated' (Rogers, 1989; UN Statistical Office Report, 1976).[29] As a result subsistence agriculture and tasks such as collecting water and housework were not traditionally (and in some cases still are not) taken into consideration. Yet, in less developed States in particular, these are vital activities which may in fact account for the largest proportion of the net benefits[30] to individuals within these States. The discounting of these benefits can have disastrous impacts, in that they may be diminished in quantity or quality as a result of new projects, yet no account might be taken of this. Van Wijk *et al.*, for example, noted that a major and potentially damaging impact of irrigation projects is that they tend to promote production of cash crops over subsistence agriculture (van Wijk *et al.*, 1996).[31] They also note that in many countries men are responsible for the production of cash crops and at times end up in direct competition with those responsible for subsistence agriculture (women) for land. This can lead in two ways to increased poverty, particularly amongst women and children. The first is that the income from cash crops is shared neither equally, nor equitably within families. Instead those that bring it in (men) get the largest share. Secondly, it can mean that families lose their ability to be self-sufficient in basic food stuffs and become reliant on the market price for the cash crops, as more and more land is bought over for cash crop production (van Wijk *et al.*, 1996).[32] Yet these negative impacts may be ignored as they fall within the informal, non-cash output sectors traditionally excluded from assessments of a project's worth; only increases in national income generated by increases in cash crop production and sale being considered in the valuation of projects.

The result is that the net assessed benefits of some irrigation projects were/are over valued, as they fail to take account of all costs. In others indirect positive impacts may be ignored leading to an undervaluing of the net worth of the project in question. So, for example, the sorts of improvements seen in the education of girls in the Bhima area might ordinarily be excluded from the evaluation of a projects net worth, as they may be regarded as being indirect, or non-cash outputs which ought to be excluded from evaluations.[33]

These impacts traditionally seem to have been regarded as falling very much in the private sphere and so to have been of no interest to those responsible for irrigation projects and, by extension, of no interest to international law.

One could, of course, argue that economic accounting is not a legal matter. The law simply provides that account must be taken of certain factors and it is up to the community to determine how those factors are weighed. But this would miss the point. The law assumes that the accounting method is neutral and that the factors being accounted are neutral and are handled in a neutral manner, when in reality there is little that is neutral about them. The mechanisms used to implement the law are skewed in favour of those with the most power in the market place, with the result that, if the law does not explicitly deal with the impacts of different methods of analysis of the worth of various uses, the impact of the law in this area will automatically be discriminatory. This is not to say that the legal principles must lose their neutrality[34] to compensate for societal imbalances, but that the mechanisms developed to *implement* them should take into account and attempt to neutralise such societal biases.[35] In turn, this may require legal provisions prescribing the mechanisms to be employed and the matters to be considered by them, but it need not require modification of the actual principles themselves.

Changes in Mechanisms

Some international actors are now adapting the mechanisms they use to assess the value of products to take account of the above issues. The World Bank,[36] for example, has introduced new policies and directives to deal with some of the inequities caused by its old policies. For example, in its 1994 Policy Paper on Women and Development it recognised that development and growth are 'best served' when public resources are invested where they yield the highest economic and social returns (World

Bank Policy Paper, 1994).

Until 1994 World Bank lending programmes, while they might consider women as a distinct group of beneficiaries, did not consider the *relative* positions of men and women (World Bank Policy Paper, 1994).[37] That is, women would be considered only if they, as a group, were intended beneficiaries. In 1994 the World Bank adopted its Operational Policy on gender, the object of which is, '[t]o reduce gender disparities and enhance women's participation in the economic development of their countries'.[38] The policy provides that the Bank will help governments, 'identify barriers ... that prevent women from participating in and benefiting from *public* policies and programs'.[39] It thus recognises the exclusion of women from the public sphere, at least in certain countries, and endeavours to ensure that their interests are included in all programmes. No positive obligations are, however, imposed upon the borrower states. Contrast this with the World Bank's Operational Directive on Indigenous Peoples which provides that, where adverse impacts on indigenous peoples are unavoidable, the borrower must find a solution to them before the Bank will consider funding the project.[40]

Impacts of Changes

Little can, however, be drawn from these changes in the World Bank's policies. Whilst it is true that the Bank has expanded its policies to take account of more than simply cash outputs, in some areas, notably in relation to gender issues, its policies are not binding. This means that, even if solutions cannot be found to noted gender inequities, the Bank may still fund the project in question, so sustaining or even promoting gender inequity. But at least it will be aware of doing so!

Two questions remain: first, are these changes in policies sufficient to meet the problems outlined above, or is more detail required in the actual law itself? and, second, what difference do the changes make to the implementation of the 'equitable and reasonable use' principle? If adhered to, this form of change in policy ought to make implementation of the 'equitable and reasonable use' principle more effective in so far as more realistic assessments of the value of projects will be reached. But whether they are sufficient on their own to lead to the eradication of bias in the system is questionable. In reality, the only conclusions we can draw are that generally there is a move towards ensuring that neutral laws lead to equitable impacts. The effects of implementing the new policies outlined above are, however, not yet clearly established. There is still a need to study their impacts to establish if further modifications to the implementing mechanisms are required.

Conclusion

The only determinate conclusion which can be drawn from our research is that although the ILC's Draft Articles may lead to 'equitable and reasonable use; they cannot ensure it.

Does the law (as reflected in the ILC's Draft Articles) discriminate against groups? It certainly appeared to in the period when the mechanism employed for determining the net benefit of projects was largely the Keynsian system of accounting. Now that the World Bank and others have adopted policies providing that account must be taken of other factors, including impacts of gender relations the answer is less obvious. These policies were adopted too recently for any definite conclusions to be drawn as to their efficacy in tackling the discriminatory impacts of projects.

One must also consider whether the policies themselves are sufficient to deal with discrimination. Consideration might be given to the positive discrimination provisions found in the World Bank policies on Indigenous Peoples. Perhaps we should go further and introduce changes in the law to ensure that the mechanisms used to value impacts are neutral and equitable in their effects. Perhaps the law should deal directly with the variety of circumstances in which people find themselves - women, children and men. The question of whether or not such changes are necessary should probably only be answered after more careful examination of *all* of the impacts of projects, not just those traditionally included in evaluation of their worth.

Notes

1. Hereafter ILC Draft Articles. These deal with non-navigational uses of international rivers in relation to rivers which flow through two or more States. The term 'river' in this paper refers to the whole watercourse. The ILC Draft Articles is being used as the basis for drafting an international convention. (Under General Assembly Resolution 49/52, December 9 1994 the GA established a working group to draft the convention on the basis of the draft articles. The convention has now completed part of the adoption process. All that remains is for it to be adopted by the General

Assembly of the United Nations.) They also represent a fairly good codification of the practice of States. (See ILC 1994 Report at 224.) As such their terms merit consideration despite having no real force in international law as yet.

2. To focus primarily on a particular use would have been too limiting as it could exclude consideration of the wider impacts on such things as education and health.
3. Harrison (1991) compares the relative economic and political situations of men and women in Oceanview, a Kingston slum. Article 6 of the World Bank OD states: '[t]he burden of poverty falls disproportionately on women', World Bank Operational Directive 4.15 on Poverty Reduction (1991) (http://www.worldbank.org/html/opr/opmanual/ods/415tx.html).
4. The World Bank has noted there is a need to go 'beyond gender-neutral policies to ensure that the *outcomes* are equally beneficial to men and women', World Bank Policy Paper (1994).
5. See also MRC Report (1996).
6. A number of the examples we refer to are exclusively national projects, but as the *impacts* of projects at the local level are not dependent on whether the project is a national or an international project this should not be problematical.
7. That is not to say that in each case examined the impacts on all individuals within these broad sectors of society will be the same, nor that the laws will always enhance the position of the more powerful sectors.
8. For example, just providing education for all will not significantly help women and girls if each family decides on its own that girls should not be educated. The public/private distinction itself need not however lead to bias or discrimination. The discrimination arises as a result of the way society is structured. Activities defined as being feminine tend also to be regarded as falling within the private sphere, those regarded as masculine as falling within the public. The exclusion of the private sphere from the law and from economic analysis can and does amount to a biased system.
9. The dichotomy is, according to a number of feminist theorists, relevant to public international law in so far as international law operates to regulate State interactions with each other (Charlesworth *et. al.*, 1991). These interactions are by their nature public activities and the law in regulating them ignores activities and matters deemed to be private. (But *c.f.* the regulation of human rights where states may be held responsible for inter-personal relations illustrating the development of International Law in spheres previously considered private. See *Plattform 'Arzte fur das leben'* v *Austria*, 21 June 1988, Series A No 139, 13 EHRR (1991), 204, and Charlesworth *et. al.* (1991), pp. 627-9.) The public/private dichotomy in public international law must be different to that found in the domestic law of states due to the difference in subjects of the two systems. Space does not permit any real consideration of these issues. What will be illustrated,

however, is the way in which the *mechanisms* used to *implement* seemingly gender-neutral laws can *create* a public/private distinction.

10. In this respect we are adopting an anti-essentialist feminist critique (see Colker, 1991-2) and are opposed to a notion of homogeneity.
11. We are aware of different perceptions operating in different parts of the world. For example, the MRC Report (1996, p.3), distinguishes between 'women development' [*sic*] and 'gender development', the latter being defined as 'activities that acknowledge the relation between roles of men and women in society and are geared to making full use of these different roles'. *C.f.*, for example, MacKinnon (1987, p.3): 'constructing gender as difference ... obscures and legitimizes the way gender is imposed by force. It hides that force behind a static description of gender as a biological or social myth or semantic partition ... The idea of gender difference helps keep the reality of male dominance in place'. See also MacKinnon *et. al.* (1985).
12. We would stress that our illustrations are not intended to justify our theoretical standpoint. Rather the results of our illustrations have led us to agree with certain feminist views.
13. That is, a debate solely between the sexes.
14. The irrigation project was completed in 1976 and the survey was conducted between 1987-88.
15. Nigerian law allowed either for compensation to be awarded, or for alternative (and often less fertile) land to be provided. Where compensation was awarded it was only for artificial additions to the land and not for the land itself.
16. Established through an Oxfam sponsored survey (Hitchcox, 1992).
17. Article 5 ILC Draft Articles.
18. Articles 12 - 17 ILC Draft Articles. See also the Lac Lannoux Arbitration (France v. Spain) Int.L.R. 24 (1957) 101.
19. Articles 12 to 17 ILC Draft Articles, see especially Article 17.
20. Article 17 ILC Draft Articles.
21. Under Article 7 ILC Draft Articles. See also the *Trail Smelter Arbitration* (Canada v. U.S.A.) (138, 1941) RIAA iii 1905; the *Corfu Channel Case* (United Kingdom v. Albania) [1949] ICJ Rep 4; and the UN Convention on the Law of the Sea 1983 21 I.L.M. 1261, Article 194. See generally Birnie and Boyle (1992).
22. This need not be the most equitable utilisation possible, just *an* equitable utilisation.
23. All other obligations are to some extent subsidiary to it. See ILC Draft Articles at 218. On state practice see also Griffith (1959).
24. As Charlesworth *et. al.* noted: 'States are patriarchal structures ... because they are based on the concentration of power in, and control by, an elite and the domestic legitimation of a monopoly over the use of force to maintain that control' (1991, p.622). Thus the state system and

international law between them support a system which is biased in favour of the most powerful groups within society, making the likelihood of bias in implementation of these laws all the greater.

25. Article 6 (1) ILC Draft Articles.
26. *Supra* notes 15 and 16 and accompanying text.
27. This reflects Scott and Coustalin's findings that the dominant principles in domestic water law have gone through a series of twists and turns over the last few centuries, each twist having been prompted by changing economic interests (1995). On evaluating projects see Dixon *et. al.* (1989).
28. This is roughly speaking the method used by international organisations and individual governments to determine the contribution of different activities to the GNPs of States (Rogers, 1989). The Keynsian method of assessing national income is illustrative of the wider public/private distinction discussed above (*supra* notes 8 and 9 and accompanying text). By designating certain activities as welfare and therefore rendering them unaccountable, it leads to bias in the system and reinforces the public/private dichotomy. See Waring (1992) on the impacts of this in practice and Charlesworth (1992).
29. Non-monetary economic activities have been defined by the UN as 'welfare' issues which should continue to be excluded from considerations of national income (UN Statistical Office Report, 1976).
30. Benefits being inputs to the body. In the Lao PDR 60% of the population are subsistence farmers with less than 10% of crops being marketed (Jacobs, 1996).
31. See also Rogers who notes that 'Investment favours export and cash crops ... with little regard for calorie output per acre or per unit of investment' (Rogers, 1989, p.42).
32. This has led to increased malnutrition and disease among children in areas of high cash crop production such as western Kenya (van Wijk *et. al.*, 1996).
33. See the text between notes 10 and 11.
34. For example, by promoting positive discrimination.
35. But see also MRC Report (1996, p.21) where it notes the importance of changing apparently neutral rules to ensure participation by both men and women. For example, the rule allowing only 1 family representative to be a member of the Water User Organisation was changed to allow 2 family representatives, as, if only 1 were allowed, the representative would always be the male head of the household. If 2 were allowed, a female representative could also join.
36. The length of this article does not permit an analysis of the policies of all of the international lending institutions, nor all States so we shall concentrate on the example provided by the World Bank as illustrative of how mechanisms of implementation can be altered to take on board and attempt to neutralise societal biases.

37. The paper emphasises the change in approach recently adopted by the Bank. Whereas earlier programmes focused on 'women in development' (where women were treated as a target group of beneficiaries), the new policy framework is broadening to encompass 'gender and development'. This latter approach focuses 'on gender differentiation and the factors underlying the structure of gender relations within households' and is said to distinguish between the practical and strategic needs of women. Practical needs encompass demand for goods and services 'arising out of women's socially acceptable roles in society' (for example health care). Strategic needs refer to requirements that will help women to achieve greater equality relative to men, (for example equal employment opportunities). Furthermore the paper recognises that the best way to involve women is to analyse their positions in relation to men.
38. World Bank **OP 4.20, The Gender Dimension of Development (1994)**, Article 1. See also *http://worldbank.org/html/opr/opmanual/ops/420tx.html.*
39. Article 2(a)(i).
40. World Bank OD 4.20, Indigenous Peoples (1991), Article 9, *http://www.worldbank.org/html/opr/opmanual/ods/420tx.html.*

Bibliography

Birnie, P. W. and Boyle, A. E. (1992), *International Law and the Environment*, Clarendon Press, Oxford.

Biswas, A. and Habr, H. N. (1993), 'Environmental and Water Resources Management: The Need for a New Holistic Approach', *Water Resources Development*, vol. 9, pp. 117-26.

Charlesworth, H. (1992), 'The Public/Private Distinction and the Right to Development in International Law', *Australian Yearbook of International Law*, vol. 12, pp. 190-204.

Charlesworth, H., Chinkin, C. and Wright, S. (1991), 'Feminist approaches to international law', *American Journal of International Law*, vol. 85, pp. 613-45.

Colker, R. (1991-2), 'The example of lesbians: A posthumous reply to Professor Mary Joe Frug', *Harvard Law Review*, vol. 105, pp. 1084-95.

Conaghan, J. (1986), 'The Invisibility of Women in Labour Law: Gender-neutrality in Model Building', *International Journal of the Sociology of Law*, vol. 18, pp. 377-392, in F. Olsen (ed.) (1995), *Feminist Legal Theory*, vol. 2, Dartmouth, Aldershot.

Dixon, J. A., Talbot, L. M. and LeMoigne, G. J.-M. (1989), *Dams and the Environment: Considerations in World Bank Projects*, The World Bank, Washington, D.C.

Dreze, J. and Sen, A. (1989), *Hunger and Public Action*, Oxford University Press, Oxford.

Griffith, W. L. (1959), 'The Use of Waters of International Drainage Basins Under Customary International Law', *American Journal of International Law*, vol. 53, pp. 50-80.

Harrison, F. V. (1991), 'Women in Jamaica's Urban Informal Economy: Insights from a Kingston Slum', in C. T. Mohanty, A. Russo, and L. Torres (eds.), *Third World Women and the Politics of Feminism*, Indian University Press, Bloomington and Indianapolis.

Hitchcox, L. (1992), 'A Water Programme in Vietnam and its Impacts on Women', *Development in Practice*, vol. 2, pp. 23-36.

International Law Commission (1994), 'Draft Articles on the Non-Navigational Use of International Watercourses', *Report of the International Law Commission on the work of its forty-sixth session* GAOR 49th Sess. Sup. No. 10 (A/49/10).

Jacobs, J. W. (1996), 'Planning for Change and Sustainability in Water Development in Lao PDR and the Mekong River Basin', *Natural Resources Forum*, vol. 20, pp. 175-87.

MacKinnon, C. A. (1983), 'Feminism, Marxism, Method, and the State: Toward Feminist Jurisprudence', *Signs: Journal of Women in Culture and Society*, vol. 8, pp. 635-58, in F. Olsen (ed.) (1995), *Feminist Legal Theory*, vol. 1, Dartmouth, Aldershot.

MacKinnon, C.A. (1987), *Feminism Unmodified Discourses on Life and Law*, Harvard University Press, Cambridge, Massachusetts and London.

MacKinnon, C.A., Dubois, E. C., Dunlap, M. C., Gilligan, C. J. and Menkel-Meadow, C. J. (1985), 'Feminist Discourse, Moral Values, and the Law - A Conversation', *Buffalo Law Review*, vol. 34, pp. 11-87, in F. Olsen (ed.) (1995), *Feminist Legal Theory*, vol. 1, Dartmouth, Aldershot.

Main, H. A. C. (1990), 'Dam Projects and Urbanization in Kano State, Nigeria', *Singapore Journal of Tropical Geography*, vol. 11, pp. 87-99.

Mekong River Commission (MRC) (1996), '*Sustainable Irrigated Agriculture Project, Special Report Gender Development in Irrigated Agriculture*', Bangkok.

Mohanty, C. (1991), 'Under Western Eyes, Feminist Scholarship and Colonial Discourse', in C. Mohanty, A. Russo and L. Torres (eds.) (1991), *Third World Women and the Politics of Feminism*, Indian University Press, Bloomington and Indianapolis.

Nicholson, L. (ed.) (1990), *Feminism/Postmodernism*, Routledge, London.

Rogers, B. (1989), *The Domestication of Women, Discrimination in Developing Societies*, Routledge, London.

Scott and Coustalin (1995), 'The Evolution of Water Rights', *Natural Resources Journal*, vol. 35, pp. 821-979.

United Nations Statistical Office (1976), *Report of the expert group on welfare-oriented supplements to the national accounts and balances and other measures of the levels of living*, UN document ESA/STAT/AC.4/5, 15 April 1976, pp. 2-3.

van Wijk, C., de Lange, L. and Saunders, D. (1996), 'Gender Aspects in the Management of Water', *Natural Resources Forum*, vol. 20, pp. 91-103.

Walker, K. (1994), 'An Exploration of Article 2(7) of the United Nations Charter as an Embodiment of the Public/Private Distinction in International Law', *New York Journal of International Law and Politics*, vol. 26, pp. 173-99.

Waring, M. (1992), 'Gender and International Law: Women and the Right to Development', *Australian Yearbook of International Law*, vol. 12, pp. 177-89.

World Bank Policy Paper (1994), *Enhancing Women's Participation in Economic Development*, The World Bank, Washington.

Wright, S. (1992), 'Economic Rights and Social Justice: A Feminist Analysis of some International Human Rights Conventions', *Australian Yearbook of International Law*, vol. 12, pp. 241-64.

9. Women's Law and Cultural Understandings of Gender in Finland

ANU PYLKKÄNEN

Introduction

Social equality and distributive justice have been the tokens of the Nordic welfare states all through the twentieth century; it has been only natural that women's rights and gender equality have been the focus of official state policies. The pursuit of equality, therefore, has been very much connected with the state, at the same time as it has become an academic discipline. Since the 1960s era of state feminism, a women's movement separate from the state has been almost non-existant. It was part of this state feminist tradition, that in 1995, the Finnish government decided to promote women's studies with three new chairs additional to the one that the University of Helsinki had founded earlier. They were finally allocated to law (Helsinki), social sciences (Tampere) and theoretical women's studies (Åbo Akademi University in Turku). There will be four more chairs in the following few years to fields such as economics and medicine.

In this chapter, I will consider the Law Faculty of Helsinki University as an example of the kind of challenges which a shift towards becoming more establishment poses, both to the male hegemony in academia, and to women's studies itself. I will discuss also the reasons why this in fact very moderate addition to the academic curriculum was not as easily accepted as it first seemed. Indeed, the Finnish 'dilemma of equality' has been much discussed and criticised. Despite early political integration and a 'women-friendly' welfare state, Finnish women are not in a better position than their sisters in other countries as concerns persistent gendered structures: the wage gap, sexual violence and so on (Holli, 1990;

Parvikko, 1991). Equality policies have concentrated on administrative measures against discrimination mostly in working life, and in allocating some resources to women's studies, but it is characteristic of Finland that a public discourse of gender equality - or rather, gender differences - has nevertheless been extremely limited.

The Women's Law Chair is one of the few in the world: in Scandinavia, it is the second after Norway, which has had its women's studies programme and professor ever since the 1970s. The uniqueness of the Chair in Women's Law lies more in its shape as a separate discipline, than in its contents as such. First developed in line with the Norwegian Women's Law, originally aiming at reshaping and systematising legal science according to women's every day experiences (Dahl, 1987), it claimed an existence as a discipline parallel to the traditional ones. Although recently moving towards a feminist theory of law, and thus to some extent assimilated to other critical approaches, its place in the legal academic curriculum is still unclear. In this chapter, I propose to argue that the considerable controversy aroused by the establishment of the Chair did, and does, reflect the ambiguity of the Finnish understandings of equality, and some of the very characteristics of the relation between gender and law in Finland.

Women and the Legal Academy

The Finnish legal culture is young, positivistic, and male. Its roots are both in German 19th century jurisprudence and Scandinavian realism, later during this century predominantly in the anglo-saxon analytical school. As a national discipline, it dates back to the second half of the 19th century and there are no more than about 190 doctorates altogether, of which women hold only little more than ten per cent (Halila, 1996). The first female to pass an exam was Agnes Lundell in 1906 and the first woman to get a PhD was Inkeri Anttila in 1946. She later became the first female Professor of Law in 1961. It was not until the 1970s however that a significant percentage of lawyers were female. As late as 1992 the number of female law school graduates was about 50 per cent. Since the 1980s, many law-related occupations in the public sector, such as lower court judges, have become to a large extent feminised. In general, women's access to legal education has not led to a more equal access to senior positions. However, it is difficult to prove any discrimination or discern gendered patterns. In practice, women are led into the legal profession and promoted to senior positions through male gatekeepers, and they must accept and adjust to the maleness of the profession (Silius, 1992).

In academia, however, the situation is different. At the moment, there are no female law professors in the Law Faculty of Helsinki University - the one in Women's Law will be the first female law professor for years, as the few female professors of the 1970s and 1980s have moved to other occupations. In the whole of Finland, there are only four or five female Professors of Law.

At the moment, the proportions of male and female students, including master's degree graduates, are equal, but there is significant selection along the gender lines in post-graduate studies. It has recently been asked why women do not want to continue their studies, or if they do, why do they prefer a career outside the academy? The very rigid and hierarchical nature of the legal academic community, as well as the maleness of the science itself, have been some of the suggested explanations. According to a recent survey in the University of Turku (Voutilainen, 1996), the attitudes to equality in academia are the harshest in Law. Amazingly enough, most people in Law thought that equality exists, whereas the women who experience discrimination were from law faculties. In other words, the tradition of Law emphasises equality and gender neutrality, and the need to adjust to that model is always strong. On the other hand, the working surroundings are least supportive and the importance of support from the family strongest. Maybe this result, among others, indicates that substantive equality requires qualitative as well as quantitative changes.

To my mind, the roots of Finnish understandings of equality can be traced both to legal culture in general, and to the relationship between women and the state. Because of our history, the emphasis on, and tradition of, formal legalism is strong. First as a part of the Swedish Empire (ca. 1100-1809), then an autonomous Grand-Duchy of Russia (1809-1917), Finland has relied on a strict interpretation of law very much as means of protecting its national interests especially towards the end of the 19th century. The national legal system was protected against Russian imperialism by emphasising the formal validity of the Swedish 18th century constitution. On the other hand, lawyers were, and are, civil servants more than anything else - less of an independent profession - and legal education has strongly favoured integration with the state (Konttinen, 1991; Pajuoja and Ervasti, 1994). It is the dominant idea of the law as a science that it should legitimate its existence by 'serving' the practice which means offering interpretations of law and suggestions for reforms. Indeed, a majority of law professors have in fact always been involved in large-scale law reforms. Many even act as judges in arbitration cases or have other similar positions. The external activities of a professor have not been limited thus far.

Nowadays, one becomes a full professor around one's early 40s, and a relatively large, if not necessarily deep, production of research is a required qualification. There is no individual promotion (tenure track), so that should one happen to fail in getting the one post available there is no hope for advancement perhaps for twenty-five years. Once a professor, one's authority is beyond question, and the hierarchical faculty structure is strict. As there is usually only one professor in a field, seldom is any real discussion or critique inside or between the disciplines encouraged. As developed in the emergence of the modern legal system in the late 19th century, the law as science concept has effectively rejected any serious demands for interdisciplinary approaches.

It is this kind of empire the Professor of Women's Law has entered. One can ask, why such a chair and what changes will occur as a result - or will there be any changes.

Finnish Understandings of Equality: the Parity Model and its Historical Background

To be a little provocative, all the controversy and contradiction connected with the Chair in Women's Law can also be, in my opinion, traced back to the peculiar features in the Finnish gender culture, namely the weak gender polarisation and the strong female integration in labour and politics. This can also be described as the lack of differentiation, being one of the many legacies from the premodern that to some extent characterise Finnish history and society even today.

The general notion of developments concerning gender equality in the West seems to be derived from the idea that men's and women's roles were polarised from the 17th Century up to the late 19th Century, when the universal legal rights (liberties) of an individual were gradually extended to women. Polarisation has been linked especially with the realm of private as the feminine sphere and clear-cut distinctions between active man/passive woman, public/private, and rational/emotional. In Finland, however, the development was quite the reverse, or, rather, late compared to other parts of Europe: gender polarisation and the distinct nuclear family with its gendered patterns were new phenomena that developed only in the late 19th and early 20th century.

Paradoxically, women were given equal and inclusive political and legal rights at the same time when their role was directed towards domestic sphere more than ever. In other words, the bourgeois family model, although introduced in Scandinavia in the early 1900s, was not adopted without modifications. The specific feature in Finland was, indeed, that the interests of the state and those of maternity were considered parallel. Women's citizenship was strongly connected with Finnish-nationalist nation-building and a concept of double citizenship has been developed to describe this phenomenon: women were entitled to citizenship as mothers. In contrast to other countries, women were themselves shaping these policies in parliament, in political parties, civic movements and in the early professionalising of care (Anttonen, 1994; Sulkunen, 1990).

Although law undoubtedly is one of the most powerful discourses in Finland, as everywhere else in the West, to define such phenomena as the state or the family or the subjectivity, and despite the fact that the formal legalist tradition has been very important in the Finnish political and legal history, I would still suggest that the importance of law in creating gender differences or gender equality has nevertheless been weak. An agricultural country up to World War II, Finland was modernised only very late in time, and the lay elements in its legal culture remained strong for a long time. In other words, the significance of legal culture was both late and weak. A change from a poor and status-bound society of estates, to a modern, democratic market society happened during the turn of the century, and an equally quick change to an industrialised economy took place only after World War II. Many legal fields, like procedural law, were reformed as late as in the 1980s and 1990s according to modern European models - more than a hundred years later than elsewhere (Nousiainen, 1993).

As regards women's status, both the vote in 1906 and the marriage laws and early welfare legislation around 1900 integrated women to the realm of the 'legal'. Formal rule-equality was the goal of the foremost feminists at that time, and critique of the problems of the private was almost insignificant - despite some critical voices such as the playwright and novelist Minna Canth who wrote about the abuse of women in families. On the other hand, there had in fact never been significant divisions, as the bourgeois family culture had until that time been a privilege of a minor elite, and ordinary women's labour had all the time been important to the agrarian subsistence economy. It was thus not the family but the work through which women were integrated in the society.

This meant also that there were no well developed doctrines of women's status in the family either; rather than individuals it was the family farm or real estate that figured most in legislation. It was other discourses such as medicine, literature and education that were more important than law, and discussions of gender in general, female sexuality, and sanctity of the family institution were in fact not uncommon in the late 19th century public debate.

As regards law and gender, women had in fact always retained a certain legal identity of their own (reflecting the power and responsibility of the agrarian household matron), however limited, and, paradoxically, a good family life was something to strive for and not to get free from. In 1929, when married women were finally granted an identical legal status with unmarried women and men, it was an era when the nuclear family emerged into the law for the first time and home culture in general was flourishing in all parts of society.

In politics, female members of parliament were actively promoting women's interests ever since the first democratic parliament gathered in 1907. Women legitimated their legal and political activities with the aims of women and family, as a parallel to, and in accordance with, those of the state. The Finnish welfare model can be claimed to be to a large extent a result of female policies. On the other hand, female politicians tended to keep to their 'proper' area, and did not question gendered power structures in general (Kuusipalo, 1993). One can say that the agrarian values and models were internalised in the politics, with a strong emphasis on women's labour, as well as on their civilising role in the upbringing of children and even men.

Finally, I will describe the way such basic concepts as state, law, and family have been perceived in the context of gender relations. Finnish women demanding equality have worked within society, and not from outside, as an external opposition. This of course has also weakened their critique. It also makes the 'progress' less visible or important, as women also joined the control that evidently was linked with the early welfare. Female citizenship has been strong but it has not altered gendered divisions of power. On the contrary, women have become dependent on the state, which is sometimes called state patriarchy (Hernes, 1984; Borchorsth and Siim, 1987; Allén, 1993). I would say that as opposed to individuals, the state has been over-emphasised in the Finnish legal and political culture, and only very recently have its critics raised their voices. The gendered and heterosexist models behind the welfare system have only recently been exposed as the welfare state in general is declining. It may be that what has motivated the system is not the equality as such but the need for female labour, and this pattern makes women vulnerable when unemployment and the public sector are at a critical stage.

Up until this century, Finnish society has thus been predominantly agrarian and characterised by the absence of bourgeois family culture. Only as late as in the beginning of this century was it common to think that people should be able to live a proper family life. Earlier, the household was more or less a production and disciplinary unit with less emphasis on its private side, and both men and women have had a crucial role in the subsistence economy. Up to the 1890s, a privatised home was a privilege of a minor elite. What had been a social reality in European family life since late 1700s was something quite extraordinary in 19th century Finland. In agrarian surroundings, the companionship of the spouses was a typical feature, and a separate home was possible only for the wealthiest farmers or bourgeoisie. Working families did not even have proper housing up until the end of the 19th century, when a dwelling with a room and a kitchen provided a working family the privacy of a family life (Markkola, 1994).

In an agrarian household, as well as in modern wage earning families, women's role has always been strong. This parity model, or symmetry, is to a large extent a result of the need for labour - which does not mean, however, that women's labour would have been in general highly valued. On the other hand, spouses have been more or less considered as members of their kinship group and inherited or family assets as the law's primary province. A nuclear family with the wife at home looking after children is a young and recent phenomenon in Finnish law: it can be situated in the decades between 1930 and 1980. Even during that era, it was not mainly a question of sacred privacy, or a private home, but of a standard or ideal of good housekeeping and childcare that both legitimated the central position of the mother at home and made homes as targets of social policies.

In today's Finland, as in many western countries, equality between the genders is based on a sameness model. For example, modern family legislation has abandoned most of the family-bound regulations and is based on market rhetoric and a minimum of substantive rules. Spouses are individuals in relation to each other and equally situated parents in relation to their children. Unlike many other countries, however, this legal construction also has a real basis: both women's (mothers') full-time employment and individual social security have made women economically more independent from men and marriage than in most western countries.

The recession and decline of the welfare state have to some extent diminished public support and de facto put stronger emphasis on private maintenance, but so far it has not been an official policy to tie women and children stronger to a private (male) source of income. 'Family values' as used in many other countries' policies simply lack the same legitimate basis in Finland. I am not saying that women's employment and economic or legal independence would not be threatened at all, but this threat is more hidden, more indirect and more linked with the reduction in the public sector in general, and less by reference to women's 'natural' caring capacities. As I tried to show earlier, private care at home has only very recent traditions in Finland (as people simply could not devote much time to it even if they wanted to) and since the late 1960s it has been replaced by public daycare systems. Professional care has in fact an even longer tradition. Caregiving at home has now become popular as a substitute to the more expensive public services, but it has not been generally accepted as a natural responsibility of women. Sufficient remuneration and social benefits are a goal in this field as well as in any caring profession, albeit that this is not yet a reality.

In Finland, the myths of the strong nordic woman and the women-friendly state - not the sanctity of the private - have for a long time hidden the problems of private life. This is one of the critical points of liberal work-based independence. Uneven division of unpaid labour, the wage-gap, sexualised violence and similar issues connected with intimate relationships have not been seriously discussed until very recently. It was only in the 1997 Programme of Equality Policies that the government declared its commitment to investigate and prevent sexualised violence against women. The Equality Act cannot be applied to private matters, and its results even in working life have been modest. It is difficult to admit discrimination and many women fear being labelled 'feminist': a label which is not generally accepted in Finland.

The Challenge of Feminist Legal Theory

Feminist approaches challenge first and foremost the distinction between theory and practice and the notion that law 'serves' the practice. The truth-creating role of law as science is one of the main targets of feminist analysis, whereas in mainstream science, despite some diverging approaches, 'law' has for more than one hundred years been seen, relatively unproblematically as an unalterable idea of written norms. In addition, there is a strong myth of law as a neutral mechanism for social change. This agenda operates mainly on the basis of the traditional division of disciplines and methods of interpretation, and for example the discrepancies between different branches of law have been little discussed.

So far, it has been one of the most important results of the Finnish feminist legal science that women are treated as both dependent and independent, at the same time, depending on which purpose a regulation is based. Women are not considered to need any support on the basis of their inferior status, but on the other hand they simply lack any legal measures to reject a presupposed responsibility for caregiving or question dependency in the intimate relationships. In practice, this can lead to the most awkward situations. Despite relative individuality in many fields of law, an old (heterosexist) construction of rights and responsibilities lies in the background of many acts regulating distribution of public resources - certain changes in other fields do not bring much change. For example, in connection with reforms of constitutional law, it has recently been asked if the equality provisions in the Form of Government have actually changed at all (Nieminen, 1996).

Women and law is called Women's Law in Scandinavia, but this does not mean that there would exist a different law or legal science for women, despite the Norwegian tradition of developing Women's Law as an independent discipline. Rather, it is a strategy within the law, a goal to become independent and get a reasonable share of the resources. On the other hand, though, it does reflect the way quests for equality are in general pursued: instead of a critique within the discipline, a separate office or chair is founded and specific legislation passed. One easily wonders if the intellectual critique is less important than administrative, measures. This is a tradition which Women's Law seeks to change. Although practitioners of women's law do also engage in official equality policies and administration, it is even more important to develop a specific critical approach to legal science and the legal system itself as a whole. We kind of try to be in and out at the same time.

As expected, women's studies as a discipline has not been welcomed because of the questions it wants to ask, and its challenge to mainstream jurisprudence. This is visible for example in the debates about the definition - what is women's law, and does anything that refers to 'women' come within the definition. Because of this ignorance or unwillingness to accept the aims of women's studies, any discussions tended to lead to a more limited defintion of women's law: one that would not challenge the basic (positivistic) understanding of the nature of the legal science. This is mainly because women's law does not tend to strengthen law's authority but instead tries to discover its hidden gendered meanings and expose them for criticism and change. It is difficult to accept this even in a country that champions equality as one of the main features of its legal culture.

The immediate response to the new chair has been varied. For most members of the faculty it is irrelevant. Very few think we really need it and even fewer know about its aims. Direct hostility is less pronounced but it does exist. What is most important, is that it is difficult to accept women's law as it challenges the dearly held neutrality of law. It also challenges the legitimate way of seeing the equality and integration of women by questioning the terms of integration in terms of men.

The Agenda for Change

In the Finnish Women's Studies programmes, a double strategy has been developed so as to have both 'a room of our own' and a possibility to influence the mainstream science. It remains to be seen if the latter goal will materialise at all. As referred to earlier, Finnish women have been integrated into society through work and politics, and less through family - the realm of 'private' has not played such a significant role as in many other parts of Europe. Women have also influenced the welfare policies, which has often been named a 'gender contract' between women and the 'women-friendly' state. These facts make it little accepted or less legitimate to challenge the system women themselves have been shaping, their inequal share of power and resources notwithstanding. The cultural understanding of weak gender polarisation seems to influence both politics and science.

Present aims are to recognise processes and mechanisms (practices) that produce and reproduce gender behind or underneath the seemingly egalitarian and neutral surface, in legal as well as in other areas, for example in working life (Rantalaiho and Heiskanen, 1997). Also the legal system and concepts themselves are subject to closer scrutiny so as to recognise their gendered nature. This may sound threatening for those who stick to the law's authority, as it critisises the often dearly held notion about law as a neutral tool for achieving social change. This may sound disappointing also for feminists, as we are not primarily suggesting new laws or policies against discrimination. But as I have tried to point out above, sexual differences do exist and are even harder to recognise as they are not overt. This is why quite a lot of new research is needed to specify and analyse especially those practices where differences are produced. No legal reforms are possible if the underlying gendered nature of law is not exposed and analysed first, as indeed widely pointed out in feminist legal scholarship (O'Donovan, 1985 and 1993; Smart, 1989 and 1995; Naffine, 1990; Graycar and Morgan, 1990; Frug, 1992; Davies, 1994). A discussion within women's studies about its own understandings of gender is also necessary: we cannot and do not want to accept one way of thinking - but how to operationalise our goals from a multitude of perspectives? (Hoskyns, 1996).

In the Finnish tradition, there is a strong tendency to negotiate and be constructive instead of being radical. Instead of strong individualism, communitarian values still dominate. I would say that a negotiation of meanings is going on all the time, not struggle. Feminist research and theory cannot develop without specific institutional forms, but unlike many others, Finns always want to integrate and avoid overt controversy. Also the tendency to generalise all women as a group (or radical feminism in general) has been uncommon in Finland, and the differences between women are always important in feminist research - except as regards race as Finland is probably one of the most homogenous and single-race cultures in the world with its 1.2 per cent of foreign residents.

With its theoretical emphasis, Finnish feminism within law is less pragmatic and in a sense less radical than in many other countries. But I would like to stress that maybe this approach is even more radical with its aims at redefining many aspects of the mainstream legal science itself. We do not want to accept descriptions of 'gender' or 'equality' as defined in current cultural and legal codes but try instead find the ways to redefine them and get distance from dichotomous heterosexist thinking of gender (Cornell, 1993) as well as rationalities inherent in the liberal thinking of justice (Frazer and Lacey, 1993; Tronto, 1993).

Conclusions

To sum up the Finnish (Nordic) gender culture, one can with reason claim that Finnish women have always been individuals relative to the independence of the family. Finnish tradition is thus very individualistic and egalitarian if understood as the absence of a distinct family culture or separate spheres of the genders. Attachment to a nuclear family has been a considerably late phenomenon, whereas strong attachment to the state characterises Finnish history ever since the centralised state of Sweden was founded in the 16th century. In the sense of the civil society, however, individualism is poorly developed. Maybe it is the absence of separate family or civic culture that has made all people subjects of the sovereign rather than subjects of their own life. Maybe it is also one reason why women, family and reproduction have never become the site of political struggle as has happened elsewhere.

The cultural norm of Woman was and is the working mother - mothering as such has been less valued. Except perhaps the short period in the first half of this century, family law has more than anything concentrated on family assets and less on the proper way of life or constructions of gender. On the other hand, women have always had a strong connection with the state and the private has in general submerged to the public. Agrarian parity and symmetry models have directly been canalised to the welfare politics so as to create a certain seamless integration of women and goals of the state. However, this 'gender contract' between women and the state has not always been favourable to women but it has sooner emphasised women's 'responsible self' rather than their autonomy or liberties. When the modern law took shape, the responsible household matron figured as the central subject in the background of rights discourse, which was largely due to the agrarian society in general and importance of real estate in specific. Up until the past few decades, individuals and their rights (subjective rights) have in fact been a weaker discourse than people's relation to real estate. Legal as well as other discourses on individual rights have thus been in general weakly developed and maybe that is why the thinking of gender has long stayed one-dimensional and the gendered structures hidden.

Bibliography

Allén, T. (1993), *The Nordic Model of Equality, The Welfare State, Patriarchy and Unfinished Emancipation*, Labour Institute for Economic Research, Helsinki.

Anttonen, A. (ed.) (1994), *Women and the Welfare State: Politics, Professions and Practices*, University of Jyväskylä.

Borchorst, A. and Siim, B. (1987), 'Women and the Advanced Welfare State - a new kind of Patriarchal Power', in A. Showstack Sassoon (ed.), *Women and the State - The Shifting Boundaries of Public and Private*, Unwin Hyman, London.

Cornell, D. (1993), *Transformations. Recollective Imagination and Sexual Difference*, Routledge, London.

Dahl, T. S. (1987), *Women's Law: An Introduction to Feminist Jurisprudence*, Oxford University Press, Oxford.

Davies, M. (1994), *Asking the Law Question*, The Law Book Company Limited, Sydney, Sweet and Maxwell.

Frazer, E. and Lacey, N. (1993), *The Politics of Community. A Feminist Critique of the Liberal-Communitarian Debate*, Harvester Wheatsheaf, New York and London.

Frug, M. J. (1993), *Postmodern Legal Feminism*, Routledge, New York and London.

Graycar, R. and Morgan J. (1990), *The Hidden Gender of Law*, The Federation Press, Leichardt.

Halila, H. (1996), *Satakahdeksankymmentäkuusi - Eräitä tietoja suomalaisista oikeustieteen tohtoreista 31.12.1995, Lakimies vol 94, 1996*:2, 274-289 (One Hundred Eighty-six. Some Information on Finnish Doctors of Laws, 31.12.1995).

Hernes, H. M. (1984), 'Women and the Welfare State: The Transition from Private to Public Dependence' in H. Holter (ed.), *Patriarchy in a Welfare Society*, Universitetsforlaget, Oslo.

Holli, A. M. (1990), 'Why the State? Reflections on the Politics of the Finnish Equality Movement Association', M. Keränen Jyväskylä (eds.), *Finnish "Undemocracy", Essays on Gender and Politics*, The Finnish Political Science Association.

Hoskyns, C. (1996), *Integrating Gender - Women, Law and Politics in the European Union*, Verso, London.

Konttinen, E. (1991), *Perinteisesti moderniin: professioiden yhteiskunnallinen synty Suomessa*, (The Emergence of Modern Professions in Finland), Tampere, Vastapaino.

Kuusipalo, J. (1993), 'Women's Positions and Strategies in Political Arenas. From representation to presence, from isolation to coming out, from feminine politics to politics on women's terms', H. Varsa (ed.), *Shaping Structural Change in Finland. The Role of Women*, Ministry of Social Affairs and Health Equality Publications, Series B: Reports 1/1993, Helsinki.

Markkola, P. (1994), *Työläiskodin synty. Tamperelaiset työläisperheet ja yhteiskunnallinen kysymys 1870-luvulta 1910-luvulle (with an English Summary: The Making of the Working-class Home. The Question of Working-class Families in Finland, 1870s through 1910s*) Helsinki; Suomen Historiallinen Seura.

Naffine, N. (1990), *Law and the Sexes. Explorations in Feminist Jurisprudence*, Allen & Unwin, Sydney.

Nieminen, L. (1996), *Perusoikeuksien yksilöllisyys ja perhekäsitykset perusoikeusjärjestelmässä. Lakimies*, vol. 94 (The Individuality of

Fundamental Rights and the Conceptions of the Family in the Finnish System of Constitutional Rights).

Nousiainen, K. (1993), *Prosessin herruus. Länsimaisen oikeudenkäytön "modernille" ominaisten piirteiden tarkastelua ja alueellista vertailua,* (with an English Summary: Rule(s) of Modern Procedure), Helsinki, Suomalainen Lakimiesyhdistys A:191.

O'Donovan, K. (1985), *Sexual Divisions in Law*, Weidenfeld, London.

O'Donovan, K. (1993), *Family Law Matters*, Pluto Press, London.

Pajuoja, J. and Ervasti, K. (1994), *Suomen Lakimiesliiton Historia, 1944-1994* (The History of Finnish Lawyers' Association), Helsinki, Lakimiesliiton Kustannus.

Parvikko, T. (1991), 'Conceptions of Gender' in E. Meehan and S. Sevenhuijsen (eds.), *Equality, Politics and Gender*, Sage, London.

Rantalaiho, L. and Heiskanen, T. (eds.) (1997), *Gendered Patterns in Working Life*, Macmillan, London.

Silius, H. (1992), *Den kringgärdade kvinnligheten. Att vara kvinnlig jurist i Finland. Åbo; Åbo Academy Press* (with an English Summary: Contracted Femininity. The Case of Women Lawyers in Finland).

Smart, C. (1989), *Feminism and the Power of the Law*, Routledge, London and New York.

Smart, C. (1995), *Law, Crime and Sexuality. Essays in Feminism*, Sage, London.

Sulkunen, I. (1990), *History of the Finnish Temperance Movement: temperance as civic religion*, Edwin Mellen Press, Lewiston (NY).

Tronto, J. (1993), *Moral Boundaries. A Political Argument for an Ethic of Care*, Routledge, New York and London.

Voutilainen, J. (1996), *Akateemisuus ja sukupuoli. Tutkimus naisten yliopistolliseen uraan vaikuttavista tekijöistä Turun yliopistossa* (Gender and the Academy), University of Turku; Hallintoviraston julkaisusarja 1/1996.

10. Special Protection of Women's Rights in China

JUNPING HE

Introduction

China has experienced more than two thousand years of feudal society. However, it established a new system of government in 1949 and began economic reform in 1979. These important social reforms affected people's lives deeply in various ways. In particular, the fate of women has improved. Chinese women, who were the footbinding[1] women, now take part in all aspects of social activities. To some extent these changes in women's roles are a result from the special protection of women's rights since 1949.

The Reasons for Special Protection of Women's Rights in China

Unequal History - Respecting Men and Discrimination Against Women

It was recorded by the ancient book of songs[2] that a new-born girl should be put under the bed. This meant that she was in a very low position. There was a spinning wheel near her, meaning that she would spin and do housework when she grows up. On the contrary, new-born boys slept on the bed surrounded by jewels. It meant that the boy was in a high position and was treasured by his family and society. A female baby's birth was not welcomed by her family, especially if she was the first child of the family. For a family, the more sons there were, the better it was. Therefore, the female was an unwelcome gender and only a supplement for a family after a son's birth. Parents thought that the daughter's birth would be their family's burden mentally and economically. There are many reasons for this. First, the parents would worry that they would be despised by their neighbours because they had no son. The neighbours might look down on this family. So it was thought to be shameful for the parents not to have a son. Secondly, the daughter was not considered to be a member of the family. She would marry a man and become a member of her husband's family. The parents could not depend on their daughter when they were old. Hence why they needed a son to support them. Thirdly, the feudal China was an agricultural society, men took part in ploughing the land. Women did housework and looked after children. A daughter only stayed at home to help her mother do housework or look after a young sister or brother. A son could help a father to plough the land and reduce the economic burden of the family when he grows up. So people thought that a daughter contributed less to the family than a son.

The feudal society ill-treated women not only regarding women's spirits, but also women's bodies. The feetbinding made women stay at home to serve a husband or a husband's parents, and do housework. They could not go out to work and take part in social activities. So women deeply relied on their husbands during that time. On women, Mao zhe dong wrote:

> A man in China is usually subjected to three systems of authority (political authority, clan authority and religious authority). As for women, in addition to being dominated by these three systems they are also dominated by men (the authority of the men). (Young, 1973, p. 73)

When a woman married a man she would belong to that man both in her body and in her spirits. The relationship between a husband and a wife was unequal. A husband was his wife's master. A wife had a duty to be loyal to her husband. The feudal morals told women that a wife could not let other men touch her body such as her hand and arm. There was an example set by the feudal morals that when a wife was walking on the road, she felt a touch on her arm, by a man's arm who was passing. She thought it was shameless and then cut off that arm which was touched by the man in order to express her loyalty to her husband. On the contrary a husband did not have a duty to be loyal to his wife. It was a legal right for the husband that if his wife had not given birth to a son he could take a second wife, while still being married to the first. The husband had a right to visit a brothel. The feudal morals encouraged widows not to remarry, and to regard the widow who had never remarried, as a good woman.

Therefore, in the feudal society, the relationship between women and men was unequal. Women were not protected by the law. They had no rights at home or in society. To some extent, they were regarded as a machine for giving birth to children.

The Situations

Although the feudal society was overthrown, and women in theory enjoy equal rights with the men under the Constitution, it is not easy to say that women enjoy equal rights with the men in practice. The following two reasons hamper the realisation of women's rights. First, the feudal ideas still influenced people who believe that 'men are better than women'. Because of such influences, a lot of women themselves also think that their ability is not as good as men's. Secondly, because of poor economic conditions, especially in rural areas, girls have little chance to finish their primary or secondary school education. Therefore, they do not know or understand their legal rights.

Women's Special Situations

As is well known, females have different physiological features to males. They may give birth to children in addition to taking part in social work. Thus, they bear a dual burden for family and society. Accordingly, the State should care for women's health and take account of women's special situations and protect their rights and interests, such as during periods of pregnancy and nursing, when women cannot be required to work as normal.

The Legislative Special Protection of Women's Rights

The legislature of China has issued a series of laws designed to protect women's rights and interests. They are the Law of Protecting Women's Rights and Interests, which is based on the Constitution, the Marriage Law, the Inheritance Law, the Law of Protection of Women's and Infants' Health, and the Regulation of Protection of Female Workers. In addition, there are many local regulations.

However, the Marriage Laws are the most important laws protecting women's rights and have made a great contribution to protect women's rights in China. Before 1992, when the Law of Protecting Women's Rights and Interests was issued, the Marriage Law was the only specific law to protect women's rights.

The Marriage Law of 1950

Important economic, political and social changes took place in China in 1949. The People's Republic of China replaced the feudal society. The land reform began first and redistributed property in the villages. Women were given rights to an equal share of land, their names were registered on family deeds. Thus, Chinese women controlled important economic resources and took steps towards economic equality and independence. In line with the land reforms another important reform was of the marriage system, the main aim of which was to get rid of the feudal marriage system, such as arranged marriages and establish a new marriage system. The first Marriage Law was formulated in 1950 and its main task was to eliminate unequal relationships in people's family or social lives and the feudal marriage system in order to establish the new, equal marriage and family system.

The marriage law stipulated specific rights. First, women enjoyed freedom of marriage. They could decide whether to marry. The marriage law saved women from the oppression of the feudal marriage system. For example, under the feudal system women could not choose boyfriends for themselves, now they had rights to choose their boyfriend according to their will. At home, they had equal rights with their husbands. Women could petition for divorce if their marriage was an arranged marriage.

In order to let more and more people know of the existence of the marriage law, there was a nationwide campaign. The marriage law was promulgated all over the country. Wide spread educational work was conducted among the people about the marriage law to let people know the importance of the law.

Couples whose marriages were 'arranged' in an arbitrary way, were encouraged to try and make a fresh start by gaining a new understanding of each other's rights and duties, but if there was no way of repairing the marriage, they might obtain a divorce if they wanted to according to the Marriage Law. During that time the principal reason of divorce was to leave an arranged marriage. The majority of divorce suits were brought by women who used the Marriage Law to free themselves from traditional restraints. It was reported that during the first year of the law in Shanghai, which is the largest city of China, 75 per cent of the 13,349 court cases were filed by women; in 32 cities and 34 county-seat towns nearly 77 per cent of the 21,433 cases were brought by women.

The Marriage Law played a key role in the protection of women's rights, so it came to be know as 'a women's law'. However, after 30 years of legal practice, the law could not meet the demands of society. It was therefore in need of modification and reform and thus the second Marriage Law was enacted with many provisions in 1980, which retains the effective provisions of the former Law and supplements it.

The Marriage Law of 1980

The Marriage Law of 1980 has a total of 37 articles being divided in 7 chapters as follows: principles, marriage, conjugal relations, family relations, divorce requirements, divorce consequences and the application of law.

Principles

The principles which regulate the marriage and family relationships are the guiding ideology of the specific articles. They can be used to deal with particular problems if there is no article or articles regulating that condition. The main principles of the Marriage Law are as follows.

Freedom of Marriage

The freedom of marriage means that a man and a women have a right to decide their marriage without other's interference and coercion. The Law prohibits compulsory marriage by arrangement. It provides for the freedom of both marriage and divorce.

The feudal ideology has deeply affected people's thoughts on marriage and family. A marriage by an arbitrary decision or by purchase was a typical marriage in the feudal society. So nowadays the Marriage Law stipulates specific principles in order to protect the freedom of people's marriage, especially women's freedom of marriage. In the feudal society the victims of compulsory marriage on account of an arrangement were women who were the objects of this marriage. They had no rights in their marriage. The law provides for effective action to punish a man who promulgated a compulsory marriage with criminal or economic sanctions.

The other important freedom is the freedom to divorce. Men and women have rights to choose to divorce if they do not want to live together. In order to protect the freedom to divorce, we should eliminate many of the feudal ideas about divorce such as 'divorce is disgraced' or a 'good wife cannot choose divorce'. Freedom of marriage might be complete if it includes these two sides: both freedom of marriage and divorce. There would be no freedom if one were lacking. Therefore the Marriage Law emphasises that both marriage and divorce constitute freedom of marriage.

Monogamy

Prior to the Marriage Law, polygamy was allowed. A husband had the right to choose more than one wife at the same time. This was a traditional marriage in China. The feudal law allowed men to own two or more wives at the same time. In order to eliminate polygamy, the Marriage Law prohibits any kind of polygamy.

Equal Rights between Men and Women

Equal rights between men and women are prescribed by the Chinese Constitution. The Constitution prescribes that women enjoy equal rights with men in all spheres of political, economic, cultural, social and family life. Women and men enjoy equal rights and perform the same obligations in family life. The Marriage Law specifically proscribes any discrimination between women and men in family life.

Protecting Women's Legal Rights and Interests

This principle is an important supplement to the former principles. Although the Law stipulates that women enjoy equal rights with men, there is also a need to stipulate special protection of women's rights. There are two major reasons for this. The first is that women have the capacity to bear children. The second is that the position of women had been lower than men's during the feudal society in China. Therefore the Marriage Law provides for the special protection of women's rights and interests in some areas, such as that a husband cannot claim for divorce in the year following a wife giving birth to a child.

Family Plan

Because of an increased population in China the government has carried out a one child policy in the majority of the Han people's areas. Both a husband and a wife have an equal duty to perform it. After a wife gives birth to one child, she has a right to leave for six months in the cities or towns, if this couple only chooses one child. During the six months, she can claim wages and welfare. A wife has a right to decide whether she would like to be pregnant or not. A husband must not ill-treat a wife who gives birth to a daughter, or who did not want to have a child.

The System of Marriage

I have already considered how women have freedom of marriage. Marriage is a legal action taken by a man and woman in order to establish conjugal relations according to law. There are three essential conditions for a legal marriage. The first is that a man and woman who want to be married should decide this completely on the basis of their own free will. The second is that a marriage should be monogamous. The third is that a man and woman should be of the minimum legal age for marriage. A husband may become a member of the wife's family. The traditional custom, of marriage was that the wife becomes a member of her husband's family after being married. The wife would live together with her husband's parents, take care of them and do a lot of housework for them. She no longer belonged to her own family. The Marriage Law allows that a husband and wife can become a member of each other's family after they are married, thus eliminating parents' worries if they have no son.

Family Relationships

The Law protects the right for women to enjoy equal rights with men in the family as the following.

Women have a right to choose their surname. Women living before 1949 did not have her own name; when a woman was young, other people called her 'little girl'. After she married, a woman could choose her husband's family name as her surname. Although the name used to distinguish people, it is a sign of independence for women to some extent. The Law stipulates that wives have a right to choose their own surname. Almost all of Chinese women do not change their surname after they are married.

Wives have a Freedom to take part in Social Activities without her Husband's Interference

More and more women want to go out and take part in social activities. Now they realise that joining all kinds of social activities will improve them. However, there are many men asking their wives to stay at home. There may be a conflict between husband and wife if the husband disagrees with a wife's wish to pursue social activities. The Law here provides that both men and women have a right to take part in social activities without interference, especially protecting the rights of women.

Wives enjoy Equal Rights with Husbands to have Ownership of Property

A wife could not own any property in the feudal society of China. The wife would be punished according to law if she took the family's property without her husband's consent. All things of the family, including his wife, where regarded as objects of property, belonging to the husband. This reflected the unequal relationship between a husband and wife. The Marriage Law provides for a system of common property. Regardless of her wealth, a wife has the same rights to family property as her husband. This protects women's rights.

A Wife and Husband have a Common Right and Responsibility to Support Each Other

A wife has a right to bring an action against her husband if her husband does not support her. The court may reduce and remit her cost of proceedings in line with her circumstances and hear the case quickly in order to protect a wife's legal interests.

A Wife and Husband have a Common Right to Inherit Property from Each Other

The Marriage Law emphasises that a widow has a right to transfer her inheritance out of her husband's family. According to traditional Chinese habits the widow could not take any property after her husband died: this violated the women's property rights. Nowadays there are two stages by which a widow can get her own property. First she can get half of the common property which belongs to her and her husband. Secondly, she can inherit her husband's properties and then deal with it without other people's interference.

Education of Children

The traditional idea about children's education was that the father should be responsible for any problems with the child, because the father had a right to educate his children. On the contrary the mother had no right to educate her children so that she need not bear any responsibility. The Marriage Law stipulates that the education of children is both a husband and wife's right and responsibility.

Surname of Children

When a child is born, its parents have a right to choose the surname of either the husband or wife for it. Only the husband's surname was used in the feudal society.

System of Divorce

Divorce is the legal termination of a marriage. Although the law allows divorce, a lot of couples do not divorce, because there remain traditional ideas against divorce. The right to divorce was conferred on a husband only in the feudal society. There were seven main reasons for men asking for divorce. The husband might choose one of the following reasons to divorce his wife:

a) his wife did not respect or care for her husband's parents;
b) his wife was jealous of the husband's second wife;
c) the husband considered that the wife was committing adultery;
d) his wife was ill which might infect husband, or the husband's family;
e) his wife was a thief who stole the family's property;
f) his wife was regarded as a gossip who might sow discord in the home; and
g) his wife had not born a son.

On the contrary the wife had no right to divorce. The system of divorce has been reformed by the Marriage Laws 1949. The freedom of divorce is an important principal in the Law. The wife enjoys equal rights to divorce with husband. The protection of women's right to divorce is concerted with the following main areas.

The Guiding Ideology of Divorce

The guiding ideology of divorce in the Marriage Law is that the freedom of divorce is protected against random divorce. One meaning is that a husband and wife can choose to divorce if there is an alienation of mutual affection between them. On the other hand, they cannot choose to divorce if there is not enough alienation of mutual affection between them. In recent years more and more women have brought an action to divorce husbands. For example, I went to Peoples Court of Chang Ping County of Beijing in 1992 and conducted a survey on divorce cases. I found that there were a total of 419 cases of divorce being heard by the court of Chang Ping County in the North of Beijing in 1991, being 287 cases prosecuted by women, nearly 70 per cent. The main reason for this is that the position of women has improved owing to the development of the social economy. Women can earn money to support themselves and depend less on men. They cannot bear a suffering marriage and pursue a happy marriage now so they go to the court to divorce their husbands.

Limitation of Husband's Right to Divorce

A court will not accept and hear a case of divorce brought by a husband during his wife's pregnancy, or one year after their baby is born, according to the Marriage Law, because during these times the health of the baby or mothers' need to be cared for. It may badly affect their health if the husband seeks a divorce. However there is an exception where it may be necessary, e.g. where a child would otherwise be illegitimate.

Protection of Women's Rights in the Division of Common Property

The general principles of separating the spouse's property is that the wife owns half of the property in common. Moreover, taking account of the phenomenon that a lot of women earn less money then men, the law stipulates that a wife may get more than half ownership of property than her husband, especially where a wife will continue to look after the child.

The Trends of Protection of Women's Property Rights in the Marriage Law

China is carrying out economic reform which bodes well for women. More and more women take part in social work and activities which broaden women's outlooks and improve their economic position. Women can now support themselves and be independent. Comparing the Marriage Law in 1980 with the law in 1950, we can find that the contents of protection of women's property are lessening. For instance, the Law of 1950 stipulated that a man's property before marriage became common property. The Law of 1980 amends this article and stipulates that the spouse's common property begins after their marriage. The Law of 1950 stipulated a wife might get financial help from her husband after the divorce for a considerable length of time. But the law of 1980 alters this article, providing only for temporary help. Those changes mean that the women are less economically dependent on men.

The Difficulty in the Protection of Women's Rights

However there are some problems affecting the realisation of women's rights. Owing to the underdevelopment of the economy in some areas, especially in rural areas, women have a heavy burden. They have little to take part in social activities and know little of what happens in the world. Their legal rights are easily violated and then they cannot protect themselves using the law, because they do not know the Marriage Law. There are nearly ten million illiterate people in China. Most of them are women. Poor families have not enough money to support all children in school. The girls usually lose their chance to go to school. They will become illiterate and lose their economic position. Parents think that a daughter will be married and become the member of the other family, so they would prefer their daughter to marry a rich man, than go to school.

In addition, violence against women in the family is usually overlooked by local administrators. They think that the conflicts between wife and husband are their private matters. Thus, they do not pay attention to violence against women.

Except the above mentioned, there are some problems in the Marriage Law itself. First, some articles are general, which cannot tackle practical problems and require judicial interpretation. Secondly, the Law lacks effective sanctions, especially economic sanctions for law-breakers. The legislature will shortly amend the Marriage Law making it meet the needs of the development of society.

Conclusion

There is a long way to go to realise the protection of women's rights in China. Although the laws stipulate some aspects to the protection of women's rights, it is very important that the laws are effective. At the same time, women also should improve themselves and be more independent at home and in society. They can protect themselves using the laws when their rights and interests are violated.

Notes

1. The term 'footbinding' refers to the Han Chinese custom of using artificial means to stunt the normal growth of women's feet and render them unnatural in shape and smallness.
2. The Advanced Chinese Dictionary, Dictionary Publish, Shang Hai, 1979.

Bibliography

Croll (1974), *The Women's Movement in China*, Russell Press, Nottingham.

Gravells, K. A. (1983), *Family Law Statutes*, Sweet and Maxwell, London.

Jaschok, M. and Miers, S. (1994), *Women and Chinese Patriarchy*, Zed Books, Hong Kong, London and New Jersey.

Marriage Law of the People's Republic of China (1950, 1980).

Young, M. B. (1973), *Women in China*, Centre for Chinese Studies, the University of Michigan, USA.

11. A Place for Maternity in the European Union

EUGENIA CARACCIOLO DI TORELLA

Introduction

Despite recent improvements, for many working women, pregnancy and maternity are still regarded as a 'penalty' and women are too often placed in the position of choosing between a family and work. This situation is not a topic of merely theoretical interest but creates concrete problems, *inter alia*, of sex equality, health and safety, democracy and fundamental rights, all of which require solutions. Over the last years pregnancy and maternity have been tackled - more or less successfully - by almost all the legal systems in Europe.[1] Recently this issue has also arisen at the European Union level.[2]

Originally EC law contemplated neither pregnancy nor maternity. Article 119 EC[3] considered sex discrimination only in so far as pay is concerned. In this context I will not explore the reasons for this situation (Barnard, 1996). Suffice it to say that it should not come as a surprise in a market-oriented Treaty, i.e. a Treaty the first aim of which was to achieve a single market. More importantly, the Treaty of Rome was market-making rather than market-correcting: it was aimed at creating an integrated labour market and enabling it to function efficiently rather than correcting its outcomes in line with political standards of social justice (Nielsen and Szyszcsak, 1993). It follows that in this context social goals were seen as merely side issues to achieving economic integration. However, following the developments of the last decade, several provisions, namely the Equal Treatment Directive,[4] Article 118a EC and the Social Policy Agreement[5] have been introduced. Using these as starting points, the EC has taken several steps to regulate this field: maternity has so far been the object of both EC legislation, and EC litigation.

In this chapter, I will attempt to consider the whole EU *corpus juris* in this field.[6] I will argue that the EC legislation so far has produced inadequate results for three main reasons. First, it has been characterised by a piecemeal approach; secondly, it has 'confined' maternity to the context of sex equality law (in particular equal treatment); and, thirdly, this legislation is 'shaped' by assumptions which reinforce stereotypes without providing an adequate solution to the problem. In contrast, I submit that the approach adopted by the European Court of Justice (ECJ) in recent years could be potentially more satisfactory. Therefore, *prima facie* an improvement in the situation is more likely to be achieved through litigation rather than legislation. Things are more complex however. This chapter will conclude by analysing the possible obstacles that a litigation strategy would encounter.

EC Legislation on Maternity

The EC legislation on maternity comprises the Equal Treatment Directive,[7] the Pregnancy and Maternity Directive[8] and the Agreement/Directive on Parental Leave.[9] Considering the scant attention originally given to pregnancy and maternity, the adoption of the EC legislation represents a development. A closer analysis of the legislation, however, provides evidence that its contribution should not be overestimated and loopholes still exist.

One of the main problems with the EC legislation is that the directives have different legal bases: the result of the different approaches is piecemeal legislation which does not help the coherent development of the area. Other problems arise from the fact that negotiations prior to the adoption of legislation involve a great deal of time and, consequently, directives leave a large discretion to the Member States who sometimes abuse it at the expense of individuals (as is well known[10]). Despite the improvements achieved, the legislation in this field is still very much a political compromise, carrying with it all the problems associated with these arrangements. Even to claim remedies before the Court of Justice has not proved to be easy.[11]

EC legislation mainly deals with pregnancy and maternity within the context of sex equality law. I submit that this approach is wrong. Pregnancy and maternity cannot be dealt by means of the Aristotelian argument 'things that are alike must be treated alike, while things that are unalike should be treated unalike in proportion to their unalikeness'

(Aristotele, Ross trans., 1925). In other words, pregnancy and maternity *per definition* are the 'exceptions' to the formal equality principle. Consequently, they raise the equal treatment *versus* special treatment debate which often results in a protectionist approach. Further, sex equality in the workplace is often the result of a balance of interests between market forces (the interests of the employer) and social concerns (the interests of the employee *in casu* working mothers).

Finally, much of EC legislation (particularly the Equal Treatment Directive) is based on an erroneous (misleading?) concept of sex equality which is based on assumptions which reinforce stereotypes, such as that women prefer to work part time because it involves less responsibility - instead of family obligations - and only a mother can take care of young children - as opposed to both parents (Bovis and Cnossen, 1996).

Instead, I submit that maternity should be viewed as something different, as a fundamental human right which goes beyond the 'equality debate'. The following sections will focus on the relevant EC legislation.

The Equal Treatment Directive

Pregnancy and maternity were explicitly considered for the first time in the European Community in the mid 1970s in the context of the Equal Treatment Directive. This Directive was issued as part of the programme to extend the non-discrimination principle established by Article 119 EC. Despite the fact that the Directive is an 'extension' of Article 119 EC, its legal basis is Article 235 EC. Article 235 EC is used when the Commission lacks any other means to achieve one of the objectives of the Community and requires unanimity.

The Directive aims to put 'into effect in the Member States the principle of equal treatment for men and women as regards access to employment ... vocational training and ... working conditions' (Art. 1). For the purpose of the Directive 'equal treatment' means that discrimination on grounds of sex, either directly or indirectly by reference in particular to the marital status or family, is forbidden. Article 2 sets out derogations to this principle and Article 2(3) specifically mentions maternity, stating that '[t]his Directive shall be without prejudice to provisions concerning the *protection*[12] of women, particularly as regards pregnancy and maternity'.

The Directive seems to be based on a paradox: maternity was introduced into EC legislation both as a part of the equal treatment principle and as a derogation from it. On the one hand it attempts to give the same rights to women and men, on the other it sets out a derogation in order to offer women 'protection'. The Directive is based on the assumption that pregnant women must enjoy special protection because they form a 'weaker category': it imposes upon women a protection which may be undesirable. In this way it establishes 'protective barriers' (Demosthenes, 1995), i.e. it protects women to the extent that they are not always able to enjoy the same freedom as given to men and it limits their opportunities in the labour market.[13] The protectionist aim of the Directive has been confirmed by the ECJ on several occasions,[14] the most well known being *Hofmann*[15] where the ECJ held that the Directive aims to protect women in two respects: '[f]irst it is legitimate to ensure the *protection* of a *woman's biological condition during pregnancy* and thereafter until such time as her physiological and mental functions have returned to normal after childbirth; secondly ... to *protect* the *special relationship between a women and her child*'.[16]

The special protection approach is no longer acceptable because it perpetuates the division between the public and the private sphere, and reinforces the idea that women 'belong' to the private sphere (Fenwick, 1996). The Pregnancy and Maternity Directive represents an attempt to move away from it.

The Pregnancy and Maternity Directive

The Pregnancy and Maternity Directive is a development of Art. 2(2) of the Equal Treatment Directive. Its adoption took a long time: it was proposed by the Commission in September 1990 as an implementing measure for Articles 16 and 28 of the Community Charter of Basic Social Rights for Workers,[17] but only in 1992 did the Member States reach an agreement. The Pregnancy and Maternity Directive aims to 'implement measures to encourage improvements in the *safety and health*[18] of pregnant workers and women workers who have recently given birth'. Although it can be regarded as a step forward from the Equal Treatment Directive, the Pregnancy and Maternity Directive still raises doubts on both institutional (Muffat-Jandet, 1991) and substantive levels (Ellis, 1993). As far as the institutional issues are concerned, the legal base of the Pregnancy and Maternity Directive is Article 118a EC (as opposed to Articles 100 and 235 EC). Article 118a EC was introduced by the Single European Act and provides that the EC Council may adopt proposals by means of a qualified majority on a proposal from the Commission, in co-operation with the Parliament and after consulting the Economic and Social Committee. In other words this Article achieves two goals. First, it provides for increased co-operation between the institutions, in particular giving more power to the Parliament, which is well-known for being the most progressive institution when it comes to social policy. Secondly, directives adopted under this procedure avoid the stumbling block of unanimity.[19] This was crucial for the adoption of the Pregnancy and Maternity Directive, which faced considerable opposition from both the UK and Italy.[20]

Paradoxically, one of the main limitations of the Directive is the legal basis itself. Article 118a EC states that: 'Member States shall pay particular attention to encouraging improvements, especially in the *working environment*, as regards the *health and safety*[21] of workers'. However, the emphasis of the Pregnancy and Maternity Directive is on health and safety (the Pregnancy and Maternity Directive was in fact introduced within the framework of the Health and Safety Framework Directive[22]) rather than on the working environment. The concept of working environment was introduced in Article 118a EC under Danish pressure. In Danish law working environment - *arbejdsmiljø* - is a very broad concept covering the performance of work, conditions at the workplace, technical equipment, and substances and materials used. Furthermore, this concept is dynamic. It reflects the social and technical evolution of society (Nielsen, 1993). In contrast, this concept has mainly been neglected by both the Council and the Commission when issuing legislation, and as a result also by the ECJ which, until recently had only considered it twice.[23] During the last few years, however, it seems that a new trend is emerging. Two recently issued directives, the Working Time Directive[24] and the Young Workers Directive[25] provide for a level of protection which goes further than merely physical hazards. Furthermore the ECJ in the *Working Time Directive* case[26] has backed an interpretation of Article 118a EC in light of the Danish concept of working environment. In the Preamble of the Pregnancy and Maternity Directive, the Commission attempts to justify the health and safety approach with 'the fatigue associated with the conditions of pregnant women ... the ergonomic difficulties faced at the workplace by women workers in late pregnancy ... the delicate conditions of women workers in late pregnancy and immediately after giving birth'. It seems however rather curious to adopt an important social policy measure under the cover of health and safety; it is arguable that this approach has undermined the social and human *status* of pregnancy and maternity by classifying them as merely 'medical provisions'. This could have been avoided if the focus had been on working environment.

As far as the substance is concerned, the Pregnancy and Maternity Directive is the result of a political compromise, carrying all the inherent problems of such arrangements. The first draft of the directive was more thorough, for example providing for 16 weeks fully paid maternity leave. In contrast, the Pregnancy and Maternity Directive mentions 14 weeks, paid at an 'adequate level'.[27] Consequently the period during which protection against unfair dismissal is guaranteed is reduced. Moreover, as some commentators (Vigerust, 1995) have remarked, since it is up to the Member State and employers to determine the amount of salary, the fact that women suffer a loss of pay in this period does not in itself constitute a breach of the Pregnancy and Maternity Directive.[28] Other provisions such as paternity leave at the time of the birth, a ban on dismissal or non-selection for a job on account of pregnancy, the reversal of the burden of proof in cases arising out of these rights, and an obligation for employers to assess the health and safety risks for their pregnant workers and to keep them informed of how to avoid these dangers were also included in the draft directive, but were not included in the final version.

Apart from the narrow scope of the final Pregnancy and Maternity Directive, there are other restrictions (Jacqmain, 1994). Art. 2 provides that the subject of the Pregnancy and Maternity Directive are pregnant workers and those who have recently given birth '*who inform their employer*[29] of their condition': does it mean that a visibly pregnant woman who has not informed the employer of her pregnancy is not protected? Further, there may be a conflict between the Pregnancy and Maternity Directive and the Equal Treatment Directive where a pregnant woman applies for a job for which she is fully qualified, but which necessarily entails exposure to a risk listed in the Pregnancy and Maternity Directive, and where there is no alternative work available (Jacqmain, 1994).

The Parental Leave Agreement

The final piece of legislation in this field is the Parental Leave Agreement/Directive which, following the procedure of the Protocol and the Agreement on Social Policy, was signed on 14 December 1995 by the Social Partners.[30] On 31 January 1996 it was adopted by the Commission as a proposal for a Directive, and on 3 June 1998 will enter into force as a

Directive. It provides that workers in the Member States (except the UK), regardless of sex, may take parental leave both to look after a child during at least three months up until the age of 8 (it is up to the Member State to set the exact length of the period), and for urgent family reasons. Another key point in the Agreement is that the leave will be flexible, i.e. full or part-time. Since it goes against the stereotype that only women can look after young children, the Agreement/Directive is an important step towards the achievement of full sex equality. Thus from the substantive point of view, the Agreement/Directive is an improvement. From the institutional point of view, however, it raises questions which are linked to the insecure legal bases of the Agreement on Social Policy.[31] Since it has been accepted as a Directive, the Parental Leave Agreement will become an 'act' within the meaning of Article 189 EC and as a directive 'binding as to the result to be achieved'. However it will be binding upon only 14 out of 15 Member States. When it is remembered that it deals with fundamental rights this approach seems highly unsatisfactory.

In summary it is my opinion that the EC legislation (at least as it is framed now) provides only weak or partial rights relating to pregnancy and maternity. Neither the protectionist approach of the Equal Treatment Directive, nor the pragmatic detailed approach of the Pregnancy and Maternity Directive can provide for a satisfactory framework. Finally to tackle this issue with a provision such as the Parental Leave Agreement/Directive the legal base of which raises doubts is arguable. In contrast, I consider that the recent approach of the ECJ offers a better alternative.

The ECJ Maternity Saga

The ECJ has, slowly but steadily, made a valuable contribution towards the establishment of a satisfactory *corpus juris* on maternity.[32] The activity of China in this field can be divided into two periods. In the first stage,[33] the ECJ clarified the (limited) meaning of the Equal Treatment Directive. Though, *prima facie,* this early contribution may seem of minimal importance, it should not be underestimated because at this point the ECJ highlighted some loopholes in the area. In the second period, the ECJ has started to construe a clear legal principle of pregnancy and maternity. In doing so the ECJ has utilised its usual technique,[34] that is to establish a broad principle and then to try to define its limits and to set out derogations. In this area, the basic principle - that discrimination on ground of pregnancy is direct discrimination - was established in *Dekker* and in the following judgments - *Hertz*,[35] *Habermann-Beltermann*,[36] *Webb*,[37] and *Gillespie*[38]- the ECJ further clarified the principle.

All of these judgments have clarified, stretched and sometimes even pre-empted EC legislation. In other words, it is my opinion that without the support of the ECJ the legislation alone would have been ineffective. The goodwill of the ECJ has been limited however, in that it has been forced to take into account considerations of policy. Consequently, the cases following the broad statement of *Dekker* contain inconsistencies and have left the more critical commentators unsatisfied (Fenwick and Hervey, 1995). In contrast, it is my opinion that the potential importance of these judgments should be emphasised. At least they must be regarded as a path towards a more coherent legislation in this field, whose first step can be identified in the Pregnancy and Maternity Directive.

The Principle in Dekker: Pregnancy and Direct Discrimination

The facts in *Dekker* are straightforward. The applicant applied for the post of instructor at the VJV, a training centre for young adults, and informed the Applications Committee that she was three months pregnant. Although she was considered by the Committee as the most suitable candidate for the job, VJV informed her that she would not be appointed. The reason given was that VJV's insurer would not reimburse the benefits that it would be obliged to pay during her maternity leave, which meant that it would be unable financially to employ a replacement during her absence and would be short-staffed. The case went before the *Hoge Raad*, the Supreme Dutch National Court, which asked the ECJ for a preliminary ruling *ex* Article 177 EC. The ECJ ruled that the refusal to engage a pregnant woman because she is pregnant was direct discrimination on grounds of sex and was therefore in breach of Arts. 2(1) and 3(1) of the Equal Treatment Directive. To classify dismissal on grounds of pregnancy as direct discrimination means that it cannot be justified in any way except via explicit legislative exemptions.[39] The test used was the causation test, according to which if the reason for dismissal applied exclusively to one sex, it would constitute direct discrimination. The ECJ also ruled upon another important principle that in certain circumstances, such as pregnancy, the absence of a male comparator is irrelevant.

Legal writers have remarked that 'now European women will look back upon these times as the years in which the European Court of Justice

... began to make good the promises of equal treatment of men and woman at work' (Rubenstein, 1991). It is submitted, however, that it is incorrect to link *Dekker* with equal treatment: in fact here the Court made a qualitative step, trying to move away from the equal treatment approach and affirming that maternity had to be protected *per se*. The statement of the ECJ according to which a (male) comparitor is irrelevant, should also be regarded as an attempt to escape the limits of sex equality law.

The Definition of the Principle - Hertz, Habermann-Beltermann, and Webb[40]

It immediately appeared that the causation principle established in *Dekker* was drafted too widely and was likely to meet many objections. National courts also needed guidance in order to apply it. The ECJ revised it in the judgments below. In doing so, however, it moved away from its former approach, that is protecting maternity *per se*, and placed pregnancy once again in the context of equal treatment. The result is that *prima facie* the importance of the principle has been watered down. In *Hertz*, the Court drew a line between *dismissal on the grounds of pregnancy* and *dismissal on the grounds of sickness related to pregnancy*. The facts of the case are straightforward. The plaintiff, Mrs. Hertz, took maternity leave. She was dismissed after failing to return to work following the expiration of the period of pregnancy, maternity and parental leave. Her absence of over 100 working days was due to an illness originating in pregnancy and childbirth. According to Danish law, it is lawful to dismiss on the grounds of prolonged absence, which can also be due to illness. The argument of the Danish Court was therefore that men who had been absent for such a long period would also have been dismissed. The case went before the *Højesteret*, which asked the ECJ for a preliminary ruling on the compatibility of Danish law with the Equal Treatment Directive. In case the answer was affirmative, the *Højesteret* further asked whether that protection applied without any time limit. The ECJ judgment reaffirmed the principle of *Dekker*, that discrimination on grounds of pregnancy is direct discrimination. However, it went further and drew a distinction between *dismissal on grounds of pregnancy* and *dismissal on grounds of illness originating in pregnancy*[41] and stated that the latter did not constitute direct discrimination. Concerning the second question, the ECJ held that during the period of maternity leave a woman must be protected against dismissal due to absence, but after the expiration of this period the distinction between pregnancy and pregnancy-related illness becomes irrelevant.[42]

It appears clearly from this case that pregnancy is no longer protected *per se*, but as a part of the equal treatment principle which requires a balancing act between the opposing interests of employers and employees. In attempting to find this balance the ECJ reached a result which is an affront to logic. The line drawn is artificial and I find it very difficult not to regard the facts in *Hertz* as direct discrimination. So far as I know it is in fact very unlikely that a man can suffer from an illness originating in pregnancy! The positive element of this case is that it highlights one of the main loopholes in the Equal Treatment Directive, which is the lack of a maternity leave period (and consequently of protection) common to all the Member States. This 'gap' has now been partially filled by the Pregnancy and Maternity Directive.

The conflict between the interests of the employers and employees is illustrated clearly in the two cases following *Dekker* where the Court considered the issue of temporary contracts and temporary staff. In *Habermann-Beltermann* the applicant had been employed under a contract of indeterminate duration to work only during the night. Shortly afterwards she became pregnant. German law[43] prohibits pregnant women from working at night. The case went before the German Court which asked the ECJ whether, in the light of the Dekker principle, the German law prohibiting night work for pregnant women was compatible with the Equal Treatment Directive. Instead of focusing on the German law, the Court held that 'the termination of a contract without a fixed term on account of the woman's pregnancy ... cannot be justified on the ground that a statutory prohibition, imposed because of pregnancy, temporarily prevents the employee from performing night-time work'.[44] In *Webb*, the plaintiff was employed to replace initially another employee, Mrs Stewart, an import operations clerk who was on maternity leave. It was anticipated that the plaintiff would stay in employment when Mrs. Stewart returned. The plaintiff was employed in advance of the maternity leave period because she would need six month's training. However, she herself became pregnant after a few weeks and was dismissed. The case came before the English courts which could not (or did not wish to) determine whether it was a case of pregnancy or illness related to pregnancy and asked the ECJ for a preliminary ruling *ex* Article 177 EC. It is my opinion that in this case the ECJ simply should have applied *Dekker*: *Webb* is a case of direct discrimination because the fundamental reason for Mrs. Webb's dismissal was her pregnancy. This however was not the reasoning of the ECJ. Instead of focusing upon the reason why Mrs. Webb was dismissed, it concentrated its efforts on the distinction between temporary and fixed staff. In light of this, the Court held that the dismissal of an employee who is recruited for an unlimited term with a view initially to replacing another employee during the latter's maternity leave, and who cannot do so because shortly after her recruitment, she is herself found to be pregnant, was contrary to the principle of equal treatment.

Habermann-Beltermann and *Webb* have caused mixed reactions. On the one hand legal writers have written that, despite their need for further clarification, the two judgments should be applauded for affirming the protection of pregnant women from being disadvantaged due to factors unique to the female sex (Bamforth, 1995). On the other hand, according to some commentators, the ECJ seems to suggest a possible justification to direct discrimination, that is the use of temporary staff or temporary contracts (Fenwick and Hervey, 1995). In theory I agree with the latter opinion. Indeed, I would go even further by saying that the ECJ has not only created justifications to direct discrimination, but in doing so has contradicted its previous position according to which the derogations listed in Art. 2 of the Equal Treatment Directive are exhaustive.[45]

From a practical point of view, however, since it unlikely that following the *Dekker* ruling any employer would ever dismiss a female employee on grounds of pregnancy, with these judgments at least the ECJ has created a form of threshold: temporary contracts and temporary staff. With that said, it is very likely that the ECJ now will be asked to clarify and to further develop these two concepts.

Gillespie

The most recent case in which the ECJ considered maternity was *Gillespie*.[46] This case differs from the others considered above as it deals with pregnancy and maternity in the context of equal pay rather than equal treatment. Here 17 women employed by the Northern Ireland Health Services took maternity leave in 1988. Under a collective agreement they received full pay for four weeks, 90 per cent for the next two weeks followed by 12 days of half pay. At the end of 1988, a pay increase backdated to 1 April was negotiated but the women were denied the benefit of the backdated rise. The case was referred to the ECJ to determine whether Article 119 EC applied to maternity pay. In addition, the ECJ was asked whether Community Law provides specific criteria for determining the amount of maternity benefits.

Commentators have said that the judgment of the ECJ is 'pragmatic but confused'.[47] On the one hand, the ECJ held that a woman on maternity leave is in a special situation which may not be compared to the situation of those workers not on maternity leave. On the other hand, it suggests that a woman who is treated differently from those workers not on maternity leave is the victim of discrimination on grounds of sex. I would rather say that the judgment of the ECJ reflects the confusion surrounding this area, and that it should be regarded as another step towards a more coherent *corpus juris* in this area. In fact, though maternity is again placed in the sex equality debate (*in casu* equal pay), at least the ECJ clearly established that maternity benefits are pay within the meaning of Article 119 EC.

Conclusion: Towards a Litigation Strategy?

In this chapter, I hope I have provided evidence that EC legislation so far has failed in its attempt to provide a sound framework for the regulation of pregnancy and maternity. One of the main limits is that this issue has been confined to sex equality law. In contrast, I submit that a 'litigation strategy'[48] would offer a better alternative. First, it would not reflect a compromise between the Member States. All of them would be forced to implement it.[49] Secondly, the ECJ has attempted to go beyond the sex equality approach. This appeared in *Dekker* where the ECJ established that discrimination on grounds of pregnancy is direct discrimination and seemed to acknowledge that maternity is a right *per se*. There is however a significant difference between a 'right *per se*' and a 'fundamental right'. Classification as a right *per se* implies that pregnancy should be protected independently from other rights, rather than as merely an appendix to them (in this case equal treatment). This protection is not however unconditional and may be overridden by other factors. In contrast a fundamental right goes to the root of the EC legal order and is impervious to alteration by other considerations. In *Dekker* the ECJ confirmed that pregnancy was a right *per se*, having a separate existence from equal treatment. Unfortunately the ECJ failed to take the further step of confirming it as a fundamental right. It is submitted that, had this enhancement taken place, it is likely that the judgments which followed

Dekker would have been decided differently. As it is, it seems that the idea of pregnancy per se has been watered down.

There are however justifications, both political and juridical/procedural for the 'limited' ('cautious'?) approach of the ECJ. First, it is not a legislator. The fact that so far it has been activist, and broadening the material scope of certain articles, has *prima facie* created law, does not mean that it cannot create fundamental rights. Further, it should be mentioned that the charge of activism has been strongly criticised (Rasmussen, 1986). Secondly, the ECJ cannot act as a 'moral body'.[50] Consequently, it cannot be required to take social decisions.[51] The ECJ has to ensure that the 'interpretation of the Treaty is observed' and even if the Maastrich Treaty aims to establish an Union which goes beyond an Economic Community, social aims seem to remain secondary to economic goals.[52] Thirdly, the ECJ is not an autonomous body but it is 'dependent' upon the request and the goodwill of the courts of the Member States. Article 177 EC states that where a question is raised before any court or tribunal of a Member State, that court or tribunal, if it considers it necessary, may request the ECJ to give a ruling; only where the question arises before a national court or a tribunal against whose decisions there is no judicial remedy under national law, shall that court or tribunal bring the matter before the ECJ. It follows that the ECJ can only respond to the questions that the national courts put forward. Accordingly it can develop a principle within the limits of those questions. In other words a successful litigation strategy needs an active ECJ as well as the co-operation of the Member States.

In spite of the analysis above, I strongly support the efforts of the ECJ, restricted as they are. Considering the scant framework in which pregnancy and maternity were originally placed, the ECJ has achieved satisfactory results and therefore its efforts should be recognised as a valuable attempt to 'reconcile professional life with motherhood'.[53]

Notes

1. For example in Italy, maternity in the workplace has been regulated since 1971 (Lex 1204/71), in Norway relevant legislation has been in force since 1977 (Arbeidsmiljoloven, 4/2/1977).
2. A. G. Darmon in his opinion in the *Dekker* and *Hertz* cases said that 'we must reconcile - with difficulty - the requirement of professional life with motherhood', case C-177/88, *Dekker v Stichting* [1990] ECR I-3941; case C-179/88, *Handels-og Konturfunctionærernes Forbund i Danmark (acting*

for B. Hertz) v Dansk Arbejdsgiverforening (acting for Aldi MarkedA/S) [1990] ECR I-3979.

3. Article 119 EC provides for equal pay for equal work. This principle has been further extended, by means of directives, to equality of treatment, equality in social security and equality in statutory schemes. For further details see Burrows and Mair (1996).
4. Council Directive 76/207, OJ 1976 L 39/40.
5. The Social Policy Agreement is one of the 'bits and pieces' which the Treaty of Maastricht has added to the European Union. Due to the opposition of the UK Government to the development of social issues within the Treaty, social policy is now divided into two parts; this division is the celebrated 'twin-track Europe'. There are a few scattered provisions, binding upon all the Member States, in the EC Treaty *plus* a Social Policy Protocol (SPP) and a Social Policy Agreement (SPA), which are not binding upon the UK, outside the Treaty. The purpose of such unusual arrangements, whose legality is questionable, is to allow 11 Member States to go along with the objectives of the European Social Charter. In other words when an agreement with the UK is impossible to reach, under the SPA and the SPP it is feasible to enact legislation binding only upon the 11 (now 14) Member States. For a more detailed discussion, see Curtin (1993) and Shaw (1994).
6. A comprehensive survey is not, of course, possible within the confines of this short article. See further Szyszczak (1996).
7. Council Directive 76/207, OJ 1976 L39/40.
8. Council Directive 92/85, OJ 1992 L 348/1.
9. Framework Agreement on Parental Leave concluded by UNICE, CEEP and the ETUC, COM(96) 26 final, 31 January 1996, Council Directive 96/34 OJ 1996 L 145/4.
10. E.g. case C-91/92, *Faccini Dori v Recreb* [1994] ECR I-3325.
11. To quote an example the *via crucis* of Ms. Gabrielle Defrenne and Ms. Helen Marshall; Case 80/70, *Defrenne (I)* [1971]ECR 445; case 43/75, *Defrenne (II)* [1976] ECR 455; case 149/77, *Defrenne (III)* [1978] ECR 1365; case 152/84, *Marshall (I)* [1986] ECR 723; case 271/91, *Marshall (II)* [1993] ECR I-4367. For a detailed comment on these cases see Cullen and Charlesworth (1995).
12. My emphasis.
13. Following this approach an English Court ruled to prevent an employee, from driving tankers containing a substance that was dangerous to women of child-bearing age, despite the fact she stated that she did not want children; *Page v Freight Hire Ltd* [1981] 1 All ER 394.
14. Case 163/82, *Commission v Italy* [1983] ECR 3273; case 312/86, *Commission v France* [1988] ECR 6315.
15. Case 184/83, *U. Hofmann v Barmer Ersatzkasse* [1984] ECR 3047.
16. My emphasis.

17. According to Article 16 'measures should also be developed enabling men and woman to reconcile their occupational and family obligations'; Article 28 of the Social Charter states that '[t]he European Council invites the Commission to submit as soon as possible initiatives which falls within its powers ... with a view to the adoption of legal instruments for the effective implementation ... of those rights which come within the Community's area of competence'.
18. My emphasis.
19. Though Article 118a EC, especially the majority system, is crucial for the development of social policy, it should not be overemphasised. Commenting on the Pregnancy and Maternity Directive, Ellis remarks that 'it is an over-simplification to say that the principle of majority voting means that a Member State can now be obliged to go along with legislation of which it disapproves: the reality remains that there is still plenty of scope for a recalcitrant Member State to obstruct proposed legislation' (Ellis, 1993).
20. On the one hand, the UK Government argued that the aim of the proposed Directive was too wide and that only the health and safety aspects justify the use of Article 118a EC as a legal base (i.e. the use of majority). The Italian Government, on the other hand abstained as a protest against the UK.
21. My emphasis.
22. Art 16(1) Directive 89/391 provides for the introduction of measures to encourage improvements in the safety and health of workers at work; OJ L 183/1, 29/06/1989.
23. Case 316/85, *Centre Public d'Aide Sociale de Courcelles v M. Christine Lebon* [1987] ECR 2811; case C-326/88, *Criminal Proceedings against Hansen & Søn* [1990] ECR 2911; see also Nielsen and Szyszczak (1993).
24. Council Directive 93/104 [1994] OJ L 307/20.
25. Council Directive 94/33 [1994] OJ 216/12.
26. Case C-84/94, *United Kingdom v Council of the European Union*, NYP; see also the Opinion of Advocate General Léger, delivered on 12 March 1996.
27. It has to be appreciated, however, that in Case 271/91 (*Marshall II*), the ECJ has broadly interpreted the term compensation. For further details see Cullen and Charlesworth (1995).
28. To a certain extent this problem has been addressed by the Court in case C-342/93, *Gillespie v Northern Ireland Health and Social Services Board*, decided on 14 February 1996 NYP.
29. My emphasis.
30. The Social Partners are the Union of Industries of the European Community (UNICE), the European Trade Union Confederation (ETUC) and the European Centre for Public Enterprises (CEEP).
31. *Supra* note 5.

32. 'The European Court has been the major driving force behind recent developments of ... anti-discrimination law, leading to crucially important changes. It is in the context of pregnancy that the EC has made greatest stride towards transcending a purely male norm' (Fredman, 1992).
33. Case 163/82, *Commission v Italy* [1983] ECR 3273; case 312/86, *Commission v France (Re Protection of Women)* [1988] ECR 6315; case 184/83, *Hofmann v Barmer Ersatzkasse* [1984] ECR 3047.
34. See e.g. the definition of measures having equivalent effect. The main principle was established in *Dassonville* as '*[a]ll* trading rules ... which are capable of hindering *directly* or *indirectly*, *actually* or *potentially* intra-Community trade'. The Court further specified in the following cases three categorises of 'measure': measures related to *characteristics of the product*, *measures related the circumstances in which goods are sold*, and recently in *Keck*, *measures related to the selling arrangements*; case 8/74, *Procureur du Roi v Dassonville* [1974] ECR 837; cases C-267-268/91, *Criminal Proceedings against Keck and Mithouard* [1993] ECR I-6097.
35. *Supra* note 2.
36. Case C-412/92, *Habermann-Beltermann v Arbeiderwohifahrt Bezirksverband* [1994] ECR I - 1657.
37. Case 32/93, *Webb v Emo Cargo* [1994] ECR I-3567.
38. Case C-342/93, *Gillespie v Northern Ireland Health and Social Services Board*, decided on 14 February 1996 NYR.
39. Case 248/83, *Commission v Germany* [1985] ECR 1459; case 22/84, *Johnston v Chief Constable RUC* [1986] ECR 1651.
40. These cases were decided before the Pregnancy and Maternity Directive came into force.
41. My emphasis.
42. The ECJ will possibly clarify this point soon. In fact, the House of Lords has recently asked the ECJ for a preliminary ruling on a case involving illness due to medical conditions arising out of the pregnancy; *M. Brown v Rentokil Ltd* (1995) Inner House Cases, 18 January, 1995; case C-394/96, NYR.
43. *Mutterschutzgesetz* (MSchG), para 8(1).
44. Case C-421/92.
45. Case 248/83, *Commission v Germany* [1985] ECR 1459; case 22/84, *Johnston v Chief Constable RUC* [1986] ECR 1651. The 'confusion' between direct and indirect discrimination also confirms the fact that sex equality law is an inappropriate context in which to place pregnancy and maternity.
46. *Supra* note 38.
47. European Court Monitor (1996), 1&2 Farmer, Moore (eds.), 103.
48. The expression is borrowed from Olsen, 1993.
49. Art. 171 EC.

50. Case C-159/90, *Society for the Protection of Unborn Children v Grogan et al* [1991] ECR I-4685, Case C-168/91 *Kostantinidis v Stadt Altensteig, Standesamt and Landrasamt Calw Ordnungsamt* [1993] ECR I-1191.
51. It is true that on certain occasions, such as *Defrenne*, the Court promoted the social dimension of the EC. A closer analysis, however, provides evidence that it was actually limited to the employment market.
52. *Contra*, Hervey, 1996.
53. A.G. Darmon, Opinion of *Dekker* and *Hertz* cases, see *supra* footnote 2.

Bibliography

Aristotele, *Etica Nicomacheoa* (W. Ross trans.,1925).

Bamforth, N. (1995), 'The Treatment of Pregnancy under Community Sex Discrimination Law', *European Public Law*, vol. 1, pp.59-68.

Barnard C. (1996), 'The Economic Objectives of Art.119' in T. Hervery and D O'Keefe (eds.), *Sex Equality Law in the European Union*, Wiley, Chancery.

Bovis, C. and Cnossen, C. (1996), 'Stereotyped Assumptions versus Sex Equality: a Socio-Legal Analysis of Equality Laws in the European Union', *The International Journal of Comparative Labour Law and Industrial Relations*, vol. 12, pp. 7-23.

Burrows, N. and Mair, J. (1996), *European Social Law*, Wiley, Chichester.

Cullen, H. and Charlesworth, A. (1995), 'Portia's Daughters: the Role of Individual Litigant in Developing Sex Discrimination Law', *West Virginia Law Review*, vol. 97, pp. 751-771.

Curtin, D. (1993), 'The Constitutional Structure of the Union: a Europe of Bits and Pieces', *Common Market Law Review*, vol. 30, pp. 17-69.

Demosthenes, S. (1995), *Protective Barriers: The Discriminatory Effects of Women Protection Laws in the European Community*, Det Juridiske Fakultets Skriftserie nr. 59, University of Bergen, Bergen.

Ellis, E. (1993), 'Protection of Pregnancy and Maternity', *Industrial Law Journal*, vol. 22, pp. 63-67.

Fenwick, H. (1996), 'Special Protection for Women in European Union Law', in T. Hervey and D. O'Keeffe (eds.), *Sex Equality Law in the European Union*, Wiley, Chichester.

Fenwick, H. and Hervey, T. (1995), 'Sex Equality in the Single Market: New Directions for the European Court of Justice', *Common Market Law Review*, vol. 32, pp. 443-470.

Fredman, S. (1992), 'European Community Discrimination Law: a Critique', *Industrial Law Journal*, vol. 21, pp. 119-134.

Hervey, T. (1996), 'The Future of Sex Equality Law in the European Union', in T. Hervey and D. O'Keeffe (eds.), *Sex Equality Law in the European Union*, Wiley, Chichester.

Jacqmain, J. (1994), 'Pregnancy as Grounds for Dismissals', *Industrial Law Journal*, vol. 23, pp. 355-359.

Muffat-Jandet, D. (1991), 'Protection of Pregnancy and Maternity', *Industrial Law Journal*, vol. 20, pp. 76-79.

Nielsen, R. (1993), *Arbejdsmiljøret*, Økonomforbundets, Forlag.

Nielsen, R. and Szyszsak, E. (1993), *The Social Dimension of the European Community*, 2nd ed., Handelshøjskolens Forlag, Copenhagen.

Olsen, F. (1993), 'Employment Discrimination in the New Europe: a Litigation Project for Women', *Journal of Law and Society*, vol. 20, pp. 131-144.

Rasmussen, H. (1986), *On Law and Policy in the European Court of Justice*, Nijihoff, Dordrecht.

Rubenstein, H. (1991), 'Highlights: January 1991', *Industrial Relations Law Reports*, vol. 20 pp. 1-3.

Shaw, J. (1994), 'Twin-Track Social Europe - the Inside Track' in D. O'Keeffe and P. Twomey (eds.), *Legal Issues of the Maastricht Treaty*, Wiley, Chichester.

Szyszczak, E. (1996), 'Community Law on Pregnancy and Maternity' in T. Hervey and D. O'Keeffe (eds.), *Sex Equality Law in the European Union*, Wiley, Chichester.

Vigerust, E. (1995), 'Graviditet, Arbeidsmiljø og Likestilling', in K. Ketscher, J. Lindgård and R. Nielsen (eds.), *Den Sociale Dimension i Kvinderetlig Perspektiv*, Copenhagen.

12. The Construction of Women in the Non-Consensual Sterilisation Debate: Why a Feminist Analysis is Needed

MARY DONNELLY

Introduction

When one approaches the considerable amount of literature in the area of non-consensual sterilisation, one is struck by two things. First, the debate centres on women both the woman whose sterilisation is proposed and quite often her mother is also a key figure. The second notable feature is that most of the debaters are not women. With a couple of notable exceptions,[1] the judiciary have been male; the medical and psychological evidence upon which the judgment is based is often given by male professionals and with some important feminist exceptions, (Peppin, 1989-90; Shaw, 1990; Kingdom, 1991; Keywood, 1995; Rhoades, 1995) many of the commentators in the area have been male (Freeman, 1988; Lee and Morgan, 1990; Kennedy, 1991). Furthermore, the legal methods used to decide whether sterilisation should take place and the underlying assumptions have failed to take account of a feminist or, often, even a female perspective.

This imbalance is evident when we consider the way in which women have been constructed in the debate. On consideration, it becomes clear that presumptions about women's essential nature and social role dominate the way in which the debate is conducted. The first part of this chapter considers the construction of women in, what might loosely be described as, the two opposing views: the anti-sterilisation, pro-motherhood stance of the Canadian courts; and, the more individualised, pro-sterilisation stance of the English and Australian judiciary. Having identified the assumptions made, it becomes evident that the debate as it is currently constituted fails to identify many features which would be fundamental to a feminist understanding of the issue. The second part of the chapter attempts to shift the focus in a way which is more centred on the reality, rather than the stereotype, of the women involved, asserting an understanding which is broadly feminist in nature.[2]

The Construction of Women

Feminists have long drawn attention to the way in which society likes to portray women in the opposing roles of madonna or whore. Woman is good and pure, or she is promiscuous and debased. Depending on the category into which she falls, either she must be protected from men or they (and society) must be protected from her. This perception of women is accentuated when the woman has learning difficulties. As her capacity to reason in the conventionally accepted sense becomes less, the association with the female body becomes more emphasised. Judicial discomfort with that body is evident in most decisions in this area. Two approaches can be identified. The first regards women with learning difficulties as innocent, asexual beings whose symbolic capacity for motherhood defines them; in short, as madonna. The second approach regards the female body as different to the male and therefore difficult and requiring control.

The Madonna

The decision of the Supreme Court of Canada in *Re Eve*[3] provides an excellent example of the 'madonna approach'. The case involved an application by the mother of a 24 year old woman (Eve) for court permission to consent to the sterilisation of her daughter who was described as 'at least mildly to moderately' disabled. The purpose of the sterilisation was contraceptive; there was no evidence that it was therapeutically necessary, nor that the act of giving birth would be any more difficult for Eve than for any woman of her age.

After more that a year of deliberation, the decision of the Supreme Court of Canada was given in a single judgment by La Forest J. The Court rejected sterilisation on the basis that it was a 'grave intrusion on a person's rights', specifically the right to reproduce, which could never be definitively said to be for the benefit of the person.[4] Thus, on the basis of the right to reproduce, all sterilisations other than those which were therapeutically necessary (defined narrowly by La Forest J)[5] were prohibited. The Court did not consider the existence of other supporting and competing rights and rejected any analysis based on interests as being 'simply not a sufficiently precise or workable tool'.[6]

The reliance on Eve's right to reproduce in this case was purely theoretical however and it is clear from the decision that it was considered that Eve should never be given the opportunity to reproduce in practice. Instead, it was envisaged that she should be subjected to a higher level of supervision in her relationships.

Two complementary priorities are at work here. The first is the maintenance of Eve's 'purity'. Her right to privacy which would allow relationships which may involve a sexual element was not considered. This would clearly interfere with the judicial perception of her as an eternal child. At one point in his judgment, La Forest J commented that Eve had a relationship with a fellow resident but remarked, evidently with satisfaction, that 'That has now been taken care of'. This relationship was elaborated upon by the trial judge who took a similar line. He stated:

> [Eve] had struck up a rather close relationship with a male student or 'trainee' as they are known at the school, who was also retarded, though somewhat less so than Eve. In fact, 'marriage' had been talked of between them. Fortunately, this situation was identified and the affair, if it can be so described, was terminated.[7]

While, as will be discussed later, there is a genuine dilemma between freedom and protection, this section is shocking in the paternalistic indifference shown towards Eve.

The second priority evident in this decision is the preservation of the capacity for motherhood. As noted above, it was the symbolic importance of motherhood, rather than the actuality, that was important. This approach is neatly summarised by Ian Kennedy, one of its leading English proponents, who argues that '[w]omanness is inextricably identified with reproductive capacity'. He continues: '[t]o destroy irrevocably this reproductive capacity is ... to destroy a fundamental, perhaps the only remaining, element of a sense of self' (1991, p.105). The argument is thus based on women's defining difference, namely their capacity (both real and symbolic) to become mothers.

The way in which symbolic importance is attached to some characteristics is not an accident. Feminists have long focused on the role of motherhood in women's lives, noting that the capacity for motherhood can simultaneously be seen as both a source of strength and of weakness (Rich, 1977). For some women, the capacity to bear children is undoubtedly a characteristic by which they would define themselves. However, there are many women for whom this capacity is not fundamental and whose sense of self is based on characteristics which they, rather than society, have chosen. The acceptance of women's definitions of themselves is fundamental to feminism. If a simple equation of motherhood with identity is not acceptable when a woman does not have learning difficulties, then it should not become so simply because she has difficulties.

The argument about motherhood is not just about symbols, however. The focus on symbolic motherhood has practical consequences for women. One of the most dangerous is the way in which it obscures the decisions made about real motherhood. These are decisions which are made on a day to day basis without recourse to the legal system or to the publicity which may ensue. The attitudes towards learning disability which leads to an automatic presumption of incapacity to be a mother go unquestioned. Furthermore, it seems to be presumed that the child's primary care-giver will be the mother.

A second factor which is hidden is the way in which other forms of prevention of child-birth also occur without judicial scrutiny. Courts, which have been very protective of the right to reproduce in relation to sterilisation, have been prepared to countenance supervision,[8] contraception and abortion[9] to ensure that a woman with learning difficulties does not have a child. There is no understanding of the effects of close supervision on a woman's life. If the decision is to opt for contraception, the health risks of long-term oral contraception are not considered before a decision is made to subject a woman to this form of treatment. Similarly, the psychological and physical impact of non-consensual abortion is completely ignored as is the effect on a woman who bears a child only to have it taken away if she is unable to care for it.

To summarise, this approach is based on an idealised and desexualized image of the female body. This is made possible only through the obfuscation of the woman who lives in that body. She is objectified, not in the traditional way as a sex-object, but as its opposite. She is the symbolic mother who is, by necessity, asexual.

The Difficult Body

Other jurisdictions, notably England[10] and Australia,[11] have adopted a more flexible policy, allowing non-consensual sterilisation if it is in the best interests of the woman involved. A subjective test involving the criteria of best interests will inevitably provide an opportunity for assumptions to masquerade as facts and the language of care and concern to mask indifference to and acceptance of discriminatory attitudes and practices. As will be discussed later, the debate about non-consensual sterilisation provides some fine examples of this danger of which all feminists espousing a greater care ethic must be aware.

Underlying all the discussions in the area is the presumption, referred to earlier, that women with a learning difficulty should not have children. This assumption, based on disability, will be considered below. Here, however, the focus is on the way this assumption combines with other assumptions based on femininity. The view of the female body evident on this side of the debate is somewhat different to the asexual mother symbol evident in the anti-sterilisation stance. This perspective views the female body as different and difficult. It can only be comprehended if it is stripped of its distinctively female features.

First, there is the view that reproduction and its regulation is exclusively a female problem which is 'solved' by invasive surgery. Although the decision is supposedly focused on the best interests of the woman, the hidden reality is that, insofar as her best interests are determined, the determination occurs within a system which is not particularly concerned with her interests in the first place. Commentators have noted the way in which the sterilisation of women with mental disabilities allows badly-funded facilities and under-resourced community care programs to remain unchallenged (Morgan and Lee, 1991).

The miraculous absence of fathers which has characterised the abortion debate is also evident in relation to sterilisation. Some commentators have noted that, where the woman has a partner, his sterilisation (or education) is not considered (Shaw, 1990; Morgan and Lee, 1991). The decision of the House of Lords in *Re F*[12] is often cited as an example of this. Here, F was an adult woman whose sterilisation was sought because she was involved in a sexual relationship with a fellow resident. However, it was her rather than his sterilisation which was sought by the Health Authority. Nor was the possibility of F's partner's sterilisation even referred to by the courts. While (as will be argued below) the sterilisation of men with learning difficulties in their own best interests cannot be treated as a simplistic equality issue, the complete incapacity of the courts to acknowledge other sources for birth-control is an indication of the unfortunate but pervasive belief that women are solely responsible for contraception.

A second discomfort with the sexed female body relates to menstruation. The leading Australian cases have involved applications for hysterectomy rather than sterilisation. The reason for opting for this, more serious operation is the facilitation of, what is described as, menstrual management. While it is stated in *P and P* that menstrual management will not, of itself, justify sterilisation, it is a factor to be taken into account in making the decision.[13] As Rhoades (1995, p.246) notes, menstruation is seen as a function which is not part of normal life and which can be eliminated without changing the way in which the woman considers herself.

In its attitude towards women, this approach might be summarised as focusing, not on female purity but, on conformity with a masculine body. However, in many ways its aim is the same, to control and androgenise the difficult female body.

Where Would a Feminist Focus?

The preceding discussion has argued that the 'woman question' has often been obscured in the debate on sterilisation. However, likewise, the 'disability question' has often been absent from feminist debate. In asking the question 'where would a feminist focus?', the dilemmas of difference as well as questions relating to freedom and protection become apparent. The following examination of the way in which a more feminist treatment of the area would operate is divided into two sections. The first relates to the framework adopted to decide the issue; the second section deals with the way in which this test is then applied in practice.

Framework for Determination

A common feminist response to issues such as this is very often to invoke a care-based, contextual approach which acknowledges the connections between the woman and others in her life (Gilligan, 1982; West, 1988). There is a level of discomfort with rights as a basis for analysis, in particular the right to reproduce which Elizabeth Kingdom describes as 'not only unconducive to engagement with practical policy formation but, deliberately or otherwise, diverts attention from it' (1991, p.94).

Certainly, the way in which rights-based analysis has been used in this debate has been problematic. The presumption of objectivity which attaches to rights has obscured the value-judgment involved. In any rights-based analysis where one right is considered to be more important than the others, the conclusion will then follow logically and without any apparent bias. However, as is evident in *Re Eve*, there is a clear value-judgment in the determination of the status of each individual right.

Secondly, as in the area of abortion, a rights analysis is insufficiently flexible to deal with an issue of this complexity.[14] While La Forest J's use of rights may have been 'precise', it also had the effect of completely obscuring the woman whose rights were at issue. Her whole life was summarised in medical and legal terms; she was simply the repository of a right which seemed to be more important than she was.

However, it would be a mistake to jettison reliance on rights entirely, particularly when we are dealing with individuals who are especially vulnerable. It is for this reason that Martha Minow argues that '[t]here is something too valuable in the aspiration of rights, and something too neglectful of the power embedded in assertions of another's need, to abandon the rhetoric of rights' (1990, p.307). While the recognition of context and connection is fundamental, it is also important not to allow the individual at the centre of the inquiry to become obscured in a maze of connections. Thus, although it can be persuasively argued that reliance on the right to reproduce is at best pointless, at worst invasive, there may be value in reliance on an individual right to bodily autonomy. If we consider (as will be argued) that non-consensual sterilisation is a procedure which is potentially invasive, then, starting from a perspective of respect for the individual's right to bodily autonomy can provide the basis for an understanding which is contextual and individualised.

This, at least in theory, is the approach taken by the High Court of Australia. In *Secretary, Department of Health and Community Services* v. *JWB*[15] the court recognised the importance of the individual's 'fundamental right to personal inviolability'.[16] However, this right did not 'trump' all other aspects of the question. Instead, it gave the Court a basis for its questioning. Because of the difficulties involved, sterilisation was seen as a step of 'last resort'.[17] In the words of Mason J:

> [S]terilisation can only be authorised in the case of a child so disabled that other procedures or treatments are or have proved inadequate, in the sense that they have failed or will not alleviate the situation so that the child can lead a life in keeping with his or her needs and capacities.[18]

This decision is not without flaws. Many questions are left unanswered and there is no feeling that the Court has come to terms with Marion as a person operating within a particular context. However, in terms of the framework it creates, this decision attempts a combination of rights and care which could provide a more suitable legal framework for determination.

Application of Test

As a preliminary, it must be noted that the simple fact that learning difficulties exist should not mean that a woman should not have a child. There are few other functions in society which are so unregulated as conception (a fact often commented upon in the right-wing media). Why should women with learning difficulties be treated differently? In its Working Paper on Sterilization, the Law Reform Commission of Canada noted that there is nothing inherent in mental disability which determines whether or not a person is competent to raise children (Law Reform Commission of Canada, 1979). Such determinations should be made the basis of each individual situation rather that on an individual's membership of a particular group.

However, it must also be accepted that there are instances in which a woman who does not have the capacity to make a decision in this regard must be protected from the consequences of conception. What is important from a feminist perspective is that the focus is genuinely on the woman and not on the cost to society or eugenics or even on the child which might be conceived. The issue which then arises is the form which this protection should take.

In this regard it is clear that, within a feminist framework, there could be no presumption that a woman must automatically be the one to take responsibility for family planning (whether this involves sterilisation or other forms of contraception). Thus, in an individual situation, a preliminary question is whether the responsibility for protection can be divided in a way which is more equal. It has been noted above that the possibility of requiring a male companion to be responsible for contraception has not been explored. In some ways, this brings us back to the issue of difference and, on closer inspection, leads to the uncomfortable question of whether it can ever be said to be in the best interests of a mentally disabled man to be sterilised without his consent in the same way as it can for a woman. It can be argued that a man is not going to experience the same physical and emotional trauma from pregnancy and child-birth which a woman will and therefore he does not need to be protected from this trauma in the same way. It is also important to remember the vulnerability of men with learning difficulties and not be satisfied with a simple shift of responsibility to greater gender equality without addressing the underlying issues including the deep-rooted discrimination in society against people with learning disabilities.

To some extent, however, this is the attitude which has allowed male abdication of responsibility for the regulation of reproduction. In most cases, it is also too simplistic an application of the difference argument. The reality is that, in most situations which involve partners with learning difficulties, both parties do not have the same level of difficulty. If the male partner is capable of taking responsibility for the prevention of pregnancy, then this is an option which should be explored. Care must be taken that sterilisation is not used as a way to avoid confronting the inequalities and exploitation which can occur in sexual relationships involving women with learning difficulties.

If, in a particular situation, the woman must be the one to take responsibility for birth control, the possibility of sterilisation must then be considered. However, the sterilisation option cannot be looked at outside of its historical context. A brief perusal of the history of the area indicates that sterilisation has been used as a way for those in power to inflict their will on the most vulnerable members of society (Freeman, 1988; Burgdorf and Burgdorf, 1977; Law Reform Commission of Canada, 1979; Williams, 1957). While the capacity to bear children should have no bearing on a person's value, the removal of this capacity has been seen as dehumanising and demeaning. Coupled with this is the practical fact that a sterilisation is most probably permanent.[19] For this reason, sterilisation should be a procedure which is considered only in very limited circumstances. This was the position of the High Court of Australia which considered sterilisation only as a step of 'last resort'.[20]

Furthermore, account must be taken of the problem of sexual abuse which is becoming central to the debate on non-consensual sterilisation. From a feminist perspective, it is difficult to see how any comprehensive determination can be made by the courts without reference to this issue. A number of those who oppose sterilisation do so on the basis that it leaves the woman more vulnerable to sexual abuse. This was the view of Moore J in *P and P*[21] who argued that, when a woman has profound learning difficulties, pregnancy is often the only way in which it can be shown that sexual abuse has occurred. With respect, however, it is not appropriate to use womens' bodies as a way of making up for the inadequacies of the legal system. If the effect of pregnancy would be sufficiently traumatic to merit steps to be taken to ensure it does not happen, then these steps should be taken rather than maintaining fertility as some sort of awkward detection device.

Having said this, however, there is justifiable cause for fear that a potential abuser would see the abuse of a woman who has been sterilised as somehow less important and that widespread sterilisation would increase the already high risk of sexual abuse of women with learning difficulties. There is an unfortunate possibility that sterilisation used to prevent pregnancy from sexual abuse may actually help give rise to the abuse because it dehumanises the woman in the eyes of the abuser and makes detection less possible. However, the solution to abuse is not found in preventing all women with learning difficulties from having a sexual relationship. The fine line between protection and repression, which has characterised aspects of feminist debate in relation to rape, arises in this situation also (Olsen, 1984). It is important not to use, this time from a feminist perspective, the same narrow reasoning as the Supreme Court of Canada in *Re Eve*. The question of non-consensual sterilisation is found somewhere in the narrow space between the avoidance of paternalism and the protection of the individual. This narrow space must be explored in each individual situation by asking whether the woman has a sexual relationship; whether she is comfortable with the relationship; whether the relationship enriches her life; whether another form of contraception would be possible. It is also important to be sensitive in a broader sense to the often patronising way in which the relationships and the sexual needs of people with learning difficulties are perceived. The imposition of a chastity requirement is not acceptable simply because the person has learning difficulties (Carson, 1989).

The problem becomes more difficult when (as in many cases) the woman is not in a relationship at the time and the purpose of the sterilisation is either to allow the development of future sexual relationships or to ensure her protection from the consequences of possible sexual abuse. For any feminist approaching this area, there is a conflict between the ideal, which in many cases would not require sterilisation, and the reality of the woman's life. In an ideal world, community care projects would be adequately funded and men would be prepared to take responsibility for birth control. However, it is also important to address the reality of the situation in which the woman is living and ask in what way would sterilisation make a difference to her life. Would she have greater freedom in a positive sense or would the sterilisation be used as a way which would allow others to avoid responsibility and put her more at risk from abuse? It is also necessary to look ahead and ask how will the woman develop and what might she feel five, ten, fifteen years in the future.

If we focus on the reality of the woman's life, we must also ask whether any interests other than the woman's should be taken into account. As was noted at the beginning of this chapter, the applications in this area are often brought by the carers, in many cases by the mother, of the woman involved. One of the few points on which the Canadian and the English judiciary agree is that carers should not be considered in making the decision. The effect of this approach has been to create a conflict between the carer and the woman. There is a presumption that they will 'want' different things and that the court must decide (in an adversarial setting) who is 'right'. While this approach does have the advantage of preventing unscrupulous parents arranging sterilisations in inappropriate circumstances, it can also have the effect of dealing with the issue on the basis of an inaccurate picture of the woman's life. She does not exist in the vacuum presumed by the courts; indeed, were it not for the role played by many carers, the lives of a large number of women with learning difficulties would be considerably impoverished. This tension between ideal and reality is difficult to resolve. However, a more inclusive approach would acknowledge the importance of relationships. Interestingly, the Antipodean approach has been to give greater importance to the views of carers. In the New Zealand case of *Re X*[22] and the Australian case of *P and P*[23] the role of the woman within her family was recognised. While the difficulties inherent in this approach are obvious, it represents an attempt at a more realistic view of the woman's life.

Conclusion

The area of non-consensual sterilisation reveals a good deal about the ways in which assumptions are imposed on a legal issue so as to predetermine the resolution of the issue. If the symbol of motherhood and the maintenance of purity is central, then sterilisation is unacceptable and unnecessary. If, on the other hand, the female body is seen as different and somehow unnatural, then removing signs of feminity is seen as simply removing unnecessary extras.

Although reliance on rights may not have served women well to date (Kingdom, 1991), recourse to a care-based analysis does not provide the ideal solution even in this most personal of areas. Rights must be tempered with care but, in this imperfect world, care must also be tempered with rights. Any decisions made will involve continual conflict between the ideal and the reality and between protection and freedom. In each situation, the resolution will often be the untidy result of compromise. However, in an area such as this, tidy solutions are very often a sign of an overly limited inquiry. As Ann Scales has noted: 'A precise picture of a fuzzy scene is a fuzzy picture' (1986, p.1373).

Notes

1. In *Re D (A Minor) (Sterilisation)* [1976] 2 W.L.R 279 was decided by Heilbron J and the judge at first instance in *P and P and Legal Aid Commission of New South Wales* (1995) 19 Fam L.R. 1 was Moore J. Both of these judges are women and both refused the application for sterilisation.
2. In describing the understanding aspired to as 'broadly feminist in nature', I am aware that this description lacks definition. For the purposes of this paper, I am taking the definition of feminist from Rosalind Delmar when she writes: 'At the very least a feminist is someone who holds that women suffer discrimination because of their sex, that they have specific needs that remain negated and unsatisfied' (1986, p.8).
3. (1986) 31 D.L.R. (4th) 1.
4. (1986) 31 D.L.R. (4th) 1, p.32.
5. *Ibid.*, p.29.
6. *Ibid.*, p.33.
7. (1980) 115 DLR (3d) 383.
8. The decision in *Re Eve* is an obvious example. See also the dissenting judgment of Brennan J in *Secretary, Department of Health and Community Services* v *JWB* (1992) 106 A.L.R. 385.
9. See Heilbron J. in *Re D* [1976] 2 W.L.R. 279, p.288.

10. The leading English cases are the decisions of the House of Lords in *Re B (A Minor) (Wardship: Sterilisation)* [1988] AC 199 and *Re F (Mental Patient) (Sterilisation)* [1990] AC 1. The principles established in these cases have been followed in *Re P* [1989] 1 F.L.R. 182; *Re E* [1991] 2 F.L.R. 585; *Re GF* [1992] 1 F.L.R. 293.
11. After a number of conflicting decisions at lower levels, the matter was resolved by the High Court of Australia in *Secretary, Department of Health and Community Services* v *JWB* (1992) 106 ALR 385; this decision was applied in *P and P and Legal Aid Commission of New South Wales* (1995) 19 Fam L.R. 1.
12. 1990] A.C. 1.
13. *Supra* note 1, p.23.
14. See McCarthy J in *Attorney General* v *X* [1992] 1 IR 1, 80. McCarthy J was working within the limits of a constitutional provision (Article 40.3.3 of Bunreacht na hEireann) which set up a direct conflict between the rights to life of the woman and of the foetus.
15. (1992) 106 A.L.R. 385.
16. *Ibid.*, p.407. The court (p.408) left open the question of whether a separate right to reproduce existed, arguing (p.407) that '[i]t is debateable whether [it] is a useful concept, when couched in terms of a basic right, and how fundamental such a right can be said to be'.
17. *Ibid.*, p.412.
18. *Ibid.* See also the very detailed guidelines laid down by the Supreme Court of Washington in *Re Hayes* (1980) 608 P. 2d 635, p.640-641.
19. As Brazier (1990) notes, even if it is medically possible to reverse the sterilisation, the chances of a person with learning difficulties having access to a reversal operation are extremely slim.
20. *Secretary, Department of Health and Community Services* v *JWB* (1992) 106 A.L.R. 385.
21. *Supra* note 1.
22. [1991] 2 NZLR 365.
23. (1995) 19 Fam L.R. 1.

Bibliography

Brazier, M. (1990), 'Sterilisation: Down the Slippery Slope', *Professional Negligence*, vol. 6, pp. 25-28.

Burgdorf, R. and Burgdorf, M. (1977), 'The Wicked Witch is Almost Dead: Buck v. Bell and the Sterilisation of Handicapped Persons', *Temple Law Quarterly*, vol. 50, pp. 995-1034.

Carson, D. (1989), 'The Sexuality of People with Learning Difficulties', *Journal of Social Welfare Law*, pp. 354-372.

Delmar, R. (1986), 'What is Feminism?' in J. Mitchell and A. Oakley (eds.), *What is Feminism?*, Blackwell, Oxford.

Douglas, G. (1991), *Law, Fertility and Reproduction*, Sweet and Maxwell, London.

Freeman, M. (1988), 'Sterilising the Mentally Handicapped' in M. Freeman (ed.), *Medicine, Ethics and the Law: Current Legal Problems*, Stevens, London.

Gilligan, C. (1982), *In a Different Voice: Psychological Theory and Women's Development*, Harvard University Press, Harvard.

Kennedy, I. (1991), 'Patients, Doctors and Human Rights' in R. Blackburn and J. Taylor (eds.), *Human Rights for the 1990s*, Mansell, London.

Keywood, K. (1995), 'Sterilising the Woman with Learning Difficulties - In her Best Interests', in J. Bridgeman and S. Millns (eds.), *Law and Body Politics*, Dartmouth, Aldershot.

Kingdom, E. (1991), 'Consent, Coercion and Consortium: the Sexual Politics of Sterilisation' in E. Kingdom (ed.), *What's Wrong With Rights*, Edinburgh University Press, Edinburgh.

Law Reform Commission of Canada (1979), *Sterilization: The Implications for Treatment of Retarded and Mentally Ill Persons*, Working Paper No. 24, Law Reform Commission, Canada.

Lee, S. and Morgan, D. (1990), 'A Lesser Sacrifice? Sterilization and Mentally Handicapped Women' in S. Lee and D. Morgan (eds.), *Birthrights: Law and Ethics at the Beginnings of Life*, Routledge, London.

Minow, M. (1990), *Making All the Difference*, Cornell University Press, Mass.

Olsen, F. (1984), 'Statutory Rape - A Feminist Critique of Rights Analysis', *Texas Law Review*, vol. 63, pp. 387-432.

Peppin, P. (1989-90), 'Justice and Care: Mental Disability and Sterilisation Decisions', *Canadian Human Rights Yearbook*, vol. 6, pp. 65-111.

Rhoades, D. (1995), 'Intellectual Disability and Sterilisation - An Inevitable Connection?', *Australian Journal of Family Law*, vol. 9, pp. 234 - 251.

Rich, A. (1977), *Of Woman Born*, Virago, London.

Scales, A. (1986), 'The Emergence of Feminist Jurisprudence: An Essay', *Yale Law Journal*, vol. 95, pp. 1373-1404.

Shaw, J. (1990), 'Sterilisation of Mentally Handicapped People: Judges Rule OK?', *Modern Law Review*, vol. 53, pp. 91-94.

West, R. (1988), *Jurisprudence and Gender*, *University of Chicago Law Review*, vol. 55, pp. 1-72.

Williams, G. (1957), *The Sanctity of Life and the Criminal Law*, Faber, London.

Index

For Product Safety Concerns and Information please contact our EU representative GPSR@taylorandfrancis.com
Taylor & Francis Verlag GmbH, Kaufingerstraße 24, 80331 München, Germany

www.ingramcontent.com/pod-product-compliance
Ingram Content Group UK Ltd.
Pitfield, Milton Keynes, MK11 3LW, UK
UKHW022203190926
475702UK00003B/174

9781138333970